Opera for Libraries

Opera for Libraries

A Guide to Core Works, Audio and
Video Recordings, Books and Serials

CLYDE T. McCANTS

McFarland & Company, Inc., Publishers
Jefferson, North Carolina, and London

Library of Congress Cataloguing-in-Publication Data

McCants, Clyde T.
Opera for libraries : a guide to
core works, audio and video recordings,
books and serials / Clyde T. McCants
p.   cm.
Includes index.

ISBN 0-7864-1442-1 (softcover binding : 50# alkaline paper) ∞

1. Opera — Bibliography.   2. Opera — Discography.
3. Music libraries — Collection development.   I. Title.
ML128.O4M21   2003   016.7821 — dc21   2002153762

British Library cataloguing data are available

On the cover: Last scene from Gounod's, *Faust* ©2003 PicturesNow.com

Manufactured in the United States of America

*McFarland & Company, Inc., Publishers
Box 611, Jefferson, North Carolina 28640
www.mcfarlandpub.com*

CONTENTS

PREFACE

This is not a highly technical book. It will not teach you how to catalogue music resources. It will not instruct you in the services available through the Online Computer Library Center (OCLC). It will not prepare you to care for rare music manuscripts entrusted to your archives. It is not designed to assist specialized libraries in conservatories and other large music schools. It's a book for plain, everyday libraries that would like to make opera available to their patrons.

My own definition of opera sets the boundaries of our subject and helps explain what is included and what is not: **An opera is a play, designed to be staged, in which the drama is communicated primarily through music and in which the characters sing all or a major portion of their roles.** In other words, an opera is not an oratorio designed for concert performance, such as Handel's *Messiah* or Mendelssohn's *Elijah*, nor is it a musical comedy or operetta like *Annie Get Your Gun* or *The Student Prince*, in which musical numbers are introduced but the main thrust of the action takes place in spoken dialogue. In some cases, the dividing line is hard to draw, and there may be some spoken dialogue in an opera. In essence, however, the drama, the plot, the story, and the characterization are communicated in an opera primarily through the music. From its beginning in Renaissance Italy, opera sought to be *dramma per musica*, drama *through* music, not merely drama *with* music.

The goal of this book is to help libraries put together a comprehensive collection of operatic materials, including sound and video recordings and other appropriate resources, and to encourage the public to use those resources and grow in their knowledge and appreciation of opera. With that purpose in mind, the largest sections of this book consist of recommendations of recordings, journals, magazines, and books. We begin in Chapter One with a basic collection of complete opera recordings. These are the works that I believe illustrate the art of opera most fully, and that have proven track records in popular acceptance and repeated performance in the world's opera houses. The next chapter goes beyond the basics for the library that can afford an even larger collection. It adds more operas to the recommended list, along with suggested "recital" recordings of great operatic singers who are either not represented at all or represented inadequately in the complete recordings. There are also a few notes on opera in English.

In Chapters One and Two I have listed without critical comment video recordings on VHS tape or DVD discs for many of the recommended operas. Unlike the sound recordings on compact discs, most of these videos I have not seen. When it comes to video tapes and DVDs, I have depended primarily on printed critiques and catalogue listings for information included in these chapters. I would be less than candid if I did not confess to you at the outset my own reservations about operas on video and their value in a library collection. Frequently, although not inevitably, there are problems in the audio and visual quality of the videos, particularly of performances recorded directly from staged productions. There are also serious artistic questions about the visual styles of many of the productions. One great concern is the contemporary movement for so-called "concept" productions, which too often deny the validity of the composer and librettist's original intentions even if the music is left unchanged. Although many excellent singers have participated in the videos, it is also true that the quality of vocalism is higher overall in sound recordings.

Chapter Three recommends books and on-line resources that will support the collection of recordings by providing additional information about the history of opera, the operatic works themselves, and their composers.

Suggested periodical publications that will keep the library up-to-date on operatic developments and new recordings are the subject of Chapter Four.

In Chapter Five I address the sometimes frustrating process of finding sources for the recordings.

Chapter Six deals with the role of the library in building interest in and appreciation of opera among patrons, and encouraging them to take full advantage of the library's collection of operatic materials.

Chapter Seven is a brief final note suggesting methods for maintenance and repair of audio and video discs, an important concern if the resources are available for the personal use of library patrons.

Developing a comprehensive opera collection obviously takes financial commitment. It also takes the time and hard work of the library staff. The inevitable and appropriate question is whether developing the collection is actually worth the investment and the effort. I believe that it is because I share with many people an old-fashioned understanding of the role of the library in our society, namely as a vast, exciting storehouse of worthwhile ideas, imaginings, discoveries, and creations of the human mind and spirit.

But is it practical, this collection of operatic materials? The good news is that filling those opera shelves is easier now than it has ever been in the past. The development of video recording on tape and DVD, and particularly the advent of compact disc sound recordings, has made it truly practical for libraries to offer large collections of operatic recordings to their patrons. The record industry has cooperated by producing high quality discs of all the standard operas, often in multiple performances, and of many of the rarer, less familiar works.

Although I am neither a trained librarian nor a professional musician, I bring to this book sixty years as an active library patron and fifty or more years of listening, looking, and reading about music in general and opera in particular. I have been a frequent speaker on operatic subjects for libraries, adult study groups, arts councils, and civic clubs since I wrote and presented a series of radio programs on the subject in the 1950s. My personal collection of operatic recordings contains over 5,000 compact discs, and unless otherwise indicated, the sound recordings recommended herein all have a place in that collection or are otherwise personally familiar to me.

I express my appreciation to the librarians, musical friends, record dealers, and the authors of the many books I have used and learned from. The information about composers, their operas, and the recordings thereof has come to me over a period of many years and from many different sources. I am grateful for all of them, particularly for *The New Grove Dictionary of Opera* and *The New Penguin Opera Guide*, both of which are basic resources in this field and should be found on the reference shelves of all libraries. Most of all, I want to express my sincere debt of gratitude to the composers, their librettists, and the performing artists who over the many years have brought me such great pleasure.

PART I

Recommended Operas

one

CORE COLLECTIONS

All opera lovers have their favorites. I am certainly no exception, but I have tried to look beyond what I like best and choose instead those works that best represent opera in its rich variety. The recommended selections range over the four hundred years of operatic history, with operas from different national backgrounds, in a variety of languages and styles. If your special favorite isn't here, you may find it in the next chapter, "Beyond the Basics," where I have included suggestions for additional operas and recommendations of recital discs by important singers of the past. My aim has been to offer enough recommendations to help you put together the strongest, most comprehensive opera collection possible for your library.

Each of the "basic" recommendations begins with a brief introduction to the special background and qualities of the opera. Next, you will find one or two or, in some cases, more recommended recordings, with brief critical comments. This chapter is arranged by composers, subarranged by their operas (listed alphabetically by title). Birth and, where appropriate, death dates are included for each composer. The dates following the titles of the operas are those of the first performance.

Recommendations for sound recordings are preceded by the recording date, label name, and the catalogue number, followed by an abbreviated cast list, including conductor and choral and orchestral ensembles. The order in which the recordings are presented is not an indication of preference but is based solely on the recording dates. Often this date is indicated in the insert flyer published with the discs, but in a few cases I have been forced to include what I hope is an educated guess. You will need the label name and number when you order, but be aware that companies occasionally change their own names and issue their recordings with revised catalogue numbers. The list of performers, however, will generally help assure that you are ordering precisely the recording you want.

Most operatic discs include printed notes about the opera and the performers, and frequently a libretto in both the original language and English. A few opera recordings come with a libretto in the original language but with no English translation, and occasionally there is no more than a brief synopsis of the action. With all operas, it is helpful to have an English language libretto, and in some cases it is virtually essential for understanding the work. You will find information about the libretto or synopsis following the name of the conductor.

Comments about the performance and sound quality appear in parentheses at the conclusion of each entry. Individual critical evaluations are, of course, never absolute and can vary widely from one person to the next, but I have tried to be as objective as possible and also to take into consideration the views of other commentators. In a few cases where I felt it would be helpful, I have mentioned recordings that I have not actually heard, always with a comment to that effect.

When I have been able to locate information about what appears to be an acceptable video VHS or DVD recording, that information is included at the end of the entry. Most of these videos, however, I have not personally reviewed. I do have reservations about operatic videos (as discussed in the Preface), but many library patrons appreciate the opportunity to see and not just to hear the opera.

Bela Bartók (1881–1945)

Duke Bluebeard's Castle (1918)

Forget your Perrault fairy tale. *Duke Bluebeard's Castle* is not a bedtime story for the nursery. It is, rather, an interior drama expressed in music of great power and sensitivity. The spoken prologue, usually omitted in recordings, asks the important question: Just where is the action on the stage happening? Is it within or without? The truth is that very little happens in the opera "without." Duke Bluebeard brings his new wife, Judith, to his castle, and at her insistence, permits her to open seven locked doors. That's about it. A great deal, however, takes place within Duke Bluebeard himself, and if we enter into the experience with him, we will find that the action may well occur within ourselves as well.

There are many ways of explaining *Duke Bluebeard's Castle*. They all no doubt have a measure of validity to them. Are we confronted here with the tragedy of rejected love? Or is it the loneliness of a life unable or unwilling to open itself to others? Are Bluebeard and Judith a kind of everyman and everywoman inviting us, warning us perhaps, to consider carefully the risks of relationship? Or do the composer and librettist urge us to accept the inevitability of, failure? These are among the issues Bartók's only opera asks us to consider.

The music is challenging for the listener, but not forbidding. Bartók understood the voice and wrote well for the vocalists. There is a strain of lyricism that runs through the opera and that demands singing that is secure and beautiful in tone. Bartók was also a master of expressive orchestration, and much of the interior action takes place in the instruments. The conductor and the orchestra are as much characters in the opera as Judith and Bluebeard are.

Duke Bluebeard's Castle has been often recorded, at least twelve versions since the first recording appeared in 1955. Each of them has something to offer to the listener, but given the colorful orchestral palette that Bartók employed, a modern stereo recording has distinct advantages. To the two versions listed here, you may want to add a recent recording on EMI 65162 which I have not heard. It has been highly praised by a number of critics.

(1965) Decca/London 466377, with Walter Berry, Christa Ludwig, London Symphony Orchestra, István Kertész, Conductor. English language libretto. (Berry and Ludwig are both in top form, vocally secure and highly dramatic. Berry's voice is unusually dark and powerful. It is good to have a genuine Hungarian conductor in this very Hungarian opera. The digitally remastered stereo sound is rich and full. The text of the spoken Prologue is helpfully included in the printed libretto.)

(1976) Sony 64110, with Siegmund Nimsgern, Tatiana Troyanos, BBC Symphony Orchestra, Pierre Boulez, Conductor. English language libretto. (Nimsgern is a gentler Bluebeard than Berry, an interesting alternative to the more forceful approach. Troyanos, a superb artist who unfortunately recorded far too little, demonstrates vocal and dramatic gifts beyond the ordinary. The recorded sound is clearly defined and brilliant. The libretto does not include the Prologue. Both performances are excellent, but I prefer the Decca/London version.)

Duke Bluebeard's Castle is available with Sylvia Sass and Kolos Kovats on VHS from Polygram/London.

Ludwig van Beethoven (1770–1827)

Fidelio (1805; 1806; 1814)

The three premiere dates for *Fidelio* are an indication of the difficulty Beethoven had with his opera. The original production was not a success and lasted but three performances. The revised version four months later was more successful, but Beethoven withdrew it after two performances, apparently because of disagreements with the director of the theater. The two earlier versions are usually referred to as *Leonore*. A further, much more extensive revision led to the 1814 *Fidelio,* the one that we hear most often today. Beethoven not only revised the opera, he also composed four different overtures, one of which — Leonore No. 1 — was written for a proposed 1807 performance in Prague which never took place. (The overture known as Leonore No. 2 was composed for the 1805 version; Leonore No. 3 for 1806; the Fidelio overture for 1814.)

Fidelio holds a special place in the operatic repertoire. It is usually approached with considerably more reverence than most other operas, in part because of the highly serious nature of much of the music and action, but also, I suspect, because Beethoven is by reputation the representative classical composer and this is his only opera. He toyed with other ideas from time to time, among them *Faust* and *Macbeth,* but none of them came to fruition. With *Fidelio,* however, he produced one of the crowning masterpieces of all opera.

The famous conductor Arturo Toscanini broadcast *Fidelio* on successive Sunday afternoons, December 10 and 17, 1944, while in Europe the "Battle of the Bulge" was beginning. Beethoven's opera celebrating the triumph of unwavering faithfulness over the force of tyranny was an appropriate and inspiring choice as we moved toward the concluding days of World War II. The Toscanini broadcast was preserved and is still available (BMG/RCA 60273). As one would expect, it is a propulsive, dramatic performance, with a particularly moving Leonore in Rose Bampton, a soprano too little recorded. Although Toscanini's recording is an important historical document, and the score is beautifully performed, the opera suffers because there is no spoken dialogue and, as a result no sense of dramatic continuity.

Many of the great conductors have committed their interpretations to disc, and I know of no recording that does not offer something of value. I, however, can vouch personally for the quality of those listed in the recommendations. One of the three modern stereo performances of the final version will certainly be the first choice for the collection, but just in case someone wants to search a little deeper into the development of *Fidelio*, I have listed as well recordings of the 1805 and 1806 versions.

(1962) EMI 67361, with Christa Ludwig, Jon Vickers, Ingeborg Hallstein, Gerhard Unger, Walter Berry, Gottlob Frick, Philharmonia Chorus and Orchestra, Otto Klemperer, Conductor. English language libretto. (This legendary performance with an escellent cast of singers is brilliantly conducted by Klemperer. Christa Ludwig is outstanding as Leonore, and Jon Vickers finds more psychological depth in Florestan than any other tenor in the recordings. The digitally remastered sound is excellent.)

(1994) Teldec or Elektra/Asylum 94560, with Charlotte Margiono, Peter Seiffert, Barbara Bonney, Deon van der Walt, Sergei Leiferkus, László Polgár, Arnold Schoenberg Choir, Chamber Orchestra of Europe, Nikolaus Harnoncourt, Conductor. English language libretto. (On the whole, these are not singers with heroic voices, but they sing well and present a more intimate view of the opera than we usually encounter. Harnoncourt is the excellent conductor. Although no one will choose a recording of Fidelio on the merits of the Marzelline, it's worth noting that Barbara Bonney is simply as good as they get.)

(1998) Naxos 8660070–71, with Inga Nielsen, Gösta Winbergh, Edith Lienbacher, Herwig Pecoraro, Alan Titus, Kurt Moll, Hungarian Radio Chorus, Nicolaus Esterházy Sinfonia, Michael Halász, Conductor. Libretto in German only. (With the exception of Kurt Moll, who is a first rate Rocco, this cast is not world famous. Windbergh and Nielsen, however, are quite good, and Alan Titus sounds uncommonly villainous as Don Pizarro. If budgetary constraints are an issue, this recording can help. It costs almost half as much as the others.)

(1996) *Leonore,* 1805 version, Deutsche Garmmophon Archiv 453461, with Hillevi Martinpelto, Kim Begley, Christiane Oelza, Michael Schade, Matthew Best, Franz Hawlata, Monteverdi Choir, Orchestre Révolutionnaire et Romantique, John Eliot Gardiner, Conductor. English language libretto. (The conductor is top drawer. The singers respond enthusiastically and sing well. The orchestra is noted for performance on authentic nineteenth century instruments or their equivalents. The only drawback here is the use of a narrator rather than the original dialogue.)

(1997) *Leonore,*1806 version, MDG Gold 3370826, with Pamela Coburn, Mark Baker, Christine Neithardt-Barbaux, Benedikt Kobel, Jean-Philippe Lafont, Victor von Halem, Kölner Rundfunkchor, Orchester der Beethovenhalle Bonn, Marc Soustrot, Conductor. English language libretto. (The value of this recording is not so much in the performance, which is acceptable but not outstanding, as in the opportunity to hear the 1806 version, which had never been previously recorded.)

Fidelio is available with Gabriela Beňačková and Joseph Protschka on DVD and VHS from Image.

Vincenzo Bellini (1801–1835)

Norma (1831)

Compared to many equally famous operas, *Norma* has only rarely found its way onto disc. The reason is not difficult to ascertain. The title role is one that challenges the most gifted sopranos, many of whom have fallen victim to its difficulties. *Norma* requires of its heroine intense dramatic conviction, superb vocal technique, and a voice that can ride the climaxes triumphantly. It is a combination not often achieved.

In the second half of the twentieth century, at least two singers met the challenge with success, Maria Callas and Joan Sutherland, although they did not bring to it precisely the same gifts. Callas found in *Norma* a psychological depth and emotional power that evaded Sutherland, but Sutherland clearly had the more even, better balanced vocal equipment, and she's never caught straining or wobbling on a high note. The critics will go right on debating the relative virtues and failures of the two, but true opera lovers will rejoice that we can enjoy both.

Each of the recommended recordings has much to offer. In general, however, both sopranos are in better voice in the earlier performances. If you can only have one *Norma,* opt for the 1984 Decca/London recording, but be aware that no true opera lover will be satisfied without at least one of the Callas performances.

(1954) EMI 56271, with Maria Callas, Ebe Stignani, Mario Filippeschi, Nicola Rossi-Lemeni, La Scala Chorus and Orchestra, Tullio Serafin, Conductor. English language libretto. (This is, of course, a monophonic recording, and the other members of the cast are not in Callas' class, although Stignani, who had been singing professionally for almost thirty years when this recording was made, can still remind us that she was the great Italian mezzo-soprano of her time. This is one of the recordings that established Callas as a reigning prima donna.)

(1960) EMI 66428, with Maria Callas, Christa Ludwig, Franco Corelli, Nicola Zaccaria, La Scala Chorus and Orchestra, Tullio Serafin, Conductor. English language libretto. (Christa Ludwig doesn't sound like an Italian mezzo, but she is an accomplished vocalist. Zaccaria and Corelli are vocally impressive, but Corelli is hardly a true bel canto stylist. Callas was vocally more secure in the 1954 version, but there is evidence of dramatic and psychological growth in this later recording. It also has the advantage of good stereo sound.)

(1964) Decca 25488, with Joan Sutherland, Marilyn Horne, John Alexander, Richard Cross, London Symphony Chorus and Orchestra, Richard Bonynge, Conductor. English language libretto. (Unlike the Callas recordings, Bonynge has opened almost all of the traditional cuts and Sutherland sings the famous "Casta diva" in the higher original key. The spectacular duets with Marilyn Horne are an outstanding feature of this recording. John Alexander and Richard Cross are both outclassed by the ladies, but they are accomplished artists, and it is particularly good to have Alexander, who recorded very little, in a complete role.)

(1984) Decca 14426, with Joan Sutherland, Montserrat Caballe, Luciano Pavarotti, Samuel Ramey, Welsh National Opera Chorus and Orchestra, Richard Bonynge, Conductor. English language libretto. (Sutherland is less fresh of voice than twenty years earlier, but the supporting cast is notable. Caballe, who also performed and

recorded the title role, is the only soprano Adalgisa on any of the four recommended recordings. Bellini would probably have approved. Pavarotti and Ramey are vocally commendable.)

Norma is available with Joan Sutherland and Tatiana Troyanos on DVD from VAI, and with Sutherland and Margreta Elkins on VHS from Kultur.

I Puritani (1835)

Some operas survive in spite of their libretti. *Puritani* is one of them. The plot is so convoluted and confusing that it makes *Finnegans Wake* read like a first-grade primer, what with Puritan and Cavalier sentiments colliding all over the place, and Elvira, the heroine, slipping in and out of sanity on the slightest excuse. If ever an opera was saved by its music, *Puritani* is the prime example.

Saved by its music? Well, yes, but when it succeeds on stage or on disc it is also saved by its singers. *I Puritani* with a substandard cast can be a dismal affair indeed, but we are fortunate to have good recordings that do justice to Bellini's musical inspiration.

As is so often true with these Italian operas of the early nineteenth century, we find both the Maria Callas and the Joan Sutherland versions. Unlike Bellini's *Norma*, however, *Puritani* cannot be carried to success by the soprano alone. It also provides important parts for baritone and bass, and one of the great bel canto tenor roles. The original cast of the 1835 premiere included Giulia Grisi, Giovanni Battista Rubini, Antonio Tamburini, and Luigi Lablache, four famous vocalists who soon became known collectively as the "*Puritani* Quartet," no doubt the popular nineteenth century version of today's "Three Tenors." Modern tenors are at a serious disadvantage since the score calls for a high "F," a note well outside the normal range of our latter day tenors. Rubini would surely have sung the note in what we know as the falsetto voice, but that produces a sound that contemporary audiences usually find either painful or exotic. Needless to say, most twentieth-century tenors avoid the note altogether.

In addition to the three recordings listed here, three other versions of the opera have been or are now available on commercial issues. The version on EMI, with Riccardo Muti as conductor, and Montserrat Caballe and Alfredo Kraus heading the cast, sticks to the score precisely as Bellini wrote it, no added cadenzas or interpolated high notes. The idea may sound wonderfully authentic, but it probably violates Bellini's own understanding of how the opera should be performed. A recent issue, which I have not been able to hear, features Edita Gruberova, an outstanding soprano, with decidedly lesser lights in the other major roles. It was apparently recorded at a live concert and is available on Nightingale 70562, and the version with Beverly Sills and Nicolai Gedda has been reissued on Universal 471207.

(1953) EMI 56275, with Maria Callas, Giuseppe di Stefano, Rolando Panerai, Nicola Rossi-Lemeni, La Scala Chorus and Orchestra, Tullio La Serafin, Conductor. English language libretto. (Callas makes Elvira believable, almost as if Freud had collaborated with Bellini and his librettist. The other cast members, including di Stefano in his dramatically involved performance, are solid Italian vocalists, even if a little bit shy of the *bel canto* ideal. The performance on this monophonic recording is severely cut.)

(1974) Decca 17588, with Joan Sutherland, Luciano Pavarotti, Piero Cappuccilli, Nicolai Ghiaurov, chorus of the Royal Opera House, London Symphony Orchestra, Richard Bonynge, Conductor. English language libretto. (This issue may be difficult to locate, but even if it is unavailable at the moment, it is bound to reappear soon. The recording is as truly complete as a *Puritani* recording can be, and the overall casting,

from Sutherland's very high top notes to Ghiaurov's low ones, is the best available. Sutherland was not the keen vocal actress that Callas was, but she is vocally superior. The overall excellence and the complete score make this the preferred recording.)

La Sonnambula (1831)

Bel canto is a term often used incautiously to mean any singing that happens to sound good; and, of course, a literal translation from the Italian is simply "beautiful singing." As a technical term, however, it refers properly to a style of singing developed primarily in Italy in the eighteenth century and carried over into the operas of the nineteenth century.

The true "*bel cantist*" will demonstrate a beautiful, even tone, with no conspicuous gear-shifting to move from the top to the bottom of the vocal range; the skill and training to handle intricate vocal ornamentation, including rapid scales and runs, pinpoint staccatos, and clearly articulated trills; and the artistic and dramatic sensitivity to sing in immaculate style with true dramatic conviction. *Bel canto* is the type of singing demanded particularly in the operas of Rossini, Donizetti, and Bellini.

For many listeners, *Sonnambula* is the opera that defines *bel canto*. Listen particularly to an outstanding performance of Amina's last act aria, "Ah! non credea mirarti," and its cabaletta (the more rapid closing sectsion), "Ah! Non giunge," and the meaning of the term is communicated far better than in mere words. The voice must be absolutely steady to stay afloat with the most meager orchestral support, able to swim without drowning in the coloratura complexities, and aware enough dramatically to communicate the sleepwalker's profound sorrow and the contrasting joy when she awakens at the call of her faithful lover.

We should hardly be surprised to find recordings by both Maria Callas and Joan Sutherland. For both sopranos, the *bel canto* repertoire was their initial claim to worldwide fame. To their recordings, however, we can in this case add a third performance to our recommendations, and that on a budget-priced label. I wish I could conscientiously recommend the old Fonit-Cetra issue from 1952, but it has long been unavailable in the United States. I cherish it for the lovable, even if not precisely perfect, singing of Lina Pagliughi, Ferruccio Tagliavini, and Cesare Siepi. It just might turn up from one of the dealers who specialize in either imports or used recordings.

(1957) EMI 56278, with Maria Callas, Nicola Monti, Nicola Zaccaria, La Scala Chorus and Orchestra, Antonio Vollo, Conductor. English language libretto. (Callas was a mistress of bel canto, although she certainly did not have the even, untroubled tone production of Sutherland. Stylistically, however, she knew how to understand dramatic situations and to color her voice to reflect her knowledge, and she was a mistress of coloratura technique. This monophonic performance is seriously cut, and her colleagues are not on her level. Her performance in this role is also available as recorded in a number of live stage performances. For general listening, however, this studio version, at least as I remember it from the old long-playing issue, is easier on the ears.)

(1980) Decca 17424, with Joan Sutherland, Luciano Pavarotti, Nicolai Ghiaurov, London Opera Chorus, National Philharmonic, Richard Bonynge, Conductor. English language libretto. (This recording replaces an earlier Sutherland 1962 issue. She may not provide the dramatic involvement of Callas, but the voice is the real thing, and the *bel canto* graces are never skirted. Her colleagues, particularly the excellent Pavarotti, help to make this the recording of choice. I have not heard the compact disc reissue and base my comments on the original long-playing version.)

(1992) Naxos 8.660042–43, with Luba Orgonasova, Raúl Giménez, Francesco Ellero D'Artegna, Netherlands Radio Chamber Orchestra, Netherlands Radio Choir, Alberto Zedda, Conductor. Italian language libretto only. (This recording on the budget Naxos label offers an impressive soprano with somewhat less impressive colleagues. Orgonasova, however, is a gifted singer and artist, and if cost is an issue, this performance represents Bellini in a respectable manner. One word of warning: it was recorded live at a concert. Audience applause is included, but when Orgonasova sings, the listener may want to join in.)

Alban Berg (1885–1935)

Lulu (1937; 1979)

Lulu is not for the easily offended. The plot, drawn by Berg from a pair of plays by Frank Wedekind, tells a thoroughly unsavory story of unbridled sexuality and its dire results among a group of people who are hardly models of conventional morality. What's more, they are not pleasant or amusing people, and Lulu herself must surely be the most destructive and morally reprehensible character in all of musical theater. I surely do not have the answer, but my guess is that the meaning of *Lulu* is concealed in the music, not in the plot or the characters that inhabit it.

That music is fascinating in and of itself. The score is composed throughout according to the dodecaphonic (twelve-tone) system, and it employs a series of formal structural features. According to Andrew Clements in *The New Grove Dictionary of Opera*, "the first two acts are dominated by the sonata and rondo structures respectively, the third by the theme and variations that first appear in its orchestral interlude."* The vocal parts are designed to be sung in that special cross between song and speech known variously as *Sprechgesang* or *Sprechstimme* (the terms are interchangeable). Berg, however, surprises us by using the clashing harmonies and the absence of

---

*Andrew Clements, "Lulu (ii)," in *The New Grove Dictionary of Opera*, ed. Stanley Sadie, III. 96.

traditional melodic patterns in such a way that we hear real music — not just technically and intellectually interesting music, but music of beauty and emotional depth. Whatever else the opera does, it clearly demonstrates the power of music to address and illuminate the most unlikely subject matter, and perhaps even to transcend it. I hear in *Lulu* the composer's mighty hymn in praise of the art that he practices.

Berg died in 1935 before completing the final act of the opera. The entire act, however, had been sketched out in short score and at least a portion had been orchestrated. In 1937 the opera was performed in a version that included only the music that Berg had himself completed. In her will, the composer's widow refused permission for the completion of Act III, but Friedrich Cerha continued to work at the project. Following a legal battle with the Alban Berg Foundation, the full three-act *Lulu* was performed in Paris in 1979. The cast of that performance committed the opera to disc, and that is the recording recommended here. I have not heard a more recent version available on Chandos 9540, but it has received favorable reviews.

(1979) Teresa Stratas, Deutsche Grammophon 463 617, Yvonne Minton, Toni Blankenheim, Robert Tear, Franz Mazura, Hanna Schwarz, Kenneth Riegel, Orchestra of the Opéra de Paris, Pierre Boulez, Condcutor. English language libretto. (The good original recording has been digitally remastered. The performance of this complex score is excellent. The cast manages their difficult assignments with great credit, and Teresa Stratas is outstanding in one of the most demanding of all roles for soprano. It is probably her best recorded performance.)

Wozzeck (1925)

Each scene of Berg's *Wozzeck* has its own predetermined musical form — pasacaglia, sonata, fantasia and fugue, invention on a note, scherzo with two trios. Submit

the score to a detailed technical analysis, and we may decide that such a formal structure is bound to produce a cold and forbidding opera. Nothing, however, could be further from the truth. For many listeners, *Wozzeck* is one of the most musically satisfying and emotionally moving operas in the entire repertoire.

We have a central character, Wozzeck himself, who, for all of his intellectual and moral failure, still touches the heart. He is a soldier at the very bottom of the military system. He is poor. He is subjected to absurd medical experiments by a frustrated physician. He is treated as an object of humorous contempt by his commanding officer. He is defeated in a fight with the Drum Major, his successful rival for the affection of Marie, Wozzeck's lover and the mother of his child. He is also the perfect operatic embodiment of every person who has ever felt alone, excluded, defeated; and Berg's music helps us to sympathize with him and, beyond that, to sympathize with all the poor, defenseless people of the world. In performance, *Wozzeck* can become an intensely humanizing experience for the audience.

It can also be a difficult experience. The music does not fall easily on the ear. The orchestra sometimes whines and grates, and the vocalists are instructed to vary between true singing, talking, and that half-song and half-speech form known as *Sprechstimme* or *Sprechgesang*. Good recordings (and there have been several) do not soften the effect. The two listed here convey the full musical impact of Berg's score, but they also enable us to enter fully into the emotionally charged world of the opera.

(1994) Teldec or Elektra/Asylum 14108, with Franz Grundheber, Waltraud Meier, Mark Baker, Graham Clark, Günter von Kannen, Siegfried Vogel, Chorus and Children's Chorus of the Deutschen Staatsopera Berlin, Staatskapelle Berlin, Daniel Barenboim, Conductor. English language libretto. (For a fair sample of Barenboim's conducting, listen to the emotional impact of the interlude before the final scene. Grundheber is a veteran of many performances of *Wozzek*, and his experience produces a convincing performance. Waltraud Meier sings extremely well and conveys the conflicting emotions effectively, particularly in the Bible reading scene. The recording quality is quite good, but it was made during a live performance and there is a great deal of stage noise.)

(1998) EMI 56865,with Bo Skovhus, Angela Denoke, Jan Blinkhof, Chris Merritt, Frode Olsen, Chorus of the Hamburg State Opera, Hamburg State Philharmonic, Ingo Metzmacher, Conductor. English language libretto. (Without softening the contours of this rugged opera, Metzmacher manages to find some gentleness in the score. The most outstanding performance is given by Angela Denoke, who communicates the conflicting emotions of Marie without distorting her beautiful voice. To a great extent, this is also the case with Skovhus. Other roles are quite well taken. This recording was also made during live performances, but there is less distraction from stage noise than in the Teldec version. By a narrow margin, this seems to me the better choice between the two recordings.)

Wozzeck is available with Philip Langridge, Franz Grundheber, and Hildegard Behrens on DVD from Image, and on VHS from Kultur.

Hector Berlioz (1803–1869)

Les Troyens (Acts 3–5, 1863; Complete, 1890)

Berlioz's opera once bore the stigma of being "unstageable." Its length seemed daunting for musicians and audiences, the orchestral and choral forces well beyond the capacities of all but the wealthiest opera companies, and the scenic demands almost impossible. When Berlioz died in 1869, he still had not seen a production of the complete *Troyens*. Even after performances in Karlsruhe in 1890, the opera as a whole languished until 1957, when Covent Garden presented a distinguished version of the entire work and demonstrated its viability in the opera house.

It is indeed a long opera, approximately four hours without taking intermissions into consideration, but Wagner's *Meistersinger* and *Götterdämerung* are even longer. Perhaps it is the epic scope of *Troyens*—encompassing the fall of Troy, the tragic love of Dido and Aeneas, and the vision of the eternal Rome—that makes it seem longer. In one sense, as much happens dramatically and musically in Berlioz's four hours as in the fourteen plus hours of Wagner's mighty *Ring des Nibelungen*.

There have been three important recordings of *Troyens*, in addition to a number of unofficial versions of various live performances. Colin Davis recorded the entire opera in 1969, a groundbreaking performance that introduced *Troyens* to the public beyond the opera houses. That recording was available on Philips 412 432–2 but is not currently listed in the domestic catalogues. For many years, Davis has been the great champion of *Troyens* and Berlioz's music in general, and his performances are as close to definitive as any recordings can possibly be. Fortunately, he has committed *Troyens* to disc a second time. That recording and the other one recommended here preserve worthy performances that would be an asset to any collection of operatic music.

(1993) Decca/London 43 693, with Françoise Pollet, Deborah Voigt, Gary Lakes, Gino Quilico, Montreal Chorus and Symphony Orchestra, Charles Dutoit, Conductor. English language libretto. (This excellent performance employs a gifted cast and has in Dutoit a conductor who understands the drama of this score fully. He tends to favor faster tempos than Davis, so that the total timing is virtually the same with the two conductors, although Dutoit adds two relatively brief passages that were not intended by Berlioz for inclusion in complete performances.)

(2000) London Symphony Orchestra 0010, with Petra Lang, Michelle DeYoung, Ben Heppner, Peter Mattei, London Symphony Chorus and Orchestra, Colin Davis, Conductor. An English language libretto is included. (Here is another first-rate performance, beautifully recorded and conducted. On the whole, it is an improvement on Davis' first recording of *Troyens*, which was also an outstanding achievement. All of the cast sing well, and Ben Hepner is particularly impressive and in control of his voice at all dynamic levels. At almost half the price of the Decca/London recording, this makes a wise first choice, both economically and artistically.)

Les Troyens is available with Plácido Domingo and Jessye Norman on DVD from Pioneer and on VHS from Paramount.

Georges Bizet (1838–1875)

Carmen (1875)

A case can be made for *Carmen* as the most popular opera in the world, although *Bohème* and *Aida* are also in the running. In any case, having long ago replaced *Faust* in the public eye, it is certainly the current crown jewel of French opera. Some critics call it "the perfect opera." Frankly, I'm not certain what the perfect opera would sound and look like, but *Carmen* is a remarkable masterpiece and truly deserves all of the favor it can garner.

It is also something of a problematic work. For many years it was regularly performed with recitatives composed a few month's after Bizet's death by Ernst Guiraud. The original version, however, was an *opéra comique* — that is, not a comic opera but an opera with spoken dialogue instead of recitatives. The score itself has been subject to additions and deletions, largely centering on the music that Bizet himself omitted from the first published edition. Adding to the confusion is the ambiguous nature of the title role, which may be sung effectively

by either a mezzo-soprano or a soprano, and, as singers have long demonstrated, may be subject to a wide variety of personal interpretations. The questions, then, that any company staging or recording *Carmen* must face are how to perform it, by whom, and with what selection of the available music.

Great Carmens of the past included sopranos Emma Calvé (whose roles rose to such high flying specialties as Ophelia in Thomas' *Hamlet*) and Emmy Destinn (who was an eloquent Aida and Butterfly, and the heroine of a more or less complete *Carmen* recorded in 1908), and, more recently, Risë Stevens, a genuine American mezzo-soprano, who for a number of years made Carmen virtually her own at the Metropolitan Opera. The recordings recommended here are evenly divided, two sopranos and two mezzo-sopranos.

(1958–59) EMI 67353, with Victoria de los Angeles, Janine Micheau, Nicolai Gedda, Ernest Blanc, Chorus and Orchestre National de la RTF, Thomas Beecham, Conductor. English language libretto. (Notice here and in the other recordings listed how few honest-to-goodness French singers appear, a comment no doubt on the absence of many truly fine French operatic voices in the last forty years or so. This recording, however, in spite of a Spanish soprano, a Swedish tenor, and a British conductor, reflects French tradition more than the others. The touch is somehow lighter, a characteristic both of de los Angeles' Carmen and Beecham's conducting. It, however, is not without its share of drama. The Guiraud recitatives are used.)

(1964) EMI 56281, with Maria Callas, Andrea Guiot, Nicolai Gedda, Robert Massard, René Duclos Chorus, Paris Opera Orchestra, Georges Prêtre, Conductor. (This is assuredly the most controversial of the *Carmen* recordings, largely because of Maria Callas, who never sang the role on stage. She has a highly individual view of the dignity, the mystery, but also the humor of the character. The other members of the cast are entirely acceptable, but this is a recording to select after you have one more traditional performance. The Guiraud recitatives are used.)

(1975) Decca 14489, with Tatiana Troyanos, Kiri Te Kanawa, Plácido Domingo, José van Dam, John Alldis Choir, London Philharmonic Orchestra, Georg Solti, Conductor. (*Carmen* is here given a most distinguished cast and conductor. It is not the most dramatic performance, but from the purely vocal standpoint this is probably the recording to choose first. Troyanos' Carmen is outstanding. Spoken dialogue, rather than the Guiraud recitatives, is used.)

(1977–78) Deutsche Grammophon 19636, with Teresa Berganza, Ileana Cotrubas, Plácido Domingo, Sherrill Milnes, Ambrosian Singers, London Symphony Orchestra, Claudio Abbado, Conductor. (Again with the spoken dialogue, this too is a lushly cast performance. For many, myself included, Berganza is the most persuasive Carmen in all of the complete recordings. Her voice is beautiful and her interpretation, exciting but also suggesting the dignity of the character, is convincing.)

Carmen is available with Julia Migenes and Plácido Domingo on VHS and DVD from Columbia/Tri-Star.

Les Pêcheurs de Perles (1863)

Orientalism was a major trend in European (particularly, but not exclusively, French) music and art during the nineteenth century. It will come as no surprise then that Bizet's *Pêcheurs de Perles* is set in exotic Ceylon. The composer creates his own, distinctively French brand of exoticism in music filled with beautiful melodies, and generally does it better than his nineteenth century French colleagues.

Les Pêcheurs, like Bizet's *Carmen,* has suffered much over the years at hands other than the composer's. A variety of changes were made and incorporated into the printed editions, and it was not until 1975 that an accurate score was available. In addition to alterations in the plot and music of the concluding scene, music by other composers was inserted (one duet, "O lumière sainte," became a trio composed by Benjamin Godard), and the original ending of the famous duet for tenor and baritone, "Au fond du temple saint," was replaced with a reprise of the familiar soaring melody heard earlier.

Recordings prior to 1975 obviously encountered insurmountable problems in any attempt to present what Bizet himself actually composed, simply because correct performing materials were not available. For the sake of authenticity, you should certainly choose one of the final two recommendations. Unfortunately, if you want the best of French singing, you will either acquire two recordings or sacrifice historical accuracy in favor of vocal beauty, but given the budget price of the Gala issue, for just a few overdue fines you can have both.

(1953) Philips 462 287–2, with Léopold Simoneau, Pierette Alarie, René Bianco, Xavier Depraz, Elisabeth Brasseur Chorus, Orchestre des Concert Lamoureux, Jean Fournet, Conductor. No libretto; only a synopsis. (Simoneau is the glory of this recording. This is what a French tenor, albeit a French Canadian in this case, should be and all too rarely is. Pierette Alarie, his wife, was much underrated, and gives a sterling performance here.)

(1959) Gala GL 100.504, with Jeanine Micheau, Alain Vanzo, Gabriel Bacquier, Lucien Lovano, Chorus of RTF, Orchestre Radio-Lyrique, Manuel Rosenthal, Conductor. No libretto; only a brief synopsis. (Gala is a budget label that specializes in issuing "live" performances, and this recording, which has appeared on other labels in the past, is from a radio broadcast in 1959. You shouldn't expect digital stereo recording, but you may be surprised with just how good the sound actually is. The cast is excellent and fully in tune with the French idiom in language and style. This performance, unlike her studio recordings, allows us an opportunity to hear Micheau at her best. Bonus tracks give us Vanzo's performances of seven arias and duets from other French language works.)

(1960) EMI 69704, with Nicolai Gedda, Jeanine Micheau, Ernest Blanc, Jacques Mars, Chorus and Orchestra of the Théâtre National de l'Opéra Comique, Pierre Dervaux, Conductor. French language libretto only. (This is not an exciting recording vocally or dramatically, in spite of the technically assured singing of Gedda and Blanc. It, however, includes approximately forty-five minutes from Bizet's *almost* completed opera *Ivan IV*.)

(1977) EMI CFP 4721, with Alain Vanzo, Ileana Cotrubas, Guillermo Sarabia, Roger Soyer, Orchestra and Chorus of the Paris Opera, Georges Prêtre, Conductor. No libretto; synopsis only. (This recording is the first to use the authentic edition of the score. Listeners who know only the famous duet for Tenor and Baritone will be disappointed to discover Bizet's own conclusion to it, which isn't half as much fun as the corrupt version. Vanzo and Cotrubas sing well, but this performance misses some of the dramatic excitement in the score.)

(1989) EMI 49837, with John Aler, Barbara Hendricks, Gino Quilico, Jean-Philippe Courtis, Chorus and Orchestra of the Théâtre du Capitole, Toulouse, Michel Plasson, Conductor. English language libretto. (I have not heard this recording and can only report that the critical reception has been mixed. On the whole, this is a cast of young singers with perhaps somewhat lighter voices than in the other recordings. I understand that the conductor opts for the traditional, rather than the authentic conclusion to the famous duet but includes the original version in an appendix, no doubt for the sake of authenticity.)

Alexander Borodin (1833–1887)

Prince Igor (1890)

When Borodin died in 1887, he left an accumulated operatic manuscript on which he had worked since 1869, some portions completed and orchestrated and others existing merely as sketches. Borodin, after all, was a distinguished scientist and pro-fessor at the Medical-Surgical Academy, and he could hardly afford the luxury of pursuing musical composition on a full-time basis. The monumental task of shaping from this material the opera we know as *Prince Igor* fell to his friend, Nicolai Rimsky-Korsakov, and to Rimsky's young student, Alexander Glazunov. Given the quality of Borodin's musical imagination, it was a task well worth undertaking.

It is only fair to say that without Rimsky and Glazunov, or some other equally committed musicians, the music would have been lost to us and we would have no *Prince Igor* today. They omitted a large portion of music, and orchestrated and completed other sections; and Glazunov, using only Borodin's fragmentary notes and sketches, composed Act III and perhaps also the Overture. By its very nature, their work was bound to stir up controversy, and other musicologists and composers have tried their hand at completing *Prince Igor* in the years since Rimsky and Glazunov. The attempt to put together the best possible musical and dramatic work will no doubt continue, probably with no foreseeable conclusion.

On the whole, *Prince Igor* has not fared well in recordings. It is an intrinsically Russian opera, and it works best when the casts are Slavic, either by birth or by vocal personality. The music demands at least six highly accomplished singers, covering the full vocal range from high soprano to low bass, and all too often the recordings have tried to get by with one or two.

The two important bass roles, Galtsky and Konchak, call for the sonority and the stylistic assurance of excellent Russian singers or their vocal and dramatic relatives. One of the best was Boris Christoff, although Bulgarian by birth, who performed both roles spectacularly in the same recording. Unfortunately, Christoff is virtually the only saving grace in this recording (EMI 63386, recently reissued), and it is ruled out of court, as are some others, because it omits Act III. Even though that section of the opera was largely the work of Glazunov, without it the already tenuous dramatic continuity is virtually destroyed. The single recording recommended here boasts a good all-around Russian cast, with excellent reproduction and conducting.

(1993) Philips 442 537–2, with Mikhail Kit, Galina Gorchakova, Gegam Grigorian, Vladimir Ognovienko, Bulat Minjelkiev, Olga Borodina, Kirov Chorus and Orchestra, St. Petersburg, Valery Gergiev, Conductor. English language libretto. (Gergiev uses a new performing edition of the score drawn from Borodin, Rimsky, and Glazunov, with some additions by Yuri Faliek. We can generally depend on good vocalism from the basses and baritones in Russian recordings. Here, however, we have also a good tenor along with a soprano and mezzo-soprano who are of true international stature.)

Prince Igor is available with Yvgeni Nesterenko and Boris Khmelnitsky on VHS from Kultur.

Benjamin Britten (1913–1976)

Billy Budd (1951; 1964)

At the end of *Billy Budd*, Captain Vere sings his last line into a void. There is no instrumental accompaniment, no orchestral comment, only silence as the stage darkens and the curtain falls. There, in brief it seems to me, is the terrifying ambiguity of this opera. Vere has told us that, "the love that passes understanding has come to me ... my mind can go back in peace." But there is no musical confirmation, and we are left to ponder the ambiguity. Britten refuses to resolve it for us. That, by the way, is par for the course in this remarkably subtle work of art, as it is in Herman Melville's novelette of the same name, which served as its source.

It is that subtlety that the conductor

and the cast must appreciate. In staged performances and on disc, *Billy Budd* has often benefited from singers who are also at home in the recital hall and who, as a result, are keenly aware of the importance of the words. The cast, however, cannot depend on communicating the meanings and emotions of the text to carry them through this opera. They must also be able to sing and to sing quite well, with all of the old *bel canto* skills in the voice, and each of the three leading roles includes a major aria-like solo. We encounter singers of just the right type in both of the recommended recordings.

Billy Budd exists in two equally authentic versions, the original four-act opera of 1951, and Britten's two-act revision performed first on television in 1961 and in the opera house in 1964. The differences are actually relatively small, primarily the omission of a major scene at the end of the first act in which Captain Vere first appears on deck. Both versions are available in superb recordings, and the choice between them is largely a matter of personal taste. The four-act recording may have a slight edge simply because it includes more of Britten's music than the two-act version. On the other hand, the revision reflects Britten's final preference for the opera.

(1997) Erato or Elektra/Asylum 21631 (four-act version), with Thomas Hampson, Anthony Rolfe-Johnson, Eric Hallvarson, Manchester Boys Choir, Gentlemen of the Hallé Choir, Northern Voices, Hallé Orchestra, Kent Nagano, Conductor. English language libretto. (Hampson and Rolfe-Johnson are both excellent as Budd and Vere. Hampson particularly demonstrates the value of a truly beautiful voice in Britten's music. Hallvarson communicates Claggart's evil forcefully, but with somewhat less vocal security than Hampson and Rolfe-Johnson. Nagano's conducting is dramatic and sensitive, and the choral passages are extremely well done.)

(1999) Chandos 9826 (two-act version), with Simon Keenlyside, Philip Langridge,

John Tomlinson, London Symphony Chorus, Tiffin Boys' Choir, London Symphony Orchestra, Richard Hickox, Conductor. English language libretto. (This is probably the best cast ever assembled for *Billy Budd*, and the excellence extends to the smaller roles. Hickox is a dynamic conductor. Tomlinson as Claggart, a role perfectly embodied in his performance, is the epitome of evil; and Keenlyside, as his opposite, Billy, radiates youth and goodness.)

Billy Budd is available with Philip Langridge and Thomas Allen on DVD from Image and on VHS from Kultur.

A Midsummer Night's Dream (1960)

Shakespeare's *A Midsummer Night's Dream* would appear to have everything in its favor as the source for an opera. It is one of Shakespeare's most musical plays, with several songs indicated in the text and other lines that seem to call out for music. For the sake of musical variety, there are the three distinct groups of characters — members of the Athenian nobility, the fairies, and the "mechanicals," whom Britten prefers to call "rustics." There are opportunities for uninhibited comic scenes, love songs and duets, and ceremonial occasions, and just think of the challenge of elaborate musical ensembles as the different characters react to one another in a variety of dramatic combinations. A number of composers have accepted the challenge and written operas based on Shakespeare's play. The wonderful music that Henry Purcell composed for *The Fairy Queen* is frequently counted among them, but actually the five masques that he contributed have little to do with Shakespeare and set none of the bard's text. Mendelssohn's delightful score is actually incidental music for the play and not in any sense an opera. Only Benjamin Britten managed to make *A Midsummer Night's Dream* into a true opera that delighted the public and the critics, and continues to hold the stage.

The opera adheres closely to the poet's text. Although approximately one-half of the play is omitted, an inevitable result of setting spoken words to music, the composer and his colleague Peter Pears added only one explanatory line to the words that Shakespeare himself wrote. The music is highly inventive and often of great beauty, particularly the evocation of the supernatural world of the fairies, all of them high voices, with Oberon sung by a countertenor; his wife, Tytania, by a light soprano with coloratura technique at her command; and the attendant fairies by children's voices. The one exception is Puck, who speaks his lines in rhythmic patterns dictated by the composer. The other voices, those who are part of the "real" world, are typical sopranos, mezzo-sopranos, tenors, baritones, and basses.

Both of the recordings listed here offer good performances of the opera. The earlier of the two is recommended as a first choice primarily because it gives us the composer's own interpretation of the score, but it may be more difficult to locate.

(1966) Decca/London 25663, with Alfred Deller, Elizabeth Harwood, John Shirley-Quirk, Helen Watts, Peter Pears, Thomas Hemsley, Josephine Veasey, Heather Harper, Owen Brannigan, Choirs of Downside and Emanuel Schools, London Symphony Orchestra, Benjamin Britten, Conductor. English language libretto. (This version is noted for the atmospheric use of recorded sound to convey the tone and action of the different scenes. The very distinguished cast, with some of the finest British singers of the 1960s, was chosen by the composer. Apparently his preference for many of the roles was for lighter, less imposing voices than we hear in the later recording. They sing the often very difficult music extremely well and manage at the same time to characterize and act with their voices.)

(1995) Philips 54122, with Brian Asawa, Sylvia McNair, Brian Bannatyne Scott, Hilary Summers, John Mark Ainsley, Paul Whelan, Ruby Philogene, Janice Watson, Robert Lloyd, New London Children's

Choir, London Symphony Orchestra, Colin Davis, Conductor. English language libretto. (Davis conducts a lively, sensitive performance. The recorded sound is excellent, but so is that on the recording from 29 years earlier. Robert Lloyd as Bottom is outstanding, as is his counterpart in the other version, Owen Brannigan. Many listeners will prefer the absolutely clear, pure sound of Sylvia McNair's Tytania and the rounder, fuller countertenor of Brian Asawa as Oberon. On the whole, the earlier recording is preferable, but this is also a good performance and certainly an acceptable alternative if Britten's own recording is not available.)

A *Midsummer Night's Dream* is available with James Bowman and Ileana Cotrubas on VHS from Kultur.

Peter Grimes (1945)

Peter Grimes was the breakthrough opera for Benjamin Britten, the work that brought him to a broad public and opened the way for the series of operas that established him as the most important British operatic composer since Purcell. For many, it was the first convincing proof that opera had not died with Puccini's *Turandot*, and *Peter Grimes* has continued to hold its place in the repertoire in the years since its premiere.

Britten and his librettists began with a character from George Crabbe's 1810 poetical work *The Borough*. Crabbe, who was something of a literary realist and refused to sentimentalize rural life, presents the fisherman Peter Grimes as a cruel, villainous person who brutalizes, even murders his apprentices. In the opera, however, Britten invites us to see him if not precisely with sympathy, at least with understanding. For the composer, Grimes is the troubled, disturbed outsider so often encountered in modern art works, one who is isolated from a narrow, closed community, ultimately even from those who, like Ellen Oxford and Balstrode, seek to help him. "I live alone," Grimes sings. "The habit grows."

The mark of Britten's artistry is the skill with which he reveals to us the community and the man himself. He uses the chorus often and effectively to represent the people of the village. Grimes comes to us primarily through his monologues, as his moods change with lightning rapidity and he moves in and out of mental reality. As in all great opera, the drama is in the hands of the composer. The drama is in the music.

Both of the recordings listed here are excellent, beautifully recorded and penetrating in their interpretation of music and character. You will not go wrong with either of them, but the earlier one has the added authenticity of the composer himself as conductor.

(1958) Decca London 14577, with Peter Pears, Claire Watson, James Pease, Lauris Elms, Jean Watson, Owen Brannigan, Orchestra and Chorus of the Royal Opera House, Covent Garden, Benjamin Britten, Conductor. English language libretto. (The sound is typical of the good work London was doing in the early years of stereo, fully as effective as that in the version recorded twenty years later. All of the roles are well taken, with particularly impressive work in the smaller roles. Peter Pears was the original Peter Grimes and had sung the role many times. His voice sounds youthful, often quite gentle, with constant care taken to maintain a beautiful tone. The interpretation is subdued but effective, keenly aware of verbal meaning and clear diction.)

(1978) Philips 462847, with Jon Vickers, Heather Harper, Jonathan Summers, Elisabeth Bainbridge, Patricia Payne, Forbes Robinson, Chorus and Orchestra of the Royal Opera House, Covent Garden, Colin Davis, Conductor. No English language libretto; there is a synopsis. (The overall performance is often gripping, highly dramatic, and there are no significant weaknesses in the cast. Jon Vickers uses his heroic, somewhat unconventional tenor voice with incredible variety in dynamics. His interpretation is far more openly emotional than Peter Pears', and that effect may not be precisely what Britten had in mind. Vickers' final scene, however, is overwhelming, heartbreaking in its intensity. I recommend the earlier performance in order to have the composer's own interpretation, but I would never want to be without Vickers' recording.)

Peter Grimes is available with Philip Langridge and Janice Cairnes on VHS from Polygram/London.

Luigi Cherubini (1760–1842)

Medée (1797)

Although Italian by birth, from his twenty-fifth year until the end of his life fifty-six years later, Cherubini was essentially a French musician. He lived in France, taught and served as Director of the Conservatoire National de Musique, and composed eighteen operas for performance in Paris. He was not always popular with the public in France, but in Germany he was greatly appreciated. There he earned the respect of other composers, including Brahms, Bruckner, and Wagner, and was imitated to the point of flattery by even more.

Medée is the only one of his thirty-five operas to gain and hold a place in the repertoire. The libretto, based on the classic drama of Euripides, presented the composer with strong, psychologically convincing characters. Cherubini then clothed the text in music that is highly dramatic but also maintains a measure of French classical restraint. *Medée* cries out for singers who can maintain a clean musical line and at the same time convey the full impact of the drama and psychological conflict. They must also be able to sing the French language eloquently and speak it as well, since in its authentic form *Medée* is an *opera comique* with spoken dialogue. Recitatives were added by Franz Paul Lachner for German performances in 1854 and later translated into Italian.

The modern popularity of the opera began with performances by Maria Callas in 1953. Although she sang the corrupt Italian version with Lachner's recitatives, her assumption of the role was sensationally successful. Callas' Medea is well documented through a series of live recordings made between 1953 and her final appearance in the role in 1961. The language, of course, is wrong, but I believe Cherubini would have approved of the way she interprets the role, underlines the meaning of the words, and communicates the drama through the music.

Unfortunately, *Medée* (or *Medea* in Italian) has not had a distinguished history on disc. The two recordings listed here have serious drawbacks; and, of course, the Callas studio version does not represent the authentic French score.

(1957) EMI 66435, with Maria Callas, Miriam Pirazzini, Renata Scotto, Mirto Picchi, Giuseppe Modesti, Chorus and Orchestra of La Scala, Milna, Tullio Serafin, Conductor. English language libretto. (This early stereo studio recording, which I know only from its long-playing issue, is only moderately effective; and aside from Callas and Scotto, the cast has little to offer. Callas, however, could give lessons to singers in any language about how to use words and voice to communicate drama. From the purely vocal standpoint, she sings better on issues of live performances, of which there are usually four or five in the catalogue at any given time. I have enjoyed particularly the 1958 performance from Dallas on Gala 100521. The sound quality is poor, with strange balances between singers and orchestra, but Callas is excellent, vocally and dramatically, and she is surrounded by colleagues far superior to those in the studio recording.)

(1995) Nuova Era 7253, with Jano Tamar, Magali Damonte, Patrizia Ciofi, Luca Lombardo, Jean-Philippe Courtis, Chorus of the Camera Stuk di Bratislava, Orchestra Internazionale d'Italia Opera, Patrick Fournillier, Conductor. French libretto only. (This is a rough and ready performance, with plenty of drama and some rather wild vocalism to go along with it. Only Patrizia Ciofi as Dircé impresses, with neat passage work and honest-to-goodness trills in her first act aria. The recording was made from live stage performances, and there is a great deal of stage noise to go along with the singing. This, however, is the only version available of the original score with the spoken dialogue.)

Claude Debussy (1862–1918)

Pelléas et Mélisande (1902)

Pelléas et Mélisande is a masterpiece of musical and dramatic half-statement and understatement. It is based on Maurice Maeterlinck's symbolist play of the same name, and rarely have libretto and musical score been closer to one another in tone and purpose.

The plot is simple enough in realistic terms: A mysterious woman marries an older man whom she does not love only to discover that she is attracted to his brother, and he to her. When their love is discovered, the husband kills his brother, and the woman herself dies after giving birth to a child. *Pelléas et Mélisande,* however, resists being confined to realistic terms. The story and the characters are revealed to us in little textual and musical hints and indirections. In Act IV, when Pelléas asks what's the matter with her, Mélisande answers, "Si, si, je suis heureuse, mais je suis triste.... I am happy, but I am sad." The opera is like Mélisande herself. It will not be pinned down.

Two recordings of *Pelléas et Mélisande* are particularly deserving of recommendation. One of them is an earlier issue of great historical and artistic significance. The other is a superb contemporary recording.

(1941) Arkadia 78018 or EMI 61038, with Irène Joachim, Jacques Jansen, Henri Etcheverry, Germaine Cernay, Paul Cabanel, Yvonne Gouverné Chorus, unidentified orchestra, Roger Desormière, Conductor.

The Arkadia has neither libretto nor synopsis. If you can secure a copy of the EMI issue as an import, you will have an English language libretto, a selection of Debussy songs performed by Maggie Teyte, and a brief selection from the opera sung by Mary Garden, the original Mélisande, accompanied by Debussy himself. (This classic version features often on lists of the world's greatest opera recordings. The cast is completely at home in the language and the style of Debussy's opera, and Desomière's conducting captures the spirit of this evasive opera. The sound is better than you might expect from wartime Paris in 1941. There is a special joy in hearing the French language sung as beautifully as these native artists do.)

(1991) Deutsche Grammophon 35344, with Maria Ewing, François le Roux, José van Dam, Christa Ludwig, Jean-Philippe Courtis, Concert Chorus of the Vienna State Opera, Vienna Philharmonic, Claudio Abbado, Conductor. English language libretto. (We live in the age of international operatic performance. Thus we have this decidedly French opera with an Italian conductor, an American Mélisande, a German Geneviève, and a Viennese orchestra and chorus. The result in this case is the best of modern *Pelléas* recordings. The singers and conductor maintain the mystery that Debussy wrote into the score. Maria Ewing is extremely sensitive as Mélisande, although she is perhaps somewhat less otherworldly than her counterpart in the earlier recording. The stereo recording quality is excellent.)

Pelléas et Mélisande is available with Colette Alliot-Lugaz and François Le Roux on VHS from Kultur.

Gaetano Donizetti (1797–1848)

Don Pasquale (1843)

Don Pasquale was an instant success when it premiered in Paris in January 1843, and before the year was out it had made its way to Italy, Austria, and Great Britain. As popular today as it was in 1843, it is one of those rare works that seem impervious to changes in musical fashion. The reasons are obvious in the work itself. It is tuneful, charming, genuinely humorous, sentimental without becoming saccharine, sophisticated without destroying our sympathy for the characters. *Don Pasquale* touches both the heart and the funny bone, and throughout, Donizetti demonstrates the artistry and skill he had acquired in the sixty-two of his operas that preceded it.

What we listen for in performance first of all is a bass or baritone for the title role who can truly sing the music and also communicate the rich humor of the character. He must be united with a spirited conductor who can maintain discipline (not always easy with singers who truly get into the spirit of the comedy) and still lead "with," rather than "against," his singers. As Malatesta, we want a baritone who can match Pasquale in wit, but also manage an appealing, even legato for "Bella siccome un angelo," and a tenor and soprano with beautiful lyric voices and reliable *bel canto* technique. If the soprano also has the spirit to stand up musically and dramatically to the Don Pasquale, the requirements of the right cast will have been fully met.

Included in the recommendations are two earlier performances that make traditional cuts in the score and are clearly not representative of good modern recorded sound. They, however, offer interesting and, with one or two of the singers, even classic performances. The more modern recording is well sung and lively. I have also included without comment two relatively recent versions that I have not heard. They have both received good critical notices. You will probably want to choose one of the modern recordings, but keep the older ones in mind as possible future additions to the collection. They offer special pleasures not otherwise available.

(1932) Opera d'Oro 1224 or Arkadia 78017; perhaps other labels as well, with Adelaide Saraceni, Tito Schipa, Afro Poli, Ernesto Badini, La Scala Chorus and Orchestra, Carlo Sabajno, Conductor. No libretto. (Schipa was one of the great lyric tenors of the twentieth century, and his performance here is a classic of the old "78" recording days. Saraceni has a little of the steam whistle about her voice, but Afro Poli's Malatesta has often been praised. As with most earlier performances, this one imposes cuts.)

(1949) Preiser 20001, with Alda Noni, Cesare Valletti, Mario Borriello, Sesto Bruscantini, Chorus and Orchestra of the RAI, Turin, Mario Rossi, Conductor. No libretto. (Valletti was Schipa's successor in many lyric tenor roles. His performance is also a classic. Bruscantini is almost his equal and proves himself an adroit comedian. This performance is also cut.)

(1982) EMI 47068, with Mirella Freni, Gösta Winbergh, Leo Nucci, Sesto Bruscantini, Ambrosian Opera Chorus, Philharmonia Orchestra, Riccardo Muti, Conductor. (I have not heard this often praised recording.)

(1990) Erato or Elektra/Asylum 45487, with Barbara Hendricks, Luca Canonici, Gino Quilico, Gabriel Bacquier, Chorus and Orchestra of the Lyons Opera, Gabriele Ferro, Conductor. (This recording also has met with critical approval. I have not heard it.)

(1993) BMG/RCA 61924, with Eva Mei, Frank Lopardo, Thomas Allen, Renato Bruson, Chorus of the Bavarian Radio, Munich Radio Orchestra, Roberto Abbado, Conductor. English language libretto. (Here is a recording that offers a thoroughly convincing performance with a strong cast. Bruson was noted primarily for the bel canto Italian roles, but he takes on the buffo Pasquale with great success. Lopardo is the lyrical and sensitive embodiment of Ernesto.)

Don Pasquale is available with Alda Noni, Cesare Valetti, and Sesto Bruscantini on VHS from Bel Canto. The Preiser recording listed above may be the sound track for the film included on this video.

L'Elisir d'Amore (1832)

L'Elisir d'Amore was originally labeled a "melodramma giocosa," an Italian term that meant little more than a play or an opera with a happy plot. *Don Pasquale*, however, was a "dramma buffo," that is, a play with a funny story. Of course, audiences are meant to laugh in both operas, but the label suggests a gentler, more romantic humor in *Elisir* than in *Pasquale*. For all the comic shenanigans of Dr. Dulcamara and the military bluster of Belcore, we have a tenor hero who wins our hearts immediately and a soprano heroine who eventually turns out to be the most sympathetic of characters. *Don Pasquale* gives us a sophisticated downtown plot. *Elisir*, although spiked with some intoxicating humor, is ultimately a pastoral love story.

Even casual opera listeners will recognize Nemorino's aria "Una furtive lagrima." Along with "Celeste Aida" and "La donna è mobile," it is one of the most famous tenor arias in all operadom and has been recorded countless times, often more than once by the same singer. Caruso put it on disc four times between 1902 and 1911, and the role of Nemorino was one of his most famous, as it has been for Luciano Pavarotti in more recent years. But there is much more to enjoy in *Elisir* than this single aria. The other three leading roles include important solos. Wonderful duets bring all of the characters fully to life. And then there is Adina's aria in the last act, "Prendi, per me sei libero," one of the sublime moments in all of Italian opera.

L'Elisir is well represented on disc. Most of the recordings made in the last thirty years, in addition to those recommended here, give a fair aural picture of Donizetti's delightful score. The earlier recordings were often severely cut, and with the one exception listed below, they do not compensate with performances of artistic interest and value.

(1952) Testament 2150, with Margherita Carosio, Nicola Monti, Tito Gobbi, Melchior Luise, Rome Opera Chorus and Orchestra, Gabriele Santini, Conductor. English language libretto. (There are many cuts in this monophonic recording, but the performance is one to cherish. Margherita Carosio was nearing the end of her career, but the voice was still true and the appropriate style was in her blood. After all, she had been singing Donizetti's music on stage since she made her debut in 1924 as Lucia di Lammermoor [at the age of 16!]. The conducting is lively and Tito Gobbi as Belcore is luxury casting indeed.)

(1970) Decca/London 14461, with Joan Sutherland, Luciano Pavarotti, Dominic Cossa, Spiro Malas, Ambrosian Opera Chorus, English Chamber Orchestra, Richard Bonynge, Conductor. English language libretto. (This recording is very much Sutherland and Pavarotti's show, but they are both at their best. The score is performed complete except that Bonynge omits the original version of Adina's last act cabaletta and inserts in its place a longer aria actually composed by Charles de Bériot for his famous wife, Maria Malibran. Donizetti was the better composer, but de Bériot supplied more of the vocal fireworks that were Sutherland's specialty. Musically it is thoroughly trivial, but Sutherland sings it spectacularly. Pavarotti in 1970 was a better and more artistic singer than later performances as one-third of the "Three Tenors" might lead us to suspect.)

(1989) Deutsche Grammophon 29744, with Kathleen Battle, Luciano Pavarotti, Leo Nucci, Enzo Dara, Metropolitan Opera Chorus and Orchestra, James Levine, Conductor. English language libretto. (An unconventional recommendation, but the singing is top drawer, the conducting energetic, and the casting solid all the way to the Giannetta, performed enchantingly by Dawn Upshaw. Pavarotti's voice is not as fresh as nineteen years earlier, but it's still better than most other tenors. Although Battle may not seem to be fully involved in the drama, only the hardest heart would fail to melt at the pure sound of her voice in Adina's last act aria.)

(1996) Decca/London 455691, with Angela Gheorghiu, Roberto Alagna, Roberto Scaltriti, Simone Alaimo, Orchestra and Chorus of Opéra de Lyon, Evelino Pidò, Conductor. English language libretto. (Alagna and Giorghiu, husband and wife in real life, play the eager young country boy and his reluctant girlfriend in this delightful performance. The vocalism throughout is of high quality. The performance is complete, but includes one important surprise. Alagna sings a version of "Una furtive," composed by Donizetti ten years after the opera was first performed. The variations are noticeable primarily in the second stanza and the concluding cadenza.)

La Favorite (1840)

Donizetti was assuredly an Italian composer, but the French title for *La Favorite* is entirely authentic. It was composed for and originally performed with great success at the Paris Opéra, where it remained in the repertoire through the early years of the twentieth century. In 1912 *Favorite* became one of the first French operas to be recorded in a more or less complete version, available now on compact discs (Marston 52010).

Donizetti reclaimed a great deal of the score from his earlier works, particularly from his 1839 opera *L'Ange de Nisida*, which was never performed in his lifetime. The result in *Favorite*, however, was more than a rehash of old ideas. It was, rather, a new, intensely dramatic, and musically exciting French grand opera. It is surely the masterpiece among the handful of operas Donizetti composed to French texts.

Outside French speaking countries, however, *La Favorite* became *La Favorita*, an Italian opera altered from the original and sung to a libretto incompetently translated from the intelligent and often eloquent French version. It is in this form that the opera has most often been performed out-

side France. Admittedly, the Italian version with a gifted cast can be an exciting experience, but it is essentially a different opera from Donizetti's original.

We are still waiting for a recording that does full justice to either *Favorite* or *Favorita*. The 1912 version has its advocates, but the sound of the old acoustic recordings is for most listeners no substitute for good modern reproduction. The one contemporary French language version listed here is acceptable without being brilliant. The problem with the Italian language performances, however, is that too often the singers provide healthy voices of the rough and ready *verismo* variety, with little understanding of the more subtle eloquence of French style. I cannot recommend enthusiastically any of the currently available recordings, but the opera itself is a winner.

(1954) Fonit-Cetra 514, with Fedora Barbieri, Gianni Raimondi, Carlo Tagliabue, Giulio Neri, Chorus and Orchestra of Torino della RAI, Angelo Questa, Conductor. No libretto; brief synopsis only. (This is a solid Italian language performance. Barbieri and Raimondi have outstanding voices and sing with intense dramatic conviction. Tagliabue and Neri are caught on disc a bit too late, as they neared the end of their distinguished careers. There's nothing subtle here, but a great deal of genuine excitement.)

(1974–77) Decca/London 30038, with Fiorenza Cossotto, Luciano Pavarotti, Gabriel Bacquier, Nicolai Ghiaurov, Chorus and Orchestra of Teatro Communale di Bologna, Richard Bonynge, Conductor. English language libretto. (This recording is in good stereo sound. The cast looks better on paper than it actually turns out to be in performance, although the young Pavarotti is in excellent form. Bacquier, a fine artist, disappoints in what is one of the greatest of the *bel canto* baritone roles. Bonynge includes the ballet music that was required for operas performed at the Paris Opéra but was not regularly part of Italian performances.)

(1999) BMG/RCA 66229, with Vesselina Kasarova, Ramon Vargas, Anthony Michaels-Moore, Carlo Colombara, Chorus of the Bavarian Radio, Munich Rundfunkorchester, Marcello Viotti, Conductor. English language libretto. (This performance of the French language version is not ideal, but it's the best of the lot. Vargas is particularly impressive and Kassarova sings effectively, but the production doesn't have much dramatic bite to it. Approximately half of the ballet music is included.)

Lucia di Lammermoor (1835)

Lucia di Lammermoor is one of many nineteenth century operas to center our attention on a suffering heroine who loses her reason amidst a turbulent shower of scales, trills, staccati, and notes well above the staff. For many opera goers of the past, Lucia's so-called "Mad Scene" was the whole show, and at some early performances the opera ended without giving the tenor an opportunity to sing his two big arias and then die tragically on stage.

Donizetti, however, composed a brilliant score from beginning to end. Salvatore Cammarano supplied him with an effective, carefully shaped libretto, much neater, in fact, than Sir Walter Scott's novel *The Bride of Lammermoor*, from which it derives. Donizetti then managed to clothe that libretto in dramatic music of the highest order. Each of the four principals is given at least a few moments in the vocal spotlight, although certainly tenor and soprano have the best of it. To reach its full effect, however, *Lucia* requires four artists with *bel canto* mastery.

It has often been said that recordings and performances in general of *Lucia* can be divided into two convenient time frames. That is B.C. and A.D., "Before Callas" and "After the Diva." It was Maria Callas who opened our eyes and ears to the dramatic potential in an opera that had too often been merely a display of fancy vocalism. Perhaps we shouldn't make too much of the division, but it is true that any Lucia after Callas was required to make a more than casual attempt to act the role as well as sing it. It's also true that Callas used the many colors of her voice to underline the drama in a way that most other singers simply couldn't manage.

I have suggested one earlier recording because it shows the B.C. approach at its best. Otherwise, here are Callas and Sutherland, each of them remarkably effective in their own way. I have not included two recordings that I have not heard. They have both won a measure of critical approval and will certainly serve as viable alternatives: Deutsche Grammophon 35309 (with Cheryl Studer, Plácido Domingo, Juan Pons, Samuel Ramey, conducted by Ion Marin) and Teldec or Elektra/Asylum 72306 (with Edita Gruberova, Neil Shicof, Alexandru Agache, Alastair Miles, conducted by Richard Bonynge).

(1942) Fonit-Cetra 517, Bongiovanni 1122, Arkadia 78021, perhaps other labels as well, with Lina Pagliughi, Giovanni Malipiero, Giuseppe Manacchini, Luciano Neroni, Orchestra and Chorus of EIAR, Torino, Ugo Tansini, Conductor. No English language libretto. (This recording, like most earlier performances, is cut in small ways and in a large one through the omission of Act III, Scene 1. The cast is typical of Italian vocalism at the time. The tenor, Malipiero, had a sound sense of style appropriate for the opera. Lina Pagliughi, the Lucia, was technically adept and had a voice that suggested Lucia's youth, all "sweetness and light," we might say. This performance reminds us that *Lucia* B.C. could provide an effective and moving operatic experience.)

(1955) EMI 66441, with Maria Callas, Giuseppe di Stefano, Rolando Panerai, Nicola Zaccaria, Chorus of La Scala, Milan, RIAS Berlin Symphony, Herbert von Karajan, Conductor. (Recorded during an actual performance in Berlin, September 29, 1955, this recording captures a performance of rare beauty and power from Callas, the other members of the cast, and Conductor

Karajan. Callas recorded the role twice under studio conditions [in 1953, EMI 66438, and in 1959, EMI 56284], and there are several other live performance recordings. This one, however, is by common critical consent the best of Callas' recordings of *Lucia*. It is cut in the typical fashion, but there is also a bit more of the opera than we're accustomed to hearing; the famous "Sextet" receives the rare distinction of an encore.)

(1971) Decca/London 10193, with Joan Sutherland, Luciano Pavarotti, Sherrill Milnes, Nicolai Ghiaurov, Chorus and Orchestra of the Royal Opera House, Covent Garden, Richard Bonynge, Conductor. (An earlier Sutherland recording on Decca/London 11622 is outclassed by the 1971 version, in part because Pavarotti makes Renato Cioni, who sang Edgardo in 1961, sound like a rank amateur. Vocally, Sutherland is virtually flawless, and although dramatically she isn't in the Callas class, she is entirely convincing. The performance is complete. For that reason — and many others — this is certainly the preferred version for a general operatic collection.)

Lucia di Lammermoor is available with Joan Sutherland and Alfredo Kraus on DVD from Pioneer and VHS from Paramount.

Antonín Dvořák (1841–1904)

Rusalka (1901)

Dvořák's operas, along with those of Smetana, have not crossed national borders as easily or as often as his symphonic and chamber music. In recent years, however, *Rusalka* has begun to garner in other parts of the world some of the popularity that it has had for a hundred years in what is now the Czech Republic. Thanks to opera companies willing to take a chance on it, and singers willing to learn the idiomatic sound if not always the precise meaning of the Czech language, *Rusalka* is making its way into the opera houses of Western Europe and even distant America.

There was already an American connection. From 1892 to 1895 Dvořák served as Director of the National Conservatory of Music of America in New York City. Those years produced his famous ninth ("New World") symphony and the "American" string quartet, but no operas. When he returned home permanently from the new world, however, he brought with him musical sketches that would eventually find their way into *Rusalka*. Perhaps the United States can claim at least a small influence on this beautiful opera after all.

Rusalka tells the tragic story of a water sprite who falls in love with a decidedly human prince, and Dvořák has clothed the libretto in music of great beauty. Rusalka's "Song to the Moon" from the first act has worked its magic on thousands of people who know nothing else of the opera itself, but there is much more in the score of equal beauty and appeal.

Both of the two recommended recordings are faithful to the letter and the spirit of Dvořák's opera. Both are beautifully recorded and performed by cast, conductor, chorus, and orchestra.

(1982–83) Supraphon 3641, with Gabriela Beňačová-Čápová, Věra Soukupová, Wiesław Ochman, Richard Novák, Drahomira Drobková, Czech Philharmonic Chorus and Orchestra, Václav Neumann, Conductor. English language libretto. (The cast includes some of the finest Czech singers of recent years working under the baton of an outstanding conductor. As a result, the performance is throroughly authentic and beautifully performed. Beňačová, particularly, is a world class singer whose tone may fall more comfortably on Western ears than that of some of her colleagues.)

(1998) Decca/London 460568, with Renée Fleming, Dolora Zajick, Ben Heppner, Franz Hawlata, Eva Urbanová, Kühn Mixed Choir, Czech Philharmonic Orchestra, Charles Mackerras, Conductor. English language libretto. (The major roles in the cast are filled by an international roster of singers — American, Canadian, German,

Czech, led by a conductor of Australian parentage. Mackerras, however, is an authority on Czech music, serves as Principal Guest Conductor of the Czech Philharmonic Orchestra, and is a recipient of the Medal of Merit from the Czech Republic. This performance yields nothing to the native cast in terms of authenticity and may offer a little extra in terms of vocal beauty. Strong men have been known to weep on first hearing Fleming's "Song to the Moon.")

Rusalka is available in an English language performance with Eilene Hannan and John Treleaven on VHS from Kultur.

Carlisle Floyd (1926–)

Susannah (1955)

Since 1950 many new American operas have appeared. Relatively few have the staying power to last beyond their initial performances. That's the way it's always been. Throughout the eighteenth and nineteenth century thousands of operas were produced in Europe. Where are they now? With the exception of the few survivors that made it into the continuing repertoires of the opera houses, they are either lost or buried away somewhere in the historical archives.

Floyd's *Susannah* is a survivor. With the possible exception of Gershwin's *Porgy and Bess*, it is the most popular American opera of the last hundred years, and unlike Gershwin's opera, which presents major casting and staging problems, it has been performed effectively by semi-professional groups in small cities all across the nation.

What are the sources of its popularity? For one thing, the plot itself is simple, earthy, a "down home" kind of story. Opera audiences may or may not be backwoods folks from the Tennessee hill country, but the setting is all–American, familiar to us from countless novels, films, and television shows. We are at home with *Susannah*.

And then there's the music — ap-

proachable, melodious, and memorable. It's the kind of music we can almost whistle as we leave the theater. There is a strong folk idiom running through the opera, although, with the exception of the "Jaybird Song" in Act I, the music and the text are entirely Floyd's own creation. What Floyd has captured in this score is a secret known and appreciated by great operatic composers through the years. The audience in the opera house may never have heard the opera before and may never have an opportunity to hear it again, and if they do not begin to grasp the beauty and truth of the score in that first encounter, the opera may be lost for all time. That is admittedly an old-fashioned approach, but I believe it rings true for Mozart, Rossini, Verdi, Puccini, and even for Wagner.

There are two available recordings of *Susannah*. The choice is between a moving performance of historical significance and a convincing, recently recorded version. My preference is for the earlier recording, but the up-to-date sound on the more recent recording may be the determining factor for many people.

(1962) VAIA 1115, with Phyllis Curtin, Norman Treigle, Richard Cassilly, Keith Kaldenberg, New Orleans Opera Orchestra and Chorus, Knud Andersson, Conductor. No libretto; synopsis only. (This performance was recorded during a performance at the New Orleans Opera, seven years after the premiere of the opera. Curtin was the original Susannah, and she was joined by Norman Treigle when *Susannah* was introduced to the New York City Opera in 1956. The performance is exciting, and Phyllis Curtin sings like the great artist she clearly is. The stereo sound is acceptable, but certainly not the equivalent of the more recent recording.)

(1993) EMD/Virgin Classics 45039, with Cheryl Studer, Samuel Ramey, Jerry Hadley, Kenn Chester, Chorus and Orchestra of L'Opéra de Lyon, Kent Nagano, Conductor. English language libretto. (Bautifully recorded and quite well performed, this recording offers a cast of international standing even in many of the smaller roles. That the performance employs the personnel of a major French opera company in no way damages the authenticity of the performance, and is a mark of Floyd's stature as a composer and the success of his opera internationally, not only on home territory.)

George Gershwin (1898–1937)

Porgy and Bess (1935)

J. Rosamond Johnson, who assisted with the choral direction and played a role in the first production of *Porgy and Bess*, whispered to the composer while the applause was still resounding in their ears, "George, you've done it — you're the Abraham Lincoln of Negro music."* In the years since the Boston premiere in 1935, there have been some dissenting voices, but critical opinion and audience approval have agreed that George Gershwin had truly "done it" with *Porgy and Bess*. Whether Gershwin was also the great liberator is another matter, but it is true that his opera was a springboard to national and international careers for some of the greatest African American vocalists.

Until relatively recent years, commentators enjoyed debating whether *Porgy and Bess* is truly an opera, or whether it is instead a Broadway musical that just happens to be sung throughout. That issue, however, has been more or less settled by performances at home and abroad in some of the major opera houses of the world, including Milan's La Scala, the prestigious Glyndebourne Opera in Great Britain, and that bastion of operatic respectability, New York's Metropolitan Opera

The recording history of *Porgy and Bess* includes countless individual selections and highlight albums, some of which are sad

distortions of Gershwin's score. The two "highlights" recordings listed here, however, are valuable documents and may prove to be of interest to library patrons.

(1941, 1942) MCA Classics 10520, selections, with Todd Duncan, Anne Brown, and others, the Eva Jessye Choir, Decca Symphony Orchestra, directed by Alexander Smallens. (Recorded with members of the original cast from 1935.)

(1963) BMG/RCA 63312, selections, with William Warfield, Leontyne Price, and others, RCA Victor Orchestra and Chorus, directed by Skitch Henderson. (Leontyne Price was closely identified with the role of Bess, and sang in many performances with the famous touring company that took *Porgy and Bess* to Europe, Latin America, and the Near East.)

If you can have only one complete recording, choose either the first or second of those listed below. The final listing is an excellent monophonic recording from 1951. There are a few cuts in this otherwise excellent performance.

(1976) BMG/RCA 2109, with Donnie Ray Albert, Clamma Dale, Wilma Shakesnider, Carol Brice, Larry Marshall, Andrew Smith, John DeMain, Conductor. English language libretto. (This recording reflects the experience of an ensemble cast who performed the opera on stage numerous times. It is excitingly dramatic and has the feel of a vital evening on Broadway. The vocalism is fully satisfying, perhaps somewhat less consciously "operatic" than on the EMI recording.)

(1988) EMI 56220, with Willard White, Cynthia Haymon, Cynthia Clarey, Harolyn Blackwell, Damon Evans, Gregg Baker, Glyndebourne Chorus, London Philharmonic, Simon Rattle, Conductor. English language libretto. (Rattle leads an outstanding cast. This is a performance that takes *Porgy* seriously in operatic terms, but

---

*Quoted in Hollis Alpert, *The Life and Times of Porgy and Bess: The Story of an American Classic* (New York: Alfred A. Knopf, 1990), p. 111.

the drama is not shortchanged. Willard White is a strong Porgy, and Damon Evans almost steals the show with his keenly vocalized "Sportin' Life.")

(1951) Sony 63322, with Lawrence Winters, Camilla Williams, Inez Matthews, June McMechen, Avon Long, Warren Coleman, Lehman Engel, Conductor. English language libretto. (The recognition of *Porgy* as a full-fledged opera virtually began with this monophonic recording. Lawrence Winters and Camilla Williams were both members of the New York City Opera at the time of the recording, and they bring with them large, beautiful operatic voices. The cast included some who had been part of the original 1935 performances. Although there are cuts, this recording has significant historical importance, and would make a good second version for a collection.)

Porgy and Bess is available with Willard White and Cynthia Haymon on DVD from EMI.

Umberto Giordano (1867–1948)

Andrea Chénier (1896)

The operatic movement known as *verismo* arose in Italy in the 1890s with such works as Mascagni's *Cavalleria Rusticana* and Leoncavallo's *I Pagliacci*. In both of these cases, the operatic plots were grimly realistic pictures of the lower strata of roughly contemporary Italian society, but *verismo* came in a very few years to present stories drawn from all social levels.

Andrea Chénier is a case in point. The setting is historical, the early years of the French Revolution, and the major characters include the daughter of a count and countess and a famous poet (the title character is based on a real person of the Revolutionary period). The plot of *Andrea Chénier* is certainly grim in its picture of the Reign of Terror, but whether or not it is truly realistic is a question only the histori-

ans can answer. What makes *Andrea Chénier* an example of *verismo*, however, is the music, which is passionate, somewhat "over the top," with strong orchestral emphases and soaring vocal lines that demand singers with the ability to project their voices over a full orchestra.

The opera has been often recorded. The title character is a rich, juicy part for the tenor, and many of those adequately ample of voice have responded to the challenge. The list of tenors who have committed their performances to disc includes Beniamino Gigli, Mario del Monaco, Franco Corelli, and each of the famous "Three Tenors"—Plácido Domingo, Luciano Pavarotti, and José Carreras. Pity the soprano and baritone without the power to hold their own in this auspicious company. There have been some poor recordings of *Andrea Chénier*, but I can vouch for those listed here that they are all strong, vital, and vocally resplendent. Two that I have not heard have appealed to the critics and should be mentioned here: José Carreras on Sony 42369 and Luciano Pavarotti on Decca/London 10117.

(1941) Arkadia 78012; Naxos 8.110066-67 (probably other labels as well), with Beniamino Gigli, Maria Caniglia, Gino Bechi, La Scala Chorus and Orchestra, Oliviero de Fabritiis, Conductor. No libretto. (This is a classic performance with an all-star lineup of stars, all at their best. Look at the smaller roles for singers who would soon climb the ladder to larger roles — Giulietta Simionato, Giuseppe Taddei, and Italo Tajo. This recording would grace any collection, but bear in mind that the 1941 sound cannot match current standards.)

(1963) EMI 65287, with Franco Corelli, Antonietta Stella, Mario Sereni, Rome Opera Chorus and Orchestra, Gabriele Santini, Conductor. English language libretto. (Corelli is the main show here, sometimes almost the only show since he tends to overshadow the others. He is an exciting singer in this *verismo* role. Stella is not one of the world's great vocalists, but she gives her all in this performance. There's nothing subtle about Corelli or Stella, but then there's nothing subtle about *Andrea Chénier*.)

(1976) BMG/RCA 39499, with Plácido Domingo, Renata Scotto, Sherrill Milnes, John Alldis Choir, National Philharmonic Orchestra, James Levine, Conductor. (This is probably the best all-round performance, with three singers well endowed vocally but not intent on shouting each other down. This is *verismo* singing and conducting without the emotional *verismo* excesses. The smaller roles, all extremely important in this opera, are quite well taken.)

(1989) Capriccio 60014, with Franco Bonisolli, Maria Gulegina, Renato Bruson, Ungarische Rundfunkchor Budapest, Radio-Sinfonie-Orchester Frankfurt, Marcello Viotti, Conductor. Libretto in Italian and German only. (This recording might be overlooked, but it is an excellent performance at a budget price. Bonisolli is no Domingo, but he makes a strong impression here. Gulegina and Bruson are both exciting. The drama is intense, the recorded sound quite good. It is listed as a "live" performance, but if an audience was present, they certainly do not make themselves known.)

Andrea Chénier is available with Plácido Domingo and Anna Tomowa-Sintow on VHS from Kultur.

Mikhail Glinka (1804–1857)

A Life for the Tsar (1836)

If Glinka is not quite the father of Russian opera, he is surely the older brother, and his influence has been felt ever since the appearance of his two great operatic works, *A Life for the Tsar* and *Ruslan and Lyudmila*. One after another, the nineteenth century Russian operas tended to follow either *A Life for the Tsar* as grand, often sprawling historical dramas or *Ruslan and Lyudmila* with fanciful, romantic, supernatural plots drawn from native folk-

lore or literature. The composers could employ their own styles, but at the same time their subject matter, and often their musical inspiration as well, looked back to Glinka.

Although the libretto of *A Life for the Tsar* (in Russian: *Zhizn'a tsarya*) was fleshed out with additional characters and incidents, the story is based on an incident in history. In 1613 Ivan Susanin lost his life when he refused to reveal to the Polish forces the hiding place of the newly chosen tsar, Mikhail Romanov. The young tsar was saved, the Polish were defeated, and Romanov was crowned in Moscow. Glinka's operatic retelling of this story is intensely patriotic, and the final scene in the original version is little more than a great hymn of praise to Tsar Mikhail I in particular, and to the reign of the Romanovs in general. The opera is dedicated to the tsar of the composer's day, Nicholas I, in whose honor Glinka changed the title of the opera, which he had originally named *Ivan Susanin*.

The communist leaders of Russia were not at all comfortable with an opera that glorified the Romanov dynasty, and in 1936 a new libretto was introduced in which the title reverted to *Ivan Susanin* and the Tsar simply isn't mentioned at all. Since the end of the communist regime, however, the original version has generally been preferred.

Glinka's vocal writing is very much in the style of nineteenth century *bel canto*, and singers equipped to handle it really well are few and far between, and more inclined to sing Bellini and Donizetti than Glinka. The singing in a 1947 Russian recording available on Preiser 90365 is loud and authentic without being beautiful, and the soprano Natalia Spiller tends to strain the listener's patience and eardrums from time to time. The sound, with the singers recorded at levels well above the orchestra, is a serious drawback. This version, as offered on the Preiser label, is also seriously cut, with Sobinin's major aria, the ballet music, and the choral epilogue all missing. Another recording on Capriccio 10783 I have not heard. The recording recommended here is not ideal, but it gives a fair representation of Glinka's opera.

(1989) Sony 46487, with Boris Martinovich, Alexandrina Pendachanska, Chris Merritt, Stefania Toczyska, Sofia National Opera Chorus, Sofia Festival Orchestra, Emil Tchakarov, Conductor. (The vocalism here is closer to Glinka's decidedly *bel canto* style than that on some of the Russian recordings. Pendachanska, Merritt, and Tocyska have the right type of voices and use them well. Only Martinovich, the Susanin, lets us down somewhat. The performance is complete in the original version, and the recording quality up to current standards.)

Ruslan and Lyudmila (1842)

Ruslan and Lyudmila is based, as much of Russian opera is, on the writings of Alexander Pushkin. Pushkin's poem, however, was considerably altered before it emerged as Glinka's opera. Characters were added and subtracted, details of the story changed, and Pushkin's humorous satire was lost in an essentially serious, even if highly fantastic, operatic plot. Three suitors for the hand of Lyudmila — Ruslan, Farlaf, and Ratmir — are challenged to rescue her from cruel supernatural powers in order to win her hand in marriage. In the process, they encounter a wicked sorceress, a giant talking head, a frightful spell that places Lyudmila in a supernatural sleep, and a magic ring by which Ruslan frees her at last. Glinka's music, however, redeems the plot and helps us, in the words of the poet Coleridge, to "willingly suspend our disbelief."

Ruslan and Lyudmila is an excessively difficult opera to cast. The *bel canto* demands of *A Life for the Tsar* are extended now to seven characters, each of whom has a major solo passage to sing. Opera houses and recording companies have trouble assembling four or even three world class singers. To bring together seven with the gifts and skills to handle Glinka's music is almost impossible. The two recordings recommended, both of them with authentic Russian casts and conductors, and representative of the two major Russian opera companies, have not quite managed the impossible, but they have probably come as close as we can realistically hope for.

(1978–79) BMG/Melodiya 29348, with Yvgeny Nesterenko, Bela Rudenko, Tamara Sinyavskaya, Boris Morozov, Nina Fomina, Alexey Maslennikov, Alesander Arkhipov, Orchestra and Chorus of the Bolshoi Theatre, Moscow, Yuri Simonov, Conductor. English language libretto. (Like many Russian recordings of the 1970s and earlier, the voices tend to be too far forward and too loud. The higher voices, particularly the sopranos, have a strong cutting edge, but that is a problem familiar from many other Russian discs. Nesterenko is the real star here, a Slavic bass with a dark, beautiful tone and keen dramatic sense. There are several small cuts in the performance, but only the omission of entr'actes in Acts III and Act V is seriously damaging. This recording is the less expensive of the two, but it may be difficult to locate.)

(1995) Philips 56248, with Vladimir Ognovienko, Anna Netrebko, Larissa Diadkova, Gennady Bezzubenkov, Galina Gorchakova, Konstantin Pluzhnikov, Yuri Marusin, Chorus and Opera of the Kirov Opera, St. Petersburg, Valery Gergiev, Conductor. English language libretto. (The singing is generally better on this recording, although none of the soloists equal Nesterenko. Gorchakova is an outstanding soprano, and the other cast members are thoroughly acceptable. The entr'actes omitted in the earlier version are restored here, and the recorded sound is considerably more realistic and better balanced.)

Christoph Willibald Gluck (1714–1787)

Iphigénie en Aulide (1774)

Through the first three quarters of the eighteenth century, opera had grown more and more bound by worn-out traditions that dictated the elaborate poetical language of the libretti, the musical shape and character of the arias and occasional duets, and their placement in the dramatic action. Gluck and his librettist, Ranieri Calzabigi, set out, apparently consciously, to reform opera by introducing eloquent but natural language, and by clothing it with music that was entirely appropriate to the drama and never merely decorative or incidental to it. What they sought was simplicity aligned with psychological and dramatic profundity. These ideals were expressed in the three operas for Vienna on which they collaborated — *Orfeo ed Euridice* (1762), *Alceste* (1767), and *Paride and Elena* (1770).

Gluck took the spirit of operatic reform with him when he traveled to Paris to continue his career in 1773. *Iphigénie en Aulide* was the first of those operas composed for the French capitol, and it was triumphant in its premiere.

The story of Iphigenia and the events and characters surrounding her came from historical legends of the Trojan War by way of the dramas of Euripides and Racine's seventeenth century play. She had been a frequent heroine in the operas of eighteenth century composers before Gluck chose her as the title character in two of his operas. The stories are themselves filled with high drama and with the torment of conflicting emotions. In other words, they are ideal operatic material, and Gluck makes the most of them, particularly in the music he composed for Iphigénie and her parents, Agamemnon and Clytemnestra.

There is only one recording of Gluck's authentic score. There was at one time a recording of the German language version edited by Richard Wagner in 1847 (RCA ARL-0114). It was not highly regarded as a performance when it was available. In any case, it had more to say about Wagner, who revised the score and the plot drastically, than it did about Gluck.

> (1987) Erato or Elektra/Asylum 45003, with Lynne Dawson, Anne Sofie von Otter, José van Dam, John Aler, Monterverdi Choir, Orchestre de l'Opéra de Lyon, John Eliot Gardiner, Conductor. English language libretto. (All four of the principal cast members are excellent, and Gardiner conducts a dramatically convincing performance. It is difficult to imagine better performances than those of Anne Sofie von Otter and José van Dam. The basic version recorded here is Gluck's 1775 revision of the 1774 original, but Gardiner has used some passages from the earlier of the two. There a cuts in some of the ballet music.)

Iphigénie en Tauride (1779)

Iphigénie en Tauride is considered by many to mark the artistic climax of Gluck's career as a composer. The score has about it the aura of maturity, particularly in the psychological sensitivity with which Gluck has portrayed Iphigénie and her brother, Orestes, in music that goes beneath the surface. It is the work of a composer who has mastered his craft and an artist who has looked long and deeply into the human mind and heart. Some people find Gluck's operas outdated, slow in movement, and devoid of action, but *Iphigénie in Tauride* is intensely dramatic, and the music constantly draws us emotionally into the action.

It ranks next to *Orfeo ed Euridice* in popularity, and that popularity has grown in recent years with a number of significant opera house revivals. One of the most interesting was at La Scala in Milan in 1957, when Maria Callas sang the title role. The performance was recorded and has been released commercially on EMI 65451. It is wrong in almost every detail. Most of the cast members are stylistically at odds with Gluck, and Dino Dondi, who sings the role of Pylades, is painful to hear. In any case, they are singing Italian, which is, of course, the wrong language, and the sound of the live recording is barely listenable. But then there's Callas, and she clearly understands what this opera is all about and how to communicate it. As a version of Gluck's opera, this recording simply will not do, but as a sample of Callas' artistry, it is well worth hearing.

Iphigénie en Tauride has been well represented on recordings in recent years. La Scala returned to the opera in 1992, and the performance found its way onto compact discs (Sony S2K 52 492). Carol Vaness sings beautifully in the title role. Riccardo Muti conducts a full modern orchestra, and the sound is impressive, but this is an opera that benefits from an historical approach in performance. Both of the recommended recordings use authentic period instruments and singers who understand Gluck's style. The results are impressive, and either recording will reward the listener with an engrossing dramatic and musical experience.

(1999) Telarc 80546, with Christine Goerke, Rodney Gilfry, Vinson Cole, Stephen Salters, Boston Baroque, Martin Pearlman, Conductor. English language libretto. (The drama is hard hitting in this performance under the committed conducting of Pearlman. It is artistically disciplined, but it sounds almost spontaneous. Christine Goerke has a strong, dramatic voice. Rodney Gilfry as Oreste conveys fully the anguish of a man suffering under a burden of guilt. The Scythian chorus sounds uncommonly bloodthirsty.)

(1999) Deutsche Grammophon Archiv 471 133-2, with Mireille Delunsch, Simon Keenlyside, Yann Beuron, Laurent Naouri, Chorus and Orchestra of Les Musiciens du Louvre, Marc Minkowski, Conductor. English language libretto. (In some ways this is the more polished performance of the two, but it is no less dramatically convincing. The singing is excellent, particularly from Simon Keenlyside as Oreste. The Scythians in this version are fully the unpleasant equals of their compatriots on the other recording.)

Orfeo ed Euridice (1762); *Orphée et Eurydice* (1774)

Gluck's operatic version of the myth of Orpheus exists in three versions made by the composer himself—the Italian original presented in Vienna in 1762, with Orfeo sung by an alto castrato; a 1769 adaptation performed in Parma, with the role arranged for soprano castrato voice; and the 1774 French version, with the role of Orphée sung by a high tenor. A further edition was prepared by Hector Berlioz in 1859 for the great mezzo-soprano Pauline Viardot. Since then, conductors and singers have far too often taken upon themselves the responsibility of determining how much of the various versions to perform in which order and from which version.

The ancient story of Orpheus and Eurydice has both the built-in appeal of a main character who is a musician and a theme that relates to the power of art and the artist. It has been one of the most popular subjects since the earliest days of opera at the beginning of the seventeenth century in Italy. Fifty or more works have been composed with Orpheus as the major character since Claudio Monteverdi in 1607 presented his *Orfeo*, the first great operatic masterpiece. Gluck's opera, however, in one or another of its versions, is the most often performed.

The complex history of the various editions of *Orfeo ed Euridice* is reflected in the recordings, and no two of those listed here present exactly the same music in the same language. There are many good versions of Gluck's opera on disc, and those who know and love *Orfeo ed Euridice* delight in debating their merits. I have included four recordings in the list here, each of them in a different version of the opera and each one a performance worth hearing.

(1956) Philips 468 537–2PM2, with Léopold Simoneau, Suzanne Danco, Pierrette Alarie, Roger Blanchard Vocal Ensemble, Lamoureux Concert Orchestra, Hans Rosbaud, Conductor. (This recording has been announced for issue in Great Britain and may be available in the United States as an import. The copy available to me is the original issue on long-playing records, and I do not know whether a libretto is included in the compact disc set. It presents the 1774 French version with a number of cuts. The role of *Orphée* was written for a *haute-contre*, an unusually high tenor voice type, and Simoneau has had to transpose some of the music downwards. Otherwise, however, he is the ideal interpreter — warm, dramatic and vocally poised. Alarie and Danco are not quite up to his standard, but theirs are good performances.)

(1982) Erato or Elektra/Asylum 45864, with Janet Baker, Elisabeth Speiser, Elizabeth Gale, Glyndebourne Chorus, London Philharmonic Orchestra, Raymond Leppard. An English language libretto is included. (Leppard has done his own version. It is sung in Italian and uses music from both the 1762 and 1774 versions with a mezzo-soprano Orfeo. Speiser and Gale are little more than adequate, but Janet Baker is an inspired performer. Unless you plan to purchase more than one recording, this is probably the best choice, particularly since it presents the opera in a form that will be familiar to many listeners.)

(1991) Philips 34093, with Derek Lee Ragin, Sylvia McNair, Cyndia Sieden, Monteverdi Choir, English Baroque Soloists, John Eliot Gardiner, Conductor. An English language libretto is included. (I have not heard this recording, but it has met with wide critical approval. The performance of the original Italian language version from 1762 is played on period instruments and uses a countertenor as Orfeo.)

(1995) Teldec or Elektra/Asylum 98418, with Jennifer Larmore, Dawn Upshaw, Alison Hagley, Chorus and Orchestra of the San Francisco Opera, Donald Runnicles, Conductor. (Here we have the Berlioz version in French, quite well performed, with Jennifer Larmore as the outstanding mezzo-soprano star. This is a moving performance, beautifully recorded. Berlioz had a great deal of respect for Gluck, and his revision reflects that respect, but Berlioz's version remains an opera at one rather large remove from the composer himself.)

Orfeo ed Euridice is available in a post-modern production with Jochen Kowalski and Gillian Webster on DVD and VHS from Kultur.

Charles Gounod (1818–1893)

Faust (1859)

Faust was at one time the world's most popular opera. It was performed so often at the Metropolitan Opera that one critic named it the *Faustspielhaus*, a pun on Wagner's famous *Festspielhaus* in Bayreuth, Germany. The reasons for its popularity are not difficult to discover. It probably has more memorable melodies than any other opera, and the music, without being easy to perform, is singable so that good voices wrap their way comfortably around the tunes. The plot is passionately dramatic without being in any way intellectually disturbing, and the overall impression is relatively uplifting, even pious.

Those are probably the same reasons that *Faust* has declined in popularity for somewhat more skeptical contemporary audiences. It is not a work of great philosophical profundity in the sense that its literary source, Goethe's *Faust,* is. Perhaps the first clue to the appreciation of Gounod's opera is not to compare it with Goethe. On the whole, Gounod and his librettists, Jules Barbier and Michel Carré, made it into a more or less conventional unhappy love story with a few spiritual overtones. If we accept it on those terms, *Faust* can still exert for us its manifold charms.

While the opera was in rehearsal prior to the premiere, Gounod removed entire sections of the score. Then, in the months and years after its first performance, Gounod made a number of revisions. Originally it had been an *opéra comique*, that is, a stage work with spoken dialogue rather than sung recitatives. Gounod first composed recitatives for performances in 1860. In 1864, for performances in Great Britain, Gounod added the famous baritone aria, "Even bravest heart may swell" ("Avant de quitter ces lieux") for the great baritone Charles Santley. The extended ballet music and an additional number for Mephistopheles were added in 1869 for performances at the Paris Opéra. The Act 4 scene in Marguerite's room and the opening section of Act 5, sometimes just the ballet and sometimes the entire *Walpurgisnacht*, are frequently omitted.

The history of *Faust* on record goes back to 1908, when a German language version was produced, with the great soprano Emmy Destinn as Marguerite. There were also French and Italian recordings prior to the introduction of electrical recording in 1925. The earliest recording among the recommendations listed here comes from Paris Opéra forces in 1930. For the first performance in your collection, you will probably choose one of the modern stereo recordings, but the 1930 version is interesting, not only as a document of historical interest, but also as a solid, valid view of the opera.

(1930) Pearl 9987, with César Vezzani, Mireille Berthon, Marthe Coiffier, Louis Musy, Marcel Journet, Chorus and Orchestra of the Paris Opéra. No libretto. (There are a number of cuts, including the entire Act IV scene in Marguerite's room, but what is here is a remarkable demonstration of true French style. Marcel Journet, who was nearing the end of his career, was a famous French bass and is clearly the most idiomatic Mephistophélès on any of the recordings. The 1930 sound has been remastered by Ward Marston, and it is remarkably clear and forceful.)

(1958) EMI 69983, with Nicolai Gedda, Victoria de los Angeles, Liliane Berton, Ernest Blanc, Boris Christoff, Orchestra and Chorus of Théâtre National de l'Opéra, André Cluytens, Conductor. English language libretto. (This stereo version replaced an earlier EMI recording with many of the same cast members. The scene in Marguerite's room is cut. Except for de los Angeles, who is a real charmer, the singing is solid, conventional, but not brilliant. De los Angeles and Gedda, although not French, have the proper sense of style. Christoff's over-the-top Mephistophélès is for some critics wonderfully effective, for others, an absolute disaster.)

(1991) EMI 56224, with Richard Leech, Cheryl Studer, Martine Mahé, Thomas Hampson, José van Dam, Chorus and Orchestra of the Capitole de Toulouse, Michel Plasson, Conductor. English language libretto. (The performance, including the singing, is strong and dramatic. On the whole, the voices are large but always under control. Van Dam is an outstanding Mephistophélès although he doesn't have the vocal weight of other singers in the role. The recording is actually more than complete since it includes in an appendix not only the ballet music, but also four additional selections drawn from the material that Gounod deleted before the premiere.)

(1993) Teldec or Elektra/Asylum 90872, with Jerry Hadley, Cecilia Gasdia, Susanne Mentzer, Alexandru Agache, Samuel Ramey, Chorus and Orchestra of the Welsh National Opera, Carlo Rizzi, Conductor. English language libretto. (To my ears, this is the most sensitive performance that we have among modern recordings. Hadley and Gasdia make the love duet sound like rare, beautiful chamber music. Ramey is the most vocally gifted of all the performers of Mephistophélès. It is a sad comment on the current state of French operatic performance that almost no one in this excellent cast is Gallic. The ballet music and two selections from the pre-premiere deletions are included in an appendix.)

Faust is available with Francisco Araiza and Gabriela Beňačková on VHS from Bel Canto Society.

Roméo et Juliette (1867)

Shakespeare has been a rich vein of source material for opera. Apparently librettists and composers have recognized a good thing when they saw it, and thus have raided the comedies, tragedies, and histories of the Bard of Avon for some of their best material. *Romeo and Juliet* alone has provided the plot, and often a portion of the words as well, for well over twenty different operas. Of these, Gounod's *Roméo et Juliette* is by far the best known and, through the years, most often performed.

Unlike some writers confronted with one of Shakespeare's dramas, Gounod's librettists, Jules Barbier and Michel Carré, treated the play with respect and turned out a libretto that is amazingly close to the original in its plot, given the necessity to condense action to accommodate musical development. The opera centers, as the play does, on the tragic love of Roméo and Juliette, and is constructed around a series of duets for the pair. Other roles are important primarily as they affect the title characters, although Mercutio, Stéphano, and Frère Laurent have a significant amount of solo music to sing. No performance of *Roméo et Juliette,* however, can succeed unless the artists in the two leading roles have the vocal gifts and verbal awareness, always a prime concern in French opera, to serve Gounod's music well.

One of the famous combinations, often spoken and written of almost with awe, was Jussi Bjoerling and Bidu Sayao, who sang their roles at the Metropolitan Opera in the 1940s. A broadcast matinee from 1947 has been recorded and appears from time to time on one or another of the labels that specialize in historical performances. It is well worth seeking out as a supplement to an operatic collection, but it is severely cut and, of course, not reproduced in modern stereo sound.

There are two generally excellent recent recordings, both of which are good recommendations for *Roméo et Juliette,* but if you insist on an absolutely complete performance, the EMI recording will have to be your choice.

(1995) BMG/RCA 68440, with Ruth Ann Swenson, Plácido Domingo, Susan Graham, Kurt Ollmann, Alastair Miles, Munich Radio Chorus and Orchestra, Leonard Slatkin, Conductor. English language libretto. (Gounod's ballet music, added to the score in 1888, along with most of Act IV, Scene 2, is omitted, as it often is in performance. Domingo and Swenson are excellent, as are the other singers, particularly Susan Graham in Stephano's aria and Kurt Ollmann in a feather light "Queen Mab" ballad. Domingo's ability to handle well this essentially lyrical role is a sign of remarkably solid vocal technique for a tenor who regularly sings Verdi's Otello.)

(1995) EMI 56123, with Angela Gheorghiu, Roberto Alagna, Marie-Ange Todorovitch, Simon Keenlyside, José Van Dam, Chorus and Orchestra of Capitole de Toulouse, Michel Plasson, Conductor. English language libretto. (This recording includes the ballet music and all of Act IV, Scene 2. Alagna is a younger sounding Roméo than Domingo and makes a wonderful partner for Gheorghiu, who sings beautifully. The rest of the cast is good, and José Van Dam makes more of Frère Laurent than is usually possible in such a thankless role. Plasson is the excellent conductor.)

Roméo et Juliette is available with Roberto Alagna and Leontina Vaduva on VHS and DVD from Kultur.

George Frideric Handel (1685–1759)

Giulio Cesare in Egitto (1724)

It was largely a matter of opportunity and obstinacy that the German Handel became the greatest British operatic composer of the eighteenth century. The opportunity was there in the fact that Italian opera had not previously been firmly established in London, and Handel realized that he was the right person for the task. The obstinacy he needed as he fought jealous rivals, recalcitrant singers, and stubborn political foes to see his thirty-nine operas for Great Britain actually performed.

After his death, Handel's operas fell into semi-obscurity. They were remembered, when they were remembered at all, through the popularity of a few of the arias, often dressed up in new arrangements and sung with texts far different from the original. The famous "Largo" from *Serse*, for example, was frequently given religious words and performed to lugubrious organ accompaniment in a radical departure from its origin as "Ombra mai fu." It was up to the twentieth century, beginning with German revivals in the 1920s, to rediscover the dramatic viability of Handel's operas.

Giulio Cesare is probably the most popular of these works. It was one of Handel's great successes, with the famous castrato Sensino as Caesar and the equally noted soprano Francesca Cuzzoni as Cleopatra. The arias that they and the other cast members were given to sing are among the most beautiful that Handel, or any other composer for that matter, ever composed.

That success was duplicated, even surpassed, in 1966 when Norman Treigle and Beverly Sills sang in a famous revival at the New York City Opera. Other members of the cast joined them in the studio in 1967 and committed the performance to disc. That recording has been available on BMG/RCA 6182–2, and it bears testimony particularly to Sills' brilliant vocalism. The opera, however, is so seriously cut and otherwise altered in a variety of ways that it cannot be recommended as an authentic version of *Giulio Cesare*. The recording recommended here is complete and raises the role of Caesar from Treigle's bass range to Jennifer Larmore's mezzo-soprano, an authentic modern equivalent of Sensino's alto castrato voice.

(1991) Harmonia Mundi 901385–7, with Jennifer Larmore, Barbara Schlick, Bernarda Fink, Marianne Rørholm, Derek Lee Ragin, Furio Zanasi, Dominique Visse, Olivier Lallouette, Concerto Köln, René Jacobs, Conductor. English language libretto. (Jacobs has been a leader in the movement to revive earlier music in authentic versions. Unlike some early music specialists, however, Jacobs brings the music to life with warmth and drama. There is nothing cold or impersonal about this recording or the singers. Larmore is excellent as Caesar and manages to sound like a genuine mezzo-soprano and also like a man. Barbara Schlick brings a clear, even soprano voice and considerable virtuosity to Cleopatra's arias.)

Rinaldo (1711)

Rinaldo was Handel's first opera for London. There had been adaptations from other Italian operas for the London stage, but now there was an Italian opera composed specifically for the British audience. They were not disappointed. Handel's score was filled with magnificent music, and the stage was filled with spectacular settings and special effects. *Rinaldo* is that kind of opera, an exciting and essentially happy retelling of events from Tasso's *Jerusalem Delivered*. It has drama, a battle, a love story, and a great deal of Armida's magic. Over the next six years, *Rinaldo* went through several new productions and revisions to suit the needs of changing casts.

Handel's accomplishment in this and several other operas was to transform the traditions of *opera seria* not by changing them, but rather by clothing them in music of such psychological appropriateness and innate beauty that those traditions became something new and wonderful. He was not a revolutionary, but he was a great and inspired composer. Listen to Almirena's "Lascia ch'io pianga" or Rinaldo's "Cara sposa," and the depth of emotion that Handel's music can inspire will become clear.

There are two exemplary studio recordings of *Rinaldo*. Both of them follow the 1711 version, with some small changes and additions. Jean-Claude Malgoire, conductor of one of the recordings, considers "that it is virtually impossible to settle on a definitive score."* Operas in the eighteenth century developed in the process of rehearsal and performance as the composer revised to suit the needs of certain singers' weaknesses and strengths so that it is often impossible to pinpoint the exact moment at which a "definitive score" came into existence.

(1977) Sony 34592, with Carolyn Watkinson, Ileana Cotrubas, Ulrik Cold, Jeanette Scovotti, Paul Esswood, Charles Brett, La Grande Écurie et la Chambre du Roy, Jean-Claude Malgoire, Conductor. Italian language libretto only. (The role of Rinaldo was originally composed for a castrato. It is sung here quite effectively by Carolyn Watkinson, a mezzo-soprano. Outstanding in the cast are Ileana Cotrubas, whose poised soprano presents an entirely sympathetic Almirena, and Jeanette Scovotti, a very light soprano who manages with precision and attack to convey the anger and power of the sorceress Armida. Malgoire obviously believes, correctly so, that this is living music and not a dead reminder of the past.)

(1999) Decca/London 467087, with David Daniels, Cecilia Bartoli, Gerald Finley, Luba Orgonasova, Bernarda Fink, Daniel Taylor, the Academy of Ancient Music, Christopher Hogwood, conductor. English language libretto. (Hogwood provides a lively, dramatic presentation of the score, with David Daniels as an excellent countertenor Rinaldo. Bartoli's singing of "Lascia ch'io pianga" would soften the heart of the cruelest Argante. This recording seems to me to have an edge on the Sony version, and it is worthwhile to have an English translation of the libretto, but either of the two recordings does honor to Handel's score.)

Engelbert Humperdinck (1854–1921)

Hänsel und Gretel (1893)

Hänsel und Gretel fits neatly into the category of *Märchenoper*. In fact, it is the principal example of fairy tale opera in the standard repertoire and certainly the most popular. Its origin is the story told in the famous collections of the Grimm brothers. Humperdinck's sister and librettist, Adelheid Wette, however, removed from the original the more disturbing violent elements and replaced the cruel mother-in-law and her acquiescent husband with parents who are essentially sympathetic. Even the wicked witch often seems in performance about as frightening as an old lady in a Halloween costume, and, after all, she ends up as a great big gingerbread cake.

Humperdinck's score is an amazing combination of folk-like melodies and complex, often contrapuntal music performed by an orchestra of Wagnerian proportions.

It is an opera for all ages. Children are delighted by the story and the memorable tunes, and more sophisticated opera aficionados, including Richard Strauss and Gustav Mahler a hundred years ago, find much in the music to admire and enjoy.

Hänsel und Greretel presents producers and performers with a number of challenges. One of the greatest is the appropriate casting of the title roles. They are children, but their music is not intended to be sung by children. Too often when adult singers try to sound like children, either they are merely overly "cute" or they miss the idea entirely and sound like seasoned opera veterans who would be more comfortable as Carmen or Aida. Choosing an artist for the witch can also prove difficult.

*Jean-Claude Malgoire, "Rinaldo — Handel's First London Opera," from the insert booklet in the Sony recording of the opera, p. 10.

Some performances have experimented with a male voice or a somewhat over-the-hill soprano or mezzo-soprano. The best solution is surely a good, solid soprano or mezzo-soprano with a sense of humor. Then there is the challenge to conductor and orchestra. *Hänsel und Gretel* is a score that demands a superb instrumental ensemble and a seasoned, sensitive conductor.

Given the challenges, it is remarkable that the opera has fared so well on disc. There have been a number of excellent recordings, along with a few that are better forgotten. The three recommended here are by no means the only good choices, but each of them has something special to offer. My personal preference is for the earliest, but if modern stereo sound is important, either of the other two will provide great pleasure for children and adults alike. The only regret is that, given the appeal of *Hänsel und Gretel* to children, there is not currently available on compact discs an acceptable English language version with a clearly articulated text.

(1953) EMI 67145, with Elisabeth Schwarzkopf, Elisabeth Grümmer, Maria von Ilosvay, Else Schürhoff, Josef Metternich, Choirs of Leighton High School for Girls and Bancroft's Schools, Philharmonia Orchestra, Herbert von Karajan, Conductor. English language libretto. (Karajan conducts Humperdinck's score as if it is great music, which it is. Grümmer is excellent as Hänsel. Schwarzkopf's Gretel will appeal to anyone who appreciates her artistry, but some find her overly precious in her treatment of the text. Metternich is an unusually strong Peter. Some listeners, myself included, believe this version to be one of great classics of recording history.)

(1971) BMG/RCA 25281, with Helen Donath, Anna Moffo, Charlotte Berthold, Christa Ludwig, Dietrich Fischer-Dieskau, Boys Choir of Tölz, Munich Radio Orchestra, Kurt Eichhorn, Conductor. English language libretto. (Beside the conductor, who paces the opera extremely well, the real star here is Christa Ludwig as the witch.

Donath is thoroughly convincing as a child; Moffo less so. Fischer-Dieskau is extravagant casting as Peter, and he lives up to his reputation. To add to the luxury, we have Arleen Augér as the Sandman and the liveliest of Dew Men in the remarkable Lucia Popp.)

(1994) Teldec or Elektra/Asylum 67145, with Ruth Ziesak, Jennifer Larmore, Hildegard Behrens, Hanna Schwarz, Bernd Weikl, Boys Choir of Tölz, Bavarian Radio Symphony, Donald Runnicles, Conductor. English language libretto. (Here is a recent performance, beautifully recorded and conducted, with an excellent cast. Larmore and Ziesak manage to sound like gifted opera singers and children at the same time. An appendix includes a brief concluding passage that Humperdinck composed for an 1894 performance directed by Cosima Wagner, Richard's widow, in Dessau.)

Hänsel und Gretel is available with Judith Blegen and Federica von Stade on VHS from Paramount and on DVD from Pioneer Video.

Leoš Janáček

The Cunning Little Vixen (1924)

An opera titled *The Cunning Little Vixen* (in Czech: *Prinody Ličky Bystroučky*) may seem to be a work for children, and on the stage it often looks like an animated cartoon, with characters dressed up like the animals, insects, and birds of the forest and farmyard. Nothing could be further from the truth. Janáček composed a decidedly adult opera with a mature and profound understanding of the cycle of life and death and the relationship of human beings to the rest of the natural world. Although the composer altered his literary source so that the vixen dies of a gunshot wound, it is not a tragic opera. Janáček, who was also his own librettist, looks at his subject from the vantage point of his almost seventy years of life, and finds in it acceptance, peace, tranquility.

Janáček composed a score of rare and

approachable beauty. The vixen, and the fox that becomes her mate, are given music that humanizes them so that we believe in them and find ourselves in their experience. The score over and over again communicates more than meets the ear at first hearing. It is the kind of music that we think about — and smile about — afterwards.

Janáček's orchestration is subtle, varied, and filled with difficulties for the instrumentalists, and it needs good modern stereo recording of a superb orchestra to produce its full effect. That is precisely what it receives in the recommended version.

> (1981) Decca/London 417129, with Lucia Popp, Dalibor Jedlička, Eva Randová, Eva Zikmundová, Vladimir Krejčik, Richard Novák, Vienna State Opera Chorus, Bratislava Children's Choir, Vienna Philharmonic, Charles Mackerras, Conductor. English language libretto. (Mackerras is a specialist in the music of Janáček, and his cast is to the manor born. The enchanting Lucia Popp is the ideal title character. The combination of a cast of good Czech singers and one of the world's greatest orchestras is an impossible combination to beat in this opera. Mackerras adds as an appendix Václav Talich's nineteen-minute orchestral suite of music from the opera. This recording may prove difficult to locate in the United States, but it should be available as an import from one of the British dealers.)

> *The Cunning Little Vixen* is available with Eva Jenis and Thomas Allen on DVD from Image.

Jenufa (1904)

Although it took twenty years and more to attract the attention it deserved, Jenufa (in Czech: *Jenůfa*) became one of the signal successes of opera in the twentieth century. Janáček was very much a composer of the human heart, but among all of his nine operas, this is the one that communicates most clearly the universal themes of forgiveness and love, and does so in a musical language that is immediately accessible to the broadest possible operatic audience.

There is violence in *Jenufa*, including a vicious attack on the title character and the murder of her child. The enduring effect of the opera, however, is not the violence, but the growth of the characters and the healing that results. *Jenufa* is not a tragedy in the ordinary sense of that term, rather a true *commedia*, a serious work that moves toward resolution and a sense of ultimate joy. The Kostelnička is indeed guilty of murder, and she is carried away at the end of the opera for trial and probable execution, but she is morally and spiritually redeemed by her act of compassion and confession, and her stepdaughter, Jenůfa, discovers "a love of such splendor that God himself smiles on us."*

As the composer saw the work, there are actually two title characters in the opera — Jenufa, of course, and also the Kostelniča, her stepmother. The title of the opera, *Její Pastorkyňa*, is difficult to translate, thus the convenient *Jenufa* for non–Czech speaking audiences, but the original suggests that both women are title characters. It means literally "not the daughter," or, as Janáček apparently preferred, "her stepdaughter." In performance, therefore, we listen particularly for strong performances in these two roles, although we always hope the other characters will be effectively performed as well.

The most highly acclaimed recording of *Jenufa* features performances by Elisabeth Södeström, Eva Randová, Wiesław Ochman, and Peter Dvorsky, conducted by Charles Mackerras. It has recently been made available again in the United States on Decca/London 414483, but I have not heard it. The version listed here, however, is one that I can recommend wholeheartedly.

---

*From the composer's libretto based on the play *Her Step-Daughter* by Gabriela Preissová, translated by Yveta Synek Graff and Robert T. Jones, copyright 1984.

(1988) BIS 449, with Gabriela Beňačová, Leonie Rysanek, Wiesław Ochman, Peter Kazaras, Schola Cantorum of New York, Opera Orchestra of New York, Eve Queler, Conductor. English language libretto. (This recording was made during a concert at New York's Carnegie Hall. Applause is included at the beginning and end of each act, but it does not intrude on the music and can be programmed out in playback. The performance has about it the immediacy of a live occasion before an audience. It is highly dramatic. Most of the singing is satisfying. Beňačková brings a gently lyric voice and sensitive interpretive gifts to the role of Jenufa. Both tenors, Ochman and Kazaras, acquit themselves well. Leonie Rysanek's performance as the Kostelnička is somewhat more controversial. The voice is hardly beautiful, but she interprets so keenly and effectively that it hardly matters. The sound quality of the recording is good but, of course, not the equivalent of a controlled studio version.)

Jenufa is available with Roberta Alexander and Anja Silja on VHS from Kultur.

Katya Kabanova (1921)

Written in Russian (original title: *Kát'a Kabanová*) this is a tragedy about guilt admitted and denied. In the case of Kát'a/Katya herself, a young woman of intense personal honesty, guilt is ultimately too great a burden to bear and she ends her life through suicide in the waters of the Volga River. On the other hand, Kabanicha, Katya's mother-in-law, who has brought about the tragedy through her cold and uncompromising attitude, is unwilling, or perhaps unable, to admit her own guilt. She tries to keep her son, Katya's husband, from aiding in the fruitless attempt to rescue his wife on the grounds that his wife really isn't worth the danger. Just as Katya is the most sympathetic, heartbreaking character in all of Janácek's operas, Kabanicha is clearly the most despicable. We look in vain for any redeeming feature in her character.

Janáček, who prepared his own libretto from Alexander Ostrovsky's Russian play

The Storm, goes beneath the surface to look deeply into the heart and mind of his heroine. She is deeply religious, almost a mystic, and in one sense her tragedy is not so much her conflict with her mother-in-law, as it is the struggle between her profound spirituality and her decidedly human emotional longings. Although Ostrovsky's play dates from 1860, there is something decidedly contemporary in the psychological and emotional complexity of Katya and the music that Janácek composed for her. Perhaps that is why this opera has attracted such a large, enthusiastic following in recent years.

I have not heard the critically praised 1976–78 recording of *Kát'a Kabanová* with Elisabeth Söderstrom, Neděžda Kniplova, and Peter Dvorsky, conducted by Charles Mackerras. It is available once more in the United States on Decca/London 4218522. Mackerras, however, conducted the opera once more in 1997 with a gifted Czech cast, and that is the version recommended here.

(1997) Supraphon 3291-2632, with Gabriela Beňačková, Eva Randová, Dagmar Pecková, Peter Straka, Miroslav Kopp, Chorus of the Prague National Theatre, Czech Philharmonic Orchestra, Charles Mackerras, Conductor. English language libretto. (Mackerras probably knows this opera better than any other conductor, and the cast is completely authentic. Beňačková is a convincing, vocally ingratiating Katya, and Randová a strong Kabanicha well able to project the vicious personality without unduly distorting the singing tone. Peter Straka is very appealing as Boris, the subject of Katya's passion and guilt. The somewhat subdued sound quality is clear and listenable.)

Katya Kabanova is available with Nancy Gustafson and Louise Winter on VHS from Kultur.

Ruggero Leoncavallo (1857–1919)

I Pagliacci (1892)

I Pagliacci has been so often performed as part of a double-bill with Mascagni's *Cavalleria Rusticana* that the two works are almost inseparable. They actually have a great deal in common as examples of the *verismo* school in full flower. Both of them present violent, hard-hitting stories of tragic life in the lower segments of nineteenth century Italian society, and both scores depend for their effect on strongly melodious music that calls for intense, immediate emotional responses. The two operas also stand as the only permanently memorable operas by their respective composers. Leoncavallo kept trying through eighteen additional works for the theater. With the exception, however, of an occasional revival of his version of *Bohème* and scattered references to *Zaza,* his operas are largely forgotten.

What is it that keeps *Pagliacci* alive and active on the stages of opera houses after a hundred years? Certainly the raw emotional drama helps, as does Leoncavallo's clever use of the play-within-a-play; but more than anything else it is music that has an immediate appeal, and a role that every tenor beyond the lightest pip-squeak aspires to sing. I might add that *Pagliacci* is also great fun, all the way from the famous Prologue to the final (spoken) line — "La commedia è finita." The comedy indeed is finished, but the melody lingers on.

Many tenors have recorded Canio, some of them unwisely so. We would have a lengthy discography indeed if we listed them all. One who was a natural for the role was Franco Corelli. His performance is available on disc (EMI 63 967), but aside from Corelli and Tito Gobbi, who sings Tonio, there is little to recommend here, and it is available only in conjunction with a recording of Mascagni's *Cavalleria Rusti-*cana that is acceptable but not a top contender in this crowded field. The three recommended recordings are all knockouts, as this opera clearly should be.

(1953) EMI 66778, with Jussi Bjoerling, Victoria de los Angeles, Leonard Warren, Robert Merrill, Paul Franke, Columbus Boys Choir, Robert Shaw Chorale, RCA Victor Orchestra, Renato Cellini, Conductor. English language libretto. (This is perhaps a more dignified and vocally resplendent performance than *Pagliacci* actually deserves, but it has the kind of cast that might make Leoncavallo's other operas resounding successes. The monophonic sound from 1953 is entirely acceptable.)

(1954) EMI 56287, with Maria Callas, Giuseppe di Stefano, Tito Gobbi, Rolando Panerai, Nicola Monti, Chorus and Orchestra of Teatro alla Scala, Milan, Tullio Serafin, Conductor. English language libretto. (This *Pagliacci* is issued only in a set along with *Cavalleria Rusticana*. Unlike the Corelli recording, however, the *Cavalleria* is also a top contender, and Gobbi is in younger, fresher voice here. Di Stefano is dramatically convincing, although the role is a trifle too heavy for his essentially lyric voice. Callas is overwhelming, and the other cast members are equal to their counterparts in any recording of the opera. The monophonic sound is good.)

(1965) Deutsche Grammophon 49727, with Carlo Bergonzi, Joan Carlyle, Giuseppe Taddei, Rolando Panerai, Ugo Benelli, Chorus and Orchestra of Teatro alla Scala, Milan, Herbert von Karajan, Conductor. English language libretto. (Recorded in good stereo sound, this recording will probably be your wisest first choice. Karajan effectively underlines the drama without taking it over the top. Bergonzi and Taddei are the center of vocal attention here, both of them singing and acting with style, voice, and conviction.)

I Pagliacci is available with Plácido Domingo and Teresa Stratas on VHS from Universal/Phillips.

Pietro Mascagni (1863–1945)

Cavalleria Rusticana (1890)

Mascagni, like Leoncavallo with *Pagliacci*, was never able to duplicate the success of *Cavalleria*. Otherwise, only his third opera, *L'Amico Fritz*, a delightful pastoral romance, continues to hold a somewhat tenuous place in opera houses today. *Cavalleria*, however, is a staple of the reportoire, as it has been since its premiere. It is a passionate, surging melodrama, set in Sicily on Easter Sunday, 1880. Mascagni provided the story with a profligate series of melodies that come so rapidly that they almost run into each other. The rush stops only once, and stops then for another good tune, the "Intermezzo," which at least provides an opportunity for audience and cast to take a breather while the Sicilians attend to their Easter worship.

Too much subtlety would destroy *Cavalleria,* but if the passion is unbridled, this tense little opera flies off in four different directions and stands in danger of becoming an operatic shouting match. As a matter of fact, there's only one place in the opera that calls for shouting at all, and that's at the very end when Turiddu's death is announced and everyone, according to the libretto, "cries out in horror." A good performance requires a strong conductor who keeps the cast in line without destroying their dramatic instincts.

The recordings recommended here include two earlier monophonic and two more recent stereo versions. Each of them is strongly and intensely sung.

(1953) BMG/RCA 6510, with Zinka Milanov, Jussi Bjoerling, Robert Merrill, Carol Smith, Robert Shaw Chorale, RCA Victor Orchestra, Renato Cellini, Conductor. English language libretto. (This recording is as close as we can come to golden-age singing. Milanov was *prima donna assoluta* at the Metropolitan Opera during the early nineteen fifties. She sings here like the great diva that she was, somewhat stately but always with feeling and in a voice that, although not perfect, conveys tremendous authority. Bjoerling is the best Turiddu in any of these recordings, and Robert Merrill is a vocal, if not always a dramatic paragon. The conducting is not equal to the vocalism. The monophonic recording is quite good.)

(1953) EMI 56287, with Maria Callas, Giuseppe di Stefano, Rolando Panerai, Anna Maria Canali, Chorus and Orchestra of Teatro alla Scala, Milan, Tullio Serafin, Conductor. English language libretto. (This monophonic recording is certainly the most dramatic of these *Cavalleria* recordings, but the drama is communicated through a large measure of musical sensitivity. Callas is passionate and vocally quite wonderful. She is also one of the most disciplined of singers, a characteristic of her artistry that often goes unnoticed. Di Stefano and Panerai are in the same league, but their batting average is a little lower than hers.)

(1965) Deutsche Garrmophon 457764, with Fiorenza Cossotto, Carlo Bergonzi, Giangiacomo Guelfi, Adriane Martino, Chorus and Orchestra of Teatro alla Scala, Milan, Herbert von Karajan, Conductor. English language libretto. (This recording is available alone or as a set with the Leoncavallo *Pagliacci*. Since both are beautifully conducted and sung, the combination makes a good first choice for the collection. Cossotto, the only mezzo-soprano Santuzza listed here, is particularly impressive.)

(1978) BMG/RCA 39500, with Renata Scotto, Plácido Domingo, Pablo Elvira, Isola Jones, Ambrosian Opera Chorus, National Philharmonic Orchestra, James Levine, Conductor. English language libretto. (Domingo contributes an extremely well sung Turridu. Scotto is in good voice and almost equals Callas in the drama of her role. If the combination recording with *Pagliacci* is not to your taste, this one is available at less than full price and makes a perfectly acceptable alternative.)

Cavalleria Rusticana is available with Plácido Domingo and Irina Obratztsova on VHS from Universal/Philips.

Jules Massenet (1842–1912)

Manon (1884)

Jules Massenet was a professional operatic composer in every sense. Writing for the lyric stage was certainly his business, and he pursued it diligently and profitably for forty years through more than thirty operas. As with anyone engaged in a professional venture, he was not always successful, but often he was, extraordinarily so. To balance such forgettable failures as *Le Mage* and *Bacchus,* there were artistic triumphs like *Manon* and *Werther.* But Massenet was a professional in another very important sense. He knew his business. He had mastered the craft of writing for the musical stage, and he was also an artist of considerable sensitivity, imagination, and artistry.

Massenet's reputation as a composer suffered badly in the years following his death in 1912. In more recent years, however, many of his operas have been successfully revived and favorably reevaluated, and a persistent collector can now accumulate almost half of his stage works on compact discs. Massenet has clearly reemerged as one of the major operatic composers of the nineteenth century.

The great lyric sopranos and tenors had enough influence to keep *Manon* alive in the repertoire through the years when Massenet's other operas were neglected. The title character herself is a figure of infinite variety, all of her changing moods fully revealed in the music; and her sometimes penitent lover, Des Grieux, expresses his conflicting emotions in a series of moving arias and duets. We listen in recordings for two singers with youthful voices, artistic maturity, and stylistic sensitivity — a rare but treasurable combination. Surprisingly, it has been realized to a greater or lesser extent in several recordings of *Manon.* The earliest dates from 1923, a pre-electrical version by the forces of the Paris Opéra Comique, and still available on Marston 52003. In 1929 the Opéra Comique provided another good recording of the opera, this time in early electrical sound (currently on The 78's 78049). These two, however, will not be acceptable for listeners who want to hear the opera in good modern sound. The three recommended versions are good performances, well recorded and with outstanding casts. Preferences will depend entirely on personal taste and interest in the specific artists involved in the recordings.

(1955) Testament SBT 3203, with Victoria de los Angeles, Henri Legay, Michel Dens, Jean Borthayre, Chorus and Orchestra of Théâtre National de l'Opéra-Comique, Pierre Monteux, Conductor. English language libretto. (Pierre Monteux was exactly the right conductor for this opera, and De los Angeles a remarkably gifted Manon, with the insight and the technique to reflect the changing lights in the character's personality. The other members of the cast were outstanding French singers of the period, and De los Angeles, although Spanish, was a mistress of French language and style. The late monophonic sound is beautifully reproduced. Standard opera house cuts are observed, but the three discs also include excellent performances of Debussy's *La Damoiselle Élue* and Berlioz's *Les Nuits d'Été.*)

(1970) EMI 69831, with Beverly Sills, Nicolai Gedda, Gérard Souzay, Gabriel Bacquier, Ambrosian Opera Chorus, New Philharmonia Orchestra, Julius Rudel, Conductor. English language libretto. (Manon is considered by many to have been Beverly Sills' finest accomplishment. This recording shows her at her vocal and dramatic best, and the other singers are all good. As Rudel conducts, this is throughout a bigger, bolder performance than Monteux's. The recording restores the traditional theater cuts and includes in an appendix the alternate aria, "Oui, dans les bois et dans la plaine," that Massenet composed apparently for Georgette Bréjean-Silver in an 1894 production.)

(1999) EMI 57005, with Angela Gheo-rghiu, Roberto Alagna, Earle Patriarco, José van Dam, Orchestra and Chorus of the Monnaie, Antonio Pappano, Conductor. English language libretto. (This is an excellent complete performance with everybody's favorite opera couple in the leading roles. They, however, are artists who, at least in this case, live up to their hype, both of them sensitive, willing to sing softly, and able to sustain the musical line without putting pressure on their voices. The effect is like heartfelt musical conversation, subtle and emotionally satisfying.)

Manon is available with Beverly Sills and Henry Price on VHS from Paramount Home Video.

Werther (1892)

In recent years, Massenet's *Werther* has come to equal, perhaps even surpass, *Manon* in popularity. It is probably the better opera of the two, with a more neatly organized dramatic structure and a flow of music that precisely expresses the complex psychological states of the two main characters at each moment. Although *Manon* is intensely personal, *Werther* is the more intimate opera, centering as it does on the private and shared emotional responses of a couple involved in what is, given their social milieu, an impossible relationship. Its source was Goethe's semi-autobiographical novel *The Sorrows of the Young Werther,* one of the works of the early Romantic movement.

There is a full measure of sorrow in the opera, but "young," it seems to me, is the true operative word in Goethe's title, and that approach should ideally carry over into performances of the opera. Werther is twenty-three, Charlotte twenty, and Albert, her fiancé, later her husband, only twenty-five, and they do not respond with the mature understanding born out of years of life experience. It isn't necessary that the singers actually be young, but they must *sound* young, young enough, that is, so that we can appreciate in them the emotional responses of youth caught in the intensity of a first love that goes tragically wrong.

Of course, on a recording the singers' appearance is not a concern. In the recordings suggested here the artists manage to communicate both the youth and the intensity through purely vocal means. *Werther* has been often recorded, and there are additional worthwhile versions not included in the list here. One that I have not heard, but which has received excellent notices is on BMG/RCA 58224, with Vesselina Kasarova and Ramon Vargas. I have included one earlier recording from 1931 because of its overall excellence, but the more recent recordings are also satisfactory. We have here a true embarrassment of riches.

(1931) The 78's 78034 or Grammofono AB 78 742/43, with Georges Thill, Ninon Vallin, Germaine Feraldy, Marcel Roque, Chorus and Orchestra of the Théâtre de l'Opéra-Comique, Elie Cohen, Conductor. No libretto. (This early recording has in the principal roles the two greatest French singers of the 1930s, Georges Thill and Ninon Vallin. The performance as a whole is stylistically completely authentic, and I can vouch for good sound for an early electrical recording — at least on the Grammofono release, which is the one I have heard. This is one of the few historical recordings that deserves consideration as your only recording of *Werther*, but the absence of a libretto is a serious drawback.)

(1968–1969) EMI 63973, with Nicolai Gedda, Victoria de les Angeles, Mady Mesplé, Roger Soyer, Children's Chorus of O.R.T.F., Orchestre de Paris, Georges Prêtre, Conductor. English language libretto. (Gedda and de los Angeles are superb. Werther's suicidal despair and Charlotte's emotional conflict are fully expressed in voices that serve the music well. The stereo sound is good. This recording has stood the test of time quite well.)

(1995) Erato or Elektra/Asylum 17790, with Jerry Hadley, Anne Sofie von Otter, Dawn Upshaw, Gêrard Thêruel, Maîtrise de l'Opéra de Lyon, Orchestra of l'Opéra de

Lyon, Ken Nagano, Conductor. English language libretto. (Von Otter presents a beautifully vocalized and dramatic Charlotte. Hadley is lyrical and powerful, but not quite the equal of the tenors in the other recordings. Charlotte is sung by both sopranos and mezzo-sopranos, and Von Otter is the only actual mezzo in the recordings listed here. In spite of the darker vocal coloration, she still sounds like a young woman.)

(1998) EMI 56820, Roberto Alagna, Angela Gheorghiu, Patricia Petibon, Thomas Hampson, Tiffin Children's Choir, London Symphony Orchestra, Antonio Pappano, Conductor. English language libretto. (With up-to-date stereo sound, this version makes an excellent choice. Alagna and Gheorghiu are well into their roles, and they both sing with conviction and ingratiating tone. The role of Charlotte is frequently done by a mezzo-soprano. Gheorghiu is another soprano heroine, but she colors her voice more darkly, at least in this role, than most sopranos.)

Werther is available with Brigitte Fassbaender and Peter Dvorsky on DVD from Images.

Gian-Carlo Menotti (1911–)

Amahl and the Night Visitors (1951)

From the beginning of his career, Gian-Carlo Menotti was successful. His first opera, *Amelia Goes to the Ball,* had its premiere in Philadelphia in 1937. Within a year, it had been performed at New York's Metropolitan Opera House, and a month later it appeared in Italy as *Amelia al Ballo.* Of course, he didn't quite equal the record achieved by Mozart, whose first opera was performed when he was eleven, but the Met is not a bad beginning for a composer still in his thirties. Menotti went on to become one of the twentieth-century pioneers in lifting opera from the opera house and transplanting it to the Broadway stage and other centers of popular theater.

How did he manage it? He did it in the most obvious way possible — by writing interesting, imaginative librettos and setting them to music that people enjoyed hearing.

His scores are accessible to a broad general public. They are tuneful even when touched by a relatively tempered modernism. Their appeal reaches a broad audience in a way that many operas of the last fifty years do not, and Menotti's "Broadway operas" of the 1940s and 1950s attracted large general audiences.

Amahl is one of those works, although it was composed not for Broadway but for the even broader audience of American television viewers. It soon found its way into the opera houses and, perhaps even more important, into the performances of a multitude of amateur groups around the world. It is probably not Menotti's best opera. Many would claim that *The Consul* is his masterpiece. But it is surely his most popular. The plot is simple, a moving Christmas "miracle" story, and the music is immediately appealing.

There are two recordings of *Amahl* currently available. Both are worth considering, but most listeners will prefer the 1986 stereo recording.

(1952) BMG/RCA 6485, with Chet Allen, Rosemary Kuhlmann, Andrew McKinley, David Aiken, Leon Lishner, Frank Monachino, Unidentified orchestra and chorus, Thomas Schippers, Conductor. English language libretto. (This performance was recorded by the original cast under Menotti's supervision two or three weeks after the first performance. The cast is excellent and certainly authentic, with special honors to Allen and Kuhlmann. The sound is acceptable, but somewhat overly resonant and cavernous.)

(1986) Jay Records 1303, with James Rainbird, Lorna Haywood, John Dobson, Donald Maxwell, Curtis Watson, Christopher Painter, Chorus and Orchestra of the Royal Opera House, David Syrus, Conductor. No libretto. (The voices are good and the singers enunciate the English text clearly so that the absence of a libretto is no problem for English-speaking listeners. Menotti himself commented on the excellent diction of James Rainbird, who sings the role of Amahl. This recording, like the one above, benefited from the composer's guidance, and he has expressed his approval of the results.)

Amahl and the Night Visitors is available with Teresa Stratas and Robert Sapolsky on VHS from Republic Studios.

Giacomo Meyerbeer (1791–1864)

Les Huguenots (1836)

Meyerbeer, who was German by birth, began his career as an operatic composer in his native land, competed successfully for several years in Italy, and eventually found his permanent artistic home in France. We remember him primarily as the most influential composer of that distinctive French form known as *grand opéra*. These massive works were frequently based on historical subjects and included spectacular scenic effects, large ensembles, elaborate vocal writing for the soloists, ballets, and almost anything else that could be added to amaze the audience. The surprising thing is that in the hands of a gifted composer like Meyerbeer this conglomeration of disparate elements could also contain interesting music and convincing dramatic situations.

One of the greatest of *grand opéras* was *Les Huguenots,* with a highly dramatic plot dealing with the personal and political conflicts between Protestants and Catholics that led to the St. Bartholomew's Day Massacre in 1572. Its premiere was a major triumph, and for many years it drew sell-out audiences in opera houses over the world. At the Metropolitan Opera, *Huguenots* performances were known as the "night of the seven stars." In December 1894 the man-

agers raised the top ticket price to seven dollars, one dollar for each of the "seven stars"—Lillian Nordica, Nellie Melba, Sofia Scalchi, Jean de Reszke, Victor Maurel, Édouard de Reszke, and Pol Plançon. The popularity of *Huguenots* faded early in the twentieth century, perhaps because opera companies were no longer willing or able to provide an equally impressive line-up.

A successful "seven-starred" revival at La Scala in 1962 has been available in a number of "live" editions, most conveniently on Opera d'Oro 1217. The sound, however, is poor, and the uneven recording quality and the Italian text disqualify it for recommendation here.

(1969) Decca/London 430549, with Joan Sutherland, Martina Arroyo, Huguette Tourangeau, Anastasios Vrenios, Gabriel Bacquier, Nicola Ghiuselev, Ambrosian Opera Chorus, New Philharmonia Orchestra, Richard Bonynge, Conductor. English language libretto. (This only partially successful recording will have to do unless an enterprising company brings together an assemblage of seven real stars and gives us a new version. Sutherland is the great attraction here, and her singing of Queen Marguerite's big aria is spectacular. Martina Arroyo as Valentine, the major soprano role, has a beautiful voice, not quite as incisive as we would like in this music. The rest of the cast is competent, except for tenor Vrenios, who is somewhat less than that. Bonynge, however, has a real feel for this music. If and when a new recording is made, he would be a likely conductor.)

Les Huguenots is available with Richard Leech and Angela Denning on DVD from Arthaus Music, and with Joan Sutherland and Anson Austin on VHS from Kultur.

Claudio Monteverdi (1567–1643)

L'Incoronazione di Poppea (1643)

Prior to 1637, opera had been essentially a privilege of the wealthy nobility.

They could afford to stage elaborate musical entertainments for such special occasions as royal weddings and to insist that the plots of the operas, almost entirely drawn from classical mythology, gave due respect to the ruling classes. When the first public opera house opened in Venice in 1637, however, audiences began to change, and opera changed with them. Producers now had to depend on a paying public, who could opt to stay home and read the latest *sermoni* of Chiabrera if the opera of the evening didn't interest them. It became essential to have subjects with popular appeal and music accessible enough to lodge in the memory.

The first masterpiece of this new type of opera was Claudio Monteverdi's *L'Incoronazione di Poppea*. Far from glorified mythological figures, the characters — the Emperor Nero, Octavia, Poppea, Seneca, and others — were familiar to any Italian who knew the national history, and the events in their lives were quite scandalous enough to make for a sensational plot. Add to the story the fact that Monteverdi was the greatest Italian composer of the seventeenth century, and here were all the ingredients for a spectacular popular success.

The libretto that Monteverdi glorified with his wonderful music remains controversial and morally ambiguous. We may expect virtue to triumph in the end, but the victors in this case are the Emperor Nero and his sometimes mistress and wife, Poppea. They conclude the opera singing a joyful and erotically charged duet (probably composed by a hand other than Monteverdi's), and we are left torn between distress at the amoral ways of human history and delight at this satirical view of life among the rich and famous. To multiply our confusion, we are led by the eloquence of the music to sympathize with all of the characters, none of whom, with the possible exception of Seneca and Drusilla, behave according to the highest standards of virtue.

Incoronazione has been a very popular opera both on the stage and on disc. There are a number of worthwhile recordings, and no two of them approach the score in the same way. The two editions listed here follow different sources, but each is based on a careful attempt to establish an accurate performing edition and to recapture authentic seventeenth century performing style. Both editions include in the printed material interesting essays on how and why the decisions concerning the version to record were made.

(1988) Virgin Veritas 561783, with Arleen Auger, Della Jones, Linda Hirst, James Bowman, Sarah Leonard, Gregory Reinhart, Adrian Thompson, City of London Baroque Sinfonia, Richard Hickox, Conductor. English language libretto. (There are two manuscript sources for *Incoronazione*, one from Venice and another from Naples, neither original with the composer. This recording follows the Venice version as closely as possible. The performance is relatively austere in effect. The drama is provided primarily by the singers, who are all quite good, through purely vocal means.)

(1993) Deutsche Grammophon Archiv 47088, with Sylvia McNair, Dana Hanchard, Anne Sofie von Otter, Michael Chance, Catherine Bott, Francesco Ellero d'Artegna, Bernarda Fink, the English Baroque Soloists, John Eliot Gardiner, Conductor. English language libretto. (The primary source for the version of the opera recorded here is the Naples manuscript. Gardiner's performance is more convincing dramatically than Hickox's. The singers are equally gifted and go a little further in communicating personality. This recording is probably the better choice for the general listener.)

L'Incoronazione di Poppea is available with Maria Ewing and Robert Lloyd on VHS from Kultur, and with Patricia Schumann and Richard Croft on DVD from Arthaus Music.

L'Orfeo (1607)

Monteverdi's *Orfeo* was the first great opera. We may applaud his contemporaries — Giacomo Peri, Giulio Caccini, Emilio dei Cavalieri, and others — for their seriousness of purpose and their ground-breaking attempts to create a persuasive form of dramatic musical declamation, but their few surviving stage works are primarily of historical rather than artistic interest. With *Orfeo* we arrive for the first time at an opera that continues to hold the stage and enthrall audiences almost four hundred years after its first performance.

The myth of Orpheus, the musician son of Apollo, has inspired composers in every age. They have found in it symbols of both the tragedy and the triumph of the artist. For Monteverdi, the triumph ultimately prevails, and the final chorus affirms that after the irretrievable loss of his beloved Euridice, Orpheus and his lyre will dwell in the heavens, where joy never draws to an end. It's as if Monteverdi is saying to us that great art is too wonderful to lose, that it must survive.

Some performances of early music give the impression of impersonal academic exercises or chilly scholarly investigations into a long dead past. *Orfeo,* however, is not a museum piece. It is a vital art work, just as exciting today as it has ever been. The best recordings, including the two recommended here, bring this masterpiece to life for us, not by trying to remake it into a contemporary opera, but rather by attempting to restore something close to the original form and style and then performing it with enthusiasm and conviction.

(1985) Deutsche Grammophon Archiv 19250, with Anthony Rolfe Johnson, Julianne Baird, Lynne Dawson, Anne Sofie von Otter, John Tomlinson, Willard White, Diana Montague, the Monteverdi Choir, the English Baroque Soloists, His Majesties Sagbutts and Cornetts, John Eliot Gardiner, Conductor. English language libretto. (Gardiner makes convincing decisions concerning instrumentation, always a controversial aspect of recordings of *Orfeo* since scoring in the early printed scores is confusing and ambiguous. He keeps the action moving. Gardiner's cast is gifted and obviously believes that there is real drama here to be communicated through music. Particularly impressive is Rolfe Johnson, who manages to persuade us of the expressive beauty of Monteverdi's vocal writing.)

(1995) Harmonia Mundi 901553, with Laurence Dale, Efrat Ben-Nun, Jennifer Larmore, Paul Gérimon, Harry Peeters, Andres Scholl, Nicolas Rivenq, Concerto Vocale, René Jacobs, Conductor. English language libretto. (Jacobs' version, based on performances at the 1993 Salzburg Festival, is large-scale and forceful, with the feel of the stage about it. The members of the excellent cast sing well, with particular strength in the smaller roles. The encounter with Charon is especially dramatic, and Paul Gérimon is wonderfully powerful and dark-hued as the guardian of the Styx. Dale is an impressive Orfeo, sensitive to emotional responses and in good control of dynamics. Both recommended recordings find drama and excitement in the score, but the Harmonia Mundi seems to me to have a slight edge.)

Orfeo is available on VHS from Universal Music and Video (no cast listing available).

Douglas Moore (1893–1969)

The Ballad of Baby Doe (1956)

A major challenge for the modern American composer is to produce an opera that will meet with the approval of professional critics and musicians, and at the same time attract an audience large and enthusiastic enough to assure a place in the continuing repertoire. Very few composers have been able to manage it. One who came close was Douglas Moore with *The Ballad of Baby Doe*, and he accomplished this feat in a score filled with easy harmony, approachable tunes, and sentimental, heart-on-the-sleeve emotional situations. It is hard to imagine a less pretentious opera, or one that is more effective in a good performance.

The plot is drawn from a series of historical events, the story of Horace Tabor, a Colorado mining millionaire who spent thirty days as a United States Senator, and his love for Elizabeth McCourt ("Baby") Doe, who became his second wife. Bankrupt after the Panic of 1893, Tabor died in 1898, but Baby Doe lived on in poverty near the old mine site. Here in 1935 she was found frozen to death. The opera is so fully grounded in history that Moore actually included among the characters President Chester Arthur and William Jennings Bryan, who sings what must be the only political speech made into an operatic aria. Much of the appeal of the opera derives from the skill with which Moore composed a score that sounds exactly right for the nineteenth century American setting. As some critics have commented, it often sounds like a Broadway musical, albeit a rather sophisticated one; but it is truly an opera, composed throughout without spoken dialogue, with the action fully communicated through music.

The recommended recording was made in 1959, not long after a revised version of the opera was first performed at the New York City Opera in 1958. Walter Cassel had appeared in the original production at Central City, Colorado, in 1956. He was joined in the New York City Opera performances and recording by Beverly Sills in one of the roles that helped establish her outstanding career.

(1959) Deutsche Grammophon 465148, with Beverly Sills, Walter Cassel, Frances Bible, Joshua Hecht, Orchestra and Chorus of the New York City Opera, Emerson Buckley, Conductor. English language libretto. (This recording is certainly the definitive version of the opera. The cast is excellent. Cassel sings with authority, and Frances Bible rises to the challenge of her Act II aria, the climax of an otherwise rather thankless role. It's exciting to hear Beverly Sills early in her career. The tone is absolutely pure, the vocal acting wonderfully effective. The recorded sound is far superior to that on the original long-playing records.)

Wolfgang Amadeus Mozart (1756–1791)

Così Fan Tutte (1790)

The nineteenth century was uncomfortable with *Così Fan Tutte*. They took their comedy seriously, and if the comedy of *Così* is taken seriously, some precious icons begin to crumble. How could two such noble ladies as Fiordiligi and Dorabella prove to be unfaithful to the men to whom they have sworn unswerving loyalty? And how could real gentlemen, as we assume Guglielmo and Ferrando to be (since they are the chosen lovers of two such noble ladies), possibly agree to play such a cruel trick on the unsuspecting ladies? Questions of morality were involved, and the result was performances with altered librettos, some of which removed even the hint of serious infidelity.

Of course, if the comedy is not taken seriously, there are no problems. Farce can cover a multitude of sins. Da Ponte's libretto is highly artificial, with one action balanced against another and the entire plot occupying a neat twenty-four hour period. Perhaps we are expected merely to laugh and let it go. The difficulty, however, is that Mozart wrote music of such profound beauty and psychological insight that we are virtually forced to take these characters seriously, even if we do so with a smile. Their emotions are complicated and real, and the characters are themselves carefully differentiated from one another in both the music and the text. We are left with an opera that is still a puzzle, although perhaps not quite so much a moral problem as it was a hundred years ago.

The great popularity of *Così Fan Tutte* is largely a twentieth-century phenomenon.

The notable production at Glyndebourne in Great Britain beginning in 1934 was recorded in 1935 (available on Arkadia 78011 and probably other labels as well). In the United States, the first performances were at the Metropolitan Opera in 1922. A popular Metropolitan Opera English-language revival in 1951 was committed to disc and is available on Sony 60652. In more recent years, *Così fan Tutte* has been recorded often and frequently quite well. The three recommended editions are representative.

(1962) EMI 67379, with Elisabeth Schwarzkopf, Christa Ludwig, Hanny Steffek, Alfredo Kraus, Giuseppe Taddei, Walter Berry, Philharmonia Orchestra and Chorus, Karl Böhm, Conductor. English language libretto. (This classic recording has an excellent conductor and cast, particularly notable for the superb performances of Elisabeth Schwarzkopf and Christa Ludwig. Two cuts, more or less traditional, are taken, but otherwise the performance is complete. The stereo recording quality is entirely acceptable.)

(1994) Decca/London 44174, with Renée Fleming, Sofie von Otter, Adelina Scarabelli, Frank Lopardo, Olaf Bär, Michele Pertusi, London Voices, Chamber Orchestra of Europe, Georg Solti, Conductor. English language libretto. (This performance is one of Solti's best. It was recorded at a pair of London concerts and employed an unusually gifted cast. The recording quality is excellent, and the performance is complete. This is probably the best choice for a collection that will contain only one recording of *Così Fan Tutte*.)

(1995) EMI 56170, with Hillevi Martinpelto, Alison Hagley, Gerald Finley, Kurt Streit, Ann Murray, Thomas Allen, Choir of the Enlightenment, Orchestra of the Age of Enlightenment, Simon Rattle, Conductor. English language libretto. (The Age of Enlightenment orchestra plays on period instruments, and Rattle keeps them moving in a performance with great dramatic thrust. There are no big names in the cast, but all sing well and are dramatically aware.

I have not heard two other period performances that rate high critical approval on Deutsche Grammophon Archiv 37829 and Harmonia Mundi 951663.)

Così Fan Tutte is available with Daniela Dessi and Delores Ziegler on DVD from Image and on VHS from Public Media.

Don Giovanni (1787)

Don Giovanni is a perennial. It blossoms again year after year in opera houses all over the world and springs up regularly in new recordings.

The popularity has a firm basis. First of all, there is the story itself and the character at its center. They were found in various forms in European folklore from several different nations before they entered the realm of literature in a 1630 Spanish play. Don Juan's (or Giovanni, in Italian) persistence over the years points to a kind of mythic significance. Apparently the character strikes at the human psyche chords of unhampered desire, unlimited freedom, and inescapable retribution. Giovanni is, perhaps subconsciously, the person we fear and the person we wish to be.

Then there is the music. Many people see Mozart as the greatest, most creative composer who ever lived, and he lavished his gifts on this opera. The music, however, is part of the puzzle of *Don Giovanni*, and the puzzle helps to make the opera interesting and challenging. It's because of the depth and ambiguity of Mozart's music that we do not always know what to make of the opera. The score is alternately delightfully humorous and deadly serious. Is it a comedy? Is it a tragedy? Is it a morality play? Certainly Leporello, Giovanni's servant, is a comic character, and a rake like Giovanni who manages so often to get away with it is one of the classic figures of humor. But there is surely nothing funny about the anguish of Donna Anna or the icy hand of the statue and the fiery fate of Giovanni himself.

Mozart prepared two versions of the opera, one for Prague in 1787 and a second for Vienna the next year. For the Vienna performances, he added a recitative and aria for Donna Elvira (In quail eccessi ... Mi tradi), wrote a new aria for Don Ottavio (Dalla sua pace) to replace the more difficult Il mio tesoro, deleted a brief aria for Leporello (Ah, pieta, signori miei), added a comic duet for Zerlina and Leporello, and made other slight changes. Modern performances, including those on disc, usually include most or all of the material, with the exception of the duet for Zerlina and Leporello.

Don Giovanni has been honored with a number of fine recordings. To the three recommended here we could easily add as many more, starting with the 1936 recording from Glyndebourne (Pearl 9369) and continuing to the famous 1956 edition conducted by Josef Krips (Decca/London 466389) and Von Karajan's 1986 version (Deutsche Grammophon 19179). There are others as well that I have not heard. Those suggested here, however, have in each case something special to recommend them.

> (1959) EMI 56232, with Eberhard Wächter, Joan Sutherland, Elisabeth Schwarzkopf, Graziella Sciutti, Luigi Alva, Giuseppe Taddei, Piero Cappuccilli, Gottlob Frick, Philharmonia Orchestra and Chorus, Carlo Maria Giulini, Conductor. English language libretto. (This distinguished recording has been around for a number of years but retains its youthful spirit. Giulini conducts a performance of spirit, drama, and wonderful ensemble. The cast is the most distinguished ever gathered for a recording of *Giovanni*. Sutherland's vocalism is spectacular; Schwarzkopf presents the most complete and detailed portrait of Donna Elvira. This performance does not include the duet for Zerlina and Leporello.)

> (1984) EMI 47036, with Thomas Allen, Carol Vaness, Maria Ewing, Elizabeth Gale, Keith Lewis, John Rawnsley, Dimitri Kavrakos, Glyndebourne Chorus, London Philharmonic Orchestra, Bernard Haitnik, Conductor. English language libretto. (Haitnik conducts an unusually balanced cast of singers in a dramatically exciting performance. Vaness is an incisive, involved Donna Anna, and Thomas Allen a suave Giovanni who could well have deceived all of the women Leporello gives him credit for. The Zerlina-Leporello duet is not performed. The recording quality is excellent.)

> (1994) Deutsche Grammophon Archiv 45870, with Rodney Gilfry, Luba Organasova, Charlotte Margiono, Eirian James, Christoph Prégardien, Ildebrando d'Arcangelo, Julian Clarkson, Monteverdi Choir, English Baroque Soloists. English language libretto. John Eliot Gardiner, Conductor. (The opera is played on period instruments. Aside from some sessions to polish, it was recorded "live," and it has the feel of a cast acting and reacting to one another in a real performance. All of the singers are vocally and dramatically assured, with particular honors for Gilfry, who provides a wonderfully varied interpretation of Giovanni, and Orgonasova, the vocally superb Donna Anna. Gardiner has chosen the complete Vienna version, including the Zerlina-Leporello duet, but the music that is different in the Prague version is included in an appendix. We have here, then, all of Mozart's *Giovanni* music. If you are to have only one *Giovanni*, you would do well to choose this version for its completeness and overall excellence.)

Don Giovanni is available with Thomas Allen and Edita Gruberova on DVD from Image and on VHS from Public Media.

Die Entführung aus dem Serail (1782)

Mozart was a young but already highly experienced musician when he composed *Die Entführung*. At twenty-six years of age, he had already completed ten and a half operas, including at least one masterpiece, *Idomeneo*. He was a notoriously fast learner, and surely he had mastered his craft by now. There are points in *Die Entführung*, however, that may cause us to wonder.

In some ways it is an awkward opera.

Perhaps it was the limited roster of singers at Vienna's Burgtheater, the site of the premiere, that dictated that the cast, aside from one bass role, would include only tenors and sopranos, and that a major character in the action would be played as a speaking role. It's also true that the position of the arias in the action doesn't always quite fit, and the length of a few of the musical numbers seems out of proportion with the situation. Conductors and producers over the years have tried all nature of revisions to whip the opera into conventional shape. On occasion they have even rewritten the libretto, and in staged performances it's always interesting to see what action the director will devise to keep Konstanze and Selim Pasha busy during the long orchestral introduction to "Martern aller Arten."

Whatever the problems, however, Mozart composed the kind of score that keeps *Die Entführung* alive on stage and disc. It is an amazing opera, filled with music that alternates between extraordinary beauty and rollicking humor. The nature of the characters assures that variety. There is Osmin, the basso profundo, who exits in a comic rage at the end of the opera, and then there are the two contrasting pairs of lovers, Konstanze and Belmonte, and their respective servants, Blonde and Pedrillo. Mozart provides them with music that fully reveals their personalities and their positions. The only musical regret is that Selim Pasha is a speaking role with no wonderful Mozartian melodies to sing.

On the whole, the singers in the two recommended recordings do justice to the wonderful music Mozart provided for them.

(1954) Deutsche Grammophon 457730, with Maria Stader, Rita Streich, Ernst Haefliger, Martin Vantin, Josef Greindl, RIAS Chamber Choir and Symphony, Ferenc Fricsay, Conductor. English language libretto. (This famous recording from a number of years ago is available now in greatly improved monophonic sound. The performance is complete with the exception of the brief Turkish march in Act I, which is often omitted. Fricsay keeps the action moving, and the cast responds with spirited performances. Stader's Konstanze isn't vocally perfect in the difficult passage work, but the voice itself is beautiful, and she really means what she sings. Haefliger is an excellent lyric tenor Belmonte. Rita Streich is the ideal Blonde, and Greindl's voluminous dark bass is just right for Osmin.)

(1991) Deutsche Grammophon Archiv 435857, with Luba Orgonasova, Cyndia Sieden, Stanford Olsen, Uwe Peper, Cornelius Hauptmann, Monteverdi Choir, English Baroque Soloists, John Eliot Gardiner, Conductor. English language libretto. (Gardiner conducts with a great deal of flexibility and strikes a good balance between the comic and the serious elements in the score. The cast on the whole is quite good, with particular honors to Luba Orgonasova, the outstanding Konstanze. Her singing of "Martern aller Arten" is surely one of the marvels of modern phonographic history. Only Cornelius Hauptmann as Osmin disappoints with a bottom-weak bass. Without the right voice for the role, he is forced to impose extra musical vocal devices in the attempt to characterize. The recording is complete, including the Turkish march. This is a logical first choice for addition to a collection.)

Die Entführung aus dem Serail is available with Inge Nielsen and Deon van der Walt on VHS from Kultur.

Le Nozze di Figaro (1786)

When opera lovers set out to determine the "perfect opera," Mozart's *Nozze di Figaro*, along with Bizet's *Carmen* and Verdi's *Otello*, is one of the prime contenders. Of course, the championship is never finally determined. How could it be when every candidate is a winner? But *Nozze* is always close to the top of the card. It has everything—a magnificent libretto from Lorenzo Da Ponte by way of Beaumarchais, characters whose humanity makes them sympathetic and immediately identifiable to the audience, and a musical score that is at once beautifully constructed, witty, deeply moving, even inspiring. It is a work of genius.

Le Nozze is now the most popular of Mozart's operas, a position once held by *Don Giovanni*. It is on the whole a brighter, sunnier work, one in which everyone and everything comes to a happy conclusion, as the closing ensemble in the opera informs us. Before that euphoria is reached, however, some darker shadows have drifted across the scene. We have shared the sadness of the Countess as she wonders what has happened to the joy and assurance of the past. We have heard the noble Count confess to us his anger that a mere commoner can enjoy the love of beautiful Susanna and he cannot. We have seen Figaro's jealousy boil over in a diatribe against women in general. All of that, and there is also running just slightly beneath the surface of the entire opera a sense of social unrest, of class against class. *Le Nozze* is certainly a comic opera, but very much a thought-provoking example of the genre.

For a Vienna revival of *Le Nozze* in 1789, Mozart composed two new arias for Susanna to replace "Venite inginocchiatevi" in Act II and "Deh vieni non tardar" in Act IV. Neither is as effective as the composer's original inspiration, but second-rate Mozart is better than the first-rate product of most other composers. These substitute arias are not included in recordings of the opera, but along with Mozart's other "concert" arias, they are available on disc (most conveniently and economically on Decca/London 455241, sung beautifully by Edita Gruberova and Teresa Berganza).

Complete recordings of *Le Nozze* are many in number and often of high quality. The three included in our list here offer uncommonly gifted singers and the direction of distinguished conductors.

(1955) Decca/London 466369, with Cesare Siepi, Lisa della Casa, Hilde Gueden, Suzanne Danco, Alfred Poell, Hilde Rössel-Majdan, Fernando Corena, Murray Dickie, Vienna State Opera Chorus, Vienna Philharmonic, Erich Kleiber, Conductor. English language libretto. (Don't let the date hold you back. The early stereo sound on this recording is quite good. The performance is complete, including the frequently omitted arias for Basilio and Marcellina. Marcellina's aria, however, is sung by Hilde Gueden, the Susanna. This is probably the best conducted *Figaro* on disc, and the cast assembled is an outstanding group of Mozart specialists. This recording is a good choice if you will only have one *Figaro* in the collection.)

(1959) EMI 63266, with Giuseppe Taddei, Elisabeth Schwarzkopf, Anna Moffo, Fiorenza Cossotto, Eberhard Wächter, Dora Gatta, Ivo Vinco, Renato Ercolani, Philharmonia Chorus and Orchestra, Carlo Maria Giulini, Conductor. English language libretto. (Here is another top-flight cast working under a gifted conductor. There has never been a more elegant Countess than Schwarzkopf. One listens with pleasure at the young Anna Moffo as Susanna. Cossotto makes a strong, lively Cherubini before she went on to such heavier Verdi roles as Lady Macbeth and Azucena. The only drawback, a serious one if you only have one recording of *Figaro*, is the absence of the arias for Marcellina and Basilio.)

(1981) Decca/London 10150, with Samuel Ramey, Kiri Te Kanawa, Lucia Popp, Frederica von Stade, Thomas Allen, Jane Berbié, Kurt Moll, Robert Tear, London Opera Chorus, London Philharmonic Orchestra, Georg Solti, Conductor. English language libretto. (Here is another complete recording with a 1980s cast that could hardly have been bettered. Ramey's Figaro and Te Kanawa's Countess are beautifully sung, and Lucia Popp is the best Susanna on any recording. Kurt Moll sings well enough to make Bartolo one of the real stars of the opera. Solti's conducting is controversial but always interesting.)

Le Nozze di Figaro is available with Bryn Terfel and Rodney Gilfry on DVD from

Universal/Deutsche Grammophon, and with Hermann Prey and Kiri Te Kanawa on VHS also from Universal/Deutsche Grammophon.

Die Zauberflöte (1791)

No opera has suffered a greater variety of interpretations than *Die Zauberflöte*. Emanuel Schikaneder, Mozart's librettist, prepared a text that is clearly allegorical. The problem is that the allegory seems at one moment to point in one direction and then to lean toward something else a moment later, and critical analysts through the years have been left scratching their heads in confusion. Is it a political satire? And if it is, toward whom is the satire aimed? Is the wicked Queen of the Night meant to be the Empress Maria Theresa? One contemporary interpretation saw the opera as a statement in support of the French Revolution, but another found in the noble Sarastro an inspiring representative of precisely the other side in that great conflict. Much of the symbolism in the opera appears to be drawn from Masonry, but whether this is merely operatic window dressing or something deeper, no one knows.

The lesson may be that *Zauberflöte* is better approached not as an exercise in interpretive cleverness, but rather as a great masterpiece in which noble sentiments are communicated in transcendent music and the deepest corners of the human heart are given lyrical expression. For all the magical trappings of the plot and hidden allegory of the characters, the people in this opera are real people. They face trials, they suffer, they love, they fail, and they triumph. As in all great operas, we find ourselves in the music.

In addition to the two recordings recommended here, you should be aware of two other versions. Neither of them, however, will serve as the only recording in a collection because they omit all of the spoken dialogue. The result is a series of wonderful musical numbers with no dramatic continuity. As performances of Mozart's score, however, both of them are well worth adding as second and third versions. In 1937 Sir Thomas Beecham recorded the opera with the Berlin Philharmonic and as fine a group of singers as he could gather in the Nazi Germany of the period. That recording is available on a number of different labels. The sound on Nimbus 7827, the version I have heard, is listenable. I understand that the recording on Dutton Laboratories 5011 is also quite good. Twenty-seven years later, the great conductor Otto Klemperer assembled a wonderful cast in which even the smaller roles were taken by world-class singers. His recording emphasizes the depth of Mozart's musical imagination, but no persuasion could convince him to include the spoken dialogue. His version of *Zauberflöte* is on EMI 55173.

(1981) EMI 47951, with Lucia Popp, Edita Gruberova, Siegfried Jerusalem, Wolfgang Brendel, Roland Bracht, Chorus and Symphony of the Bavarian Radio, Bernard Haitink, Conductor. English language libretto. (On the whole, the women outdo the men in this performance, although Siegfried Jerusalem sings an uncommonly strong, manly Tamino. Gruberova has no problems with the Queen of the Night's treacherous arias, and at the right moments she truly sounds vengeful. Lucia Popp is an eloquent Pamina, surely one of the best. This recording offers a middle-of-the-road, traditional approach to the opera that many listeners will prefer.)

(1995) Erato or Elektra/Asylum 12705, with Rosa Mannion, Natalie Dessay, Hans Peter Blochwitz, Anton Scharinger, Reinhard Hagen, Maîtrise de l'Opera de Lyon, Les Arts Florissants, William Christie, Conductor. English language libretto. (Christie's version is one of several good recordings using period instruments. The smaller orchestra produces a clear sound, forceful when required, but never covering the singers. These are rather small voices, but pure in tone, and the cast is fully involved in the drama and comedy. The performance has the feel of spontaneity and discovery, a virtue that Christie encourages.)

Die Zauberflöte is available with Francisco Araiza and Kathleen Battle on VHS and DVD from Universal/Deutsche Grammophon.

Modest Mussorgsky (1839–1881)

Boris Godunov (1874; 1908)

A word of explanation about the dates is in order. Mussorgsky's first version of *Boris* was completed 1869, but it was not performed at the time. Mussorgsky revised the opera extensively, and in that form it was presented in 1874. There were no further performances until 1896, when Nikolai Rimsky-Korsakov's revised *Boris* was introduced. Rimsky then reworked the opera once more for performance in 1908, and it was in this version that *Boris* became known outside of Russia. Dimitri Shostakovich (1939–40) and Karol Rathaus (1952; for the Metropolitan Opera) carried out later revisions.

The logical question at this point is "Why?" From Rimsky on, why did anyone think it necessary to change what Mussorgsky composed in the first place? The answer is that Mussorgsky was too original, too much his own man as a composer, and in its two original forms the orchestration seemed primitive and the vocal lines eccentric. We really shouldn't blame poor Rimsky and the others. Their versions kept *Boris* before the public until the public was ready to accept pure Mussorgsky. There is now, however, a good authentic performing edition, and recent years have proved that Mussorgsky's original is not so primitive and forbidding after all.

Boris is a big opera in every sense. As we know it, particularly in the 1874 version, it's a great, sprawling historical masterpiece. We have a psychologically complex central character, a large assortment of other characters with personal and political agendas of their own, and a love story with decidedly monarchical overtones. Most of all, we have the suffering Russian people, and they speak to us eloquently in Mussorgsky's magnificent choruses.

There have been a number of Russian recordings of *Boris,* the earlier ones in Rimsky's version. They appear from time to time on the labels that specialize in historical recordings and are worth seeking out primarily for the strength of some of the individual performances. If you're interested, look for editions in which Boris is sung by Alexander Pirogov, Mark Reizen, or Ivan Petrov. The recommended versions are all recorded in excellent stereo sound.

(1970) Decca/London 11862, with Nicolai Ghiaurov, Galina Vishnevskaya, Martti Talvela, Ludovic Spiess, Anton Diakov, Zoltan Kélémén, Wiener Sängerknaben, Sofia Radio Chorus, Chorus of the Vienna State Opera, Vienna Philharmonic, Herbert von Karajan, Conductor. English language libretto. (The Rimsky version still has its advocates, and Karajan's recording presents it in memorable fashion. Ghiaurov is a convincing Boris with an outstanding voice. Some of the other roles are less effectively taken, but the overall production is excellent. For all the virtues of this recording, however, your first choice should surely be a version of Mussorgsky's score the way it stood prior to Rimsky's revisions.)

(1993) Sony 58977, with Anatoly Kotcherga, Marjana Lipovsek, Samuel Ramey, Sergei Larin, Gleb Nikolsky, Sergei Leiferkus, Tölzer Knabenchor, Slovak Philharmonic Chorus Bratislava, Berlin Radio Chorus, Berlin Philharmonic, Claudio Abbado, Conductor. English language libretto. (Abbado's version is essentially Mussorgsky's 1874 revision. The recording reproduces Abbado's superb orchestra and gifted soloists in sumptuous sound. Kotcherga is a musical Boris who sings the role beautifully, unlike many who declaim as much as they vocalize. There are excellent performances also from Samuel Ramey as Pimen and Sergei Larin as perhaps the best Grigory on any of the recordings. If you do not acquire the version listed next, this is clearly the one to have.)

(1997) Philips 462230, with (1869 version) Nikolai Putilin, Nikolai Ohotnikov, Viktor Lutsuk, Vassily Gerello; (1874 version) Vladimir Vaneev, Olga Borodina, Nikolai Ohotnikov, Vladimir Galusin, Evgeny Nikitin, Fyodor Kuznetsov; Kirov Chorus and Orchestra, St. Petersburg, Valery Gergiev, Conductor. English language libretto. (There are significant differences between the 1869 version and the 1874 version of *Boris*. Here are both of them in excellent performances by an outstanding Russian cast under a leading Russian conductor. Putilin and Vaneev are sensitive, secure vocalists who reflect in their performances the differences in the picture of Boris in the two operas. Borodina is a wonderful Marina. On all counts this recording is the preferred first choice for *Boris*.)

Boris Godunov is available with Robert Lloyd and Olga Borodina on VHS from Universal/London.

Khovanshchina (1886)

Khovanshchina is an opera that could not be played until somebody made it playable. Mussorgsky died before completing the opera. Only two brief passages were orchestrated, there was no conclusion for Act II, and Act V existed only in assorted musical sketches. Unlike *Boris Godunov*, there are no original performing versions of *Khovanshchina*. If the opera is to be performed at all, someone must take on the task of orchestrating and completing the score. Rimsky-Korsakov was the first to attempt this difficult task, and there have been several Russian recordings using Rimsky's version. For performances in Paris, Stravinsky and Ravel revised Rimsky's version, and between 1952 and 1958, Shosta-

kovich prepared a completely new orchestration. Given the difficulty of arriving at a viable performing edition of the opera, we may well wonder if it was worth it. Four great composers, however, apparently felt that it was, and in whatever version we hear the opera, there is a wealth of impressive music in *Khovanshchina*.

It's a good thing that the opera is musically worthwhile. If *Khovanshchina* had to depend on the libretto alone, it's unlikely that anyone would have bothered to save it. The historical material on which the plot is based is incredibly confusing to anyone who has not studied the history of seventeenth century Russia in some detail. It was a time of great turmoil, as those favoring reform struggled with those who wished to preserve "old Russia" from all change. Young Peter I shared the position of Tsar with his half brother, but he faced opposition from the regent, who was Sophia, his half sister; from the *streltsy,* a Moscow-based military force (the title of the opera derives from the Khovansky family, leaders of the *streltsy*); and at least passively from the "Old Believers," a nonconformist religious group. All of these are entwined in the complicated plot of an opera that succeeds because of Mussorgsky's wonderful music and the dedication of those who completed and orchestrated it.

Both recommended recordings use the Shostakovich orchestration, although they adopt different conclusions to the last act. Gergiev ends abruptly after the self-immolation of the Old Believers. Tchakarov follows the full Shostakovich conclusion and rings down the curtain with a recollection of the peaceful "Dawn Over the River Moscow" from the Overture. Unless you have a preference concerning the conclusion, either of these recordings will make a good addition to the collection.

(1986) Sony 45831, with Nicolai Ghiaurov, Zdravko Gadjev, Kaludi Kaludov, Soyan

Popov, Nicola Ghiiuselev, Alexandrina Milcheva, Sofia National Opera Chorus and Orchestra, Emio Tchakarov, Conductor. English language libretto. (This effectively conducted and recorded version presents a musically satisfying performance. The basses, Nicolai Ghiaurov as Ivan Khovansky and Nicola Ghisuelev as Dosifey, use their impressive voices in the service of the drama. Kaludi Kaludov, as Vasily Golitsin, has a pleasant, strong tenor voice, and Alexandrina Milcheva is an excellent Marfa, the equal of her more famous counterpart on the Gergiev recording. There is a great deal of choral music in *Khovanshchina*, effectively performed by the Sofia Opera Chorus.)

(1991) Philips 32147, with Bulat Minjelkeiv, Vladimir Galusin, Alexei Steblianko, Nikolai Ohotnikov, Valery Alexeev, Olga Borodina, Chorus and Orchestra of the Kirov, St. Petersburg, Valery Gergiev, Conductor. English language libretto. (Gergiev conducts the opera with a keen sense of drama, and the sound of the recording is quite good. The final scene is particularly impressive. On the whole, the vocalism is not so good as the Sony recording, although there's nothing distressing and the voices are authentically Russian. Borodina, like Milcheva on Sony, is an excellent Marfa. Orchestral and choral forces do not let us down.)

Khovanshchina is available with Nicolai Ghiaurov and Vladimir Atlantov on DVD from Image and VHS from Kultur.

Jacques Offenbach (1819–1880)

Les Contes d'Hoffmann (1881)

Fifty years ago opera lovers thought they knew *Les Contes d'Hoffmann*. The music was familiar, particularly the famous "Barcarolle," and an evening at the opera offered an opportunity to hear not one diva, but three. Then the musicological scholars intervened and told us that our familiar *Les Contes d'Hoffmann* wasn't Offenbach's opera at all, rather a conglomeration put together over the years by a number of different composers and producers. The problem was that when Offenbach died four months before the premiere, the opera was left incomplete, with no conclusion for the "Giulietta" act or the finale. Ernest Guiraud was assigned the task of preparing a score for the initial performances.

Without Guiraud's help there would have been no performance, but with his help there began a process that would radically alter the overall shape of *Les Contes d'Hofmann*. First the "Giulietta" act was omitted, later to be restored but in the wrong place in the opera, and that was just the beginning of the changes. Eventually André Bloch added an aria for Dapertutto, taken from one of Offenbach's operettas, and composed a sextet with chorus drawing on Offenbach themes to fill out the incomplete "Giulietta" act. Other changes were made as well. In more recent years, numerous new manuscript sources have been discovered, and musicologists have published editions that incorporate these additions, too many of them some would say.

Nobody is happy. Singers complain that as they go from one opera house and conductor to another they don't know how much of which music they're going to sing. Designers and directors trouble over the order in which to play the scenes, whether "Giulietta" should come before or after "Antonia." If one of the new, more authentic versions is performed, audiences complain because they lose the beautiful baritone aria "Scintille, diamant" and Bloch's spurious but exciting sextet. Collectors puzzle over which recording to buy in order to have the best performance of the best version of the opera. The wonderful thing is that Offenbach's opera survives it all and continues to delight.

Our recommendations suggest three possibilities. One is a modern performing edition that makes more or less arbitrary decisions about what to include, but offers a performance by outstanding vocalists. Another records an acceptable but lengthy version containing almost all of Offenbach's music that has been discovered to date, with the sextet added for good measure. A third, the 1948 EMI version, gives us the opera in the version that was accepted fifty or more years ago in a performance that is inauthentic in content but absolutely authentic in style.

(1948) EMI Import 5 65260, also Preiser 20004, with Raoul Jobin, Renée Doria, Vina Bovy, Géori Boué, Louis Musy, André Pernet, Charles Soix, Roger Revoil, Chorus and Orchestra of Théâtre de l'Opéra-Comique, André Cluytens, Conductor. A French language libretto only is included with the EMI edition, but this recording may not be available domestically. (This is the best performance of *Les Contes d'Hoffmann,* the only one that employs a French cast throughout and a native conductor, chorus, and orchestra. The voices are lighter and brighter in tone than singers in the other casts. In some cases, they do not offer the beautiful vocalism that we have in the other recordings, but they know how to sing this music. This is, of course, the opera without the benefit of modern manuscript discoveries and resulting revisions. The monophonic recorded sound is acceptable.)

(1971) Decca/London 417363, with Plácido Domingo, Joan Sutherland, Huguette Tourangeau, Gabriel Bacquier, Choruses of Radio de la Suisse Romande, Pro Arte de Lausanne, Du Brassus, Orchestre de la Suisse Romande, Richard Bonynge, Conductor. English language libretto. (This is certainly the best sung version of the opera. Sutherland is in her element as Olympia and has the lyrical line for a very good Antonia. She is less comfortable dramatically as the seductive Giulietta. Domingo sings beautifully as Hoffmann. Bacquier is more comfortably stylistically than he is vocally. Bonynge's version uses spoken dialogue and some of the rediscovered material, but also includes *"Scintille, diamant"* and the sextet, although reworked as a quartet for the final scene.)

(1996?) Erato or Elektra/Asylum 14330, with Roberto Alagna, Natalie Dessay, Leontina Vaduva, Sumi Jo, José van Dam, Chorus and Orchestra of L'Opéra National de Lyon, Kent Nagano, Conductor. English language libretto. (Nagano's recording includes a great deal of material not to be heard in the other two recommended versions. It also plays thirty minutes longer than the Decca/London version and forty minutes longer than the EMI, and for many listeners that's going to be several minutes too long. There's no *"Scintille, diamant,"* but the sextet is included with different words. Most of the singing is good. Alagna is vocally secure and the voice is the real thing. Van Dam gives a virtuoso performance of the villains.)

Les Contes d'Hoffmann is available with Plácido Domingo and Ileana Cotrubas on VHS from Kultur.

Amilcare Ponchielli (1834–1886)

La Gioconda (1876)

Gioconda has been the butt of many an opera joke. On the "Quiz" portion of the Saturday afternoon Metropolitan Opera broadcasts, the light-hearted answer to any obscure question was often *"La Gioconda"*— on the grounds that it has everything in it that an opera can possibly have. It truly does. There are six big roles, each with its own aria to sing. There are massive ensembles and a large-scale ballet. There is spectacle — an on-stage ship devoured in flames, for example. There are love affairs, illicit and otherwise, a suffering blind mother, a suicidal heroine, poison, drowning, concealed identities, extreme jealousy, and a race on the Grand Canal in Venice to boot. You name it, and *Gioconda* has it.

In all candor, it truly is a little bit comical, this dramatic concoction that Arrigo Boito, writing under a pseudonym, stirred up from a Victor Hugo original, but it also gave the composer just what he needed for an exciting, old-fashioned grand opera. Ponchielli was an accomplished musician, a member of the faculty of the Milan Conservatory, where his students included Giacomo Puccini and Pietro Mascagni. Accomplishment and inspiration, however, do not always go hand in hand, and too often in his other operas there are pages where the music seems more workmanlike than inspired. With *Gioconda*, however, Ponchielli was able to sustain the dramatic and musical flow almost from beginning to end. It is the only one of his ten operas that has demonstrated lasting power.

What *Gioconda* requires on stage and on disc is a cast of dramatically aware singers with outstanding vocal gifts. Unfortunately, the handful of available recordings provide that combination only partially. The best all around performance is the 1931 version with a prime-time La Scala cast. Only the Barnaba, Gaetano Viviani, lets us down with a bland approach to his role. Giannina Arangi-Lombardi, who sings Gioconda, was surely one of the best Italian sopranos of the twentieth century. This recording is available on Naxos 8110112 in sound that is relatively good for the date, but it will not be entirely satisfying to most contemporary listeners. The only possible recommendation otherwise is one or the other of the recordings made by Maria Callas. On the basis of recorded sound, the 1959 version is probably the better choice.

> (1952) Opera Hommage 1837, perhaps still available also on Fonit-Cetra 8, with Maria Callas, Fedora Barbieri, Maria Amadini, Gianni Poggi, Paolo Silveri, Giulio Neri, Italian Radio Chorus and Orchestra, Turin, Antonio Votto, Conductor. Probably no libretto. (Maria Callas was the outstanding Gioconda of the 1950s. She made the role her own by taking it seriously dramatically and by faithfulness to the composer's intentions. She is in fresh voice in this recording, and she meets her vocal match in Fedora Barbieri, the Laura. Otherwise the cast is just acceptable, Poggi as Enzo less than that. The monophonic sound is listenable.)

> (1959) EMI 56291, with Maria Callas, Fiorenza Cossotto, Irene Companeez, Pier Miranda Ferraro, Piero Cappuccilli, Ivo Vinco, Orchestra and Chorus of Teatro alla Scala, Milan, Antonio Votto, Conductor. English language libretto. (The intervening years since her first recording had taken their toll on Callas' voice, but she remains dramatically and musically convincing. Once again, most of her colleagues are unable to rise to her level. Cossotto shows promise that would soon blossom, although she's not quite ready at this stage of her career to stand up to Callas. The stereo sound is a great improvement over the 1952 recording.)

La Gioconda is available with Eva Marton and Plácido Domingo on VHS from Kultur.

Francis Poulenc (1899–1963)

Les Dialogues des Carmélites (1957)

Poulenc dedicated his opera to Mussorgsky, Monteverdi, Debussy, and Verdi. He chose an interesting list of composers, and *Dialogues* owes something to each of them and honors each one in his choice. The careful and effective word setting of the text, the broad sweep of a powerful historical movement, the feel for aching, arching melody, and the use of simplest possible musical means — all of it does credit to Poulenc's great predecessors.

Dialogues is one of the few twentieth century operas to retain a place in the repertoire. The appeal begins with a simple, emotionally charged plot drawn from an historical event and its elaboration in a play by Georges Brentanos. Blanche, a shy, easily frightened young woman from the nobility, enters a Carmelite convent, but when the revolutionary powers during the Reign of Terror dissolve the convent and threaten the lives of the nuns, she flees. As the nuns, singing a "Salve Regina," march one by one to the guillotine, however, she rejoins them, enters at the end of the line, and walks bravely to her own death.

The composer clothed this story in a score that is musically satisfying, emotionally and dramatically appropriate, and sophisticated as only Poulenc could be, but at the same time approachable and relatively uncomplicated in harmonic and melodic development. The final scene is one of the outstanding moments in all of modern opera and a masterstroke of emotional power as we hear the hymn that the nuns sing grow fainter with each execution until only the voice of Blanche remains.

The two recommended recordings are both excellent. The choice is between a 1958 version in good monophonic sound with a group of vocalists who were in many cases Poulenc's own choices for their roles, and one from 1990 in superb stereo sound with a fine cast of French speaking singers.

(1958) EMI 567135, with Denise Duval, Régine Crespin, Denise Scharley, Liliane Berton, Rita Gorr, Xavier Depraz, Paul Finel, Chorus and Orchestra of Théâtre de l'Opéra de Paris, Pierre Dervaux, Conductor. English language libretto. (This powerful performance enlisted a cast chosen for the opera by Poulenc himself. Denise Duval, who sings Blanche, was a specialist in the music of Poulenc. Régine Crespin as Madame Lidoine and Rita Gorr as Mère Marie are also outstanding, and Denise Scharley sings beautifully and more subtly than many in Madame de Croissy's death scene. Unless contemporary stereo sound is a determining factor, this version makes a good first choice, but both versions truly are excellent.)

(1990) Virgin Classics 59227, with Catherine Dubosc, Rachel Yakar, Rita Gorr, Brigitte Fournier, Martine Dupuy, José van Dam, Jean Luc Viala, London Chorus, Chorus and Orchestra of Opéra de Lyon, Kent Nagano, Conductor. English language libretto. (Nagano conducts an intense, dramatic performance with excellent singers in all roles. The two men's parts are particularly well taken in this recording. Dubosc sings Blanche with clear tone and great simplicity. Rita Gorr, Mère Marie in the earlier recording, sings Madame de Croissy to

equal effect here. The excellent stereo sound makes for a chilling final scene.)

Les Dialogues des Carmélites is available with Anne Sophie Schmidt and Nadine Denize on DVD from Arthaus Music, and with Joan Sutherland and Isobel Buchanan on VHS from Kultur.

Sergei Prokofiev (1891–1953)

The Love for Three Oranges (1921)

There was something absurd about *The Love for Three Oranges* from the very beginning—a Russian opera premiered in the United States and sung in French. And the absurdity didn't end there. It continued in the orchestra pit and on the stage of the Auditorium in Chicago on the night of December 30, 1921, and it wasn't the result of the kind of mishaps and mistakes that have been known to plague opera performances. It was all on purpose, precisely the way Prokofiev had planned it. That's the kind of opera *The Love for Three Oranges* is.

Its source, by a rather roundabout route, was a play by the eighteenth century Italian author Carlo Gozzi, a comical fantasy that poked fun at some of his fellow authors. By the time Prokofiev set it to music 160 years later, the satire now took aim at what he considered to be outworn operatic conventions. The final irony may be that later in his career, Prokofiev embraced some of those same conventions that he attacks in *The Love for Three Oranges* (in Russian: *Lubov k tryam apel'sinam*).

Don't look for philosophical depth in this opera. One of the purposes of Prokofiev's opera is to destroy philosophical speculation set to music in operatic form. Don't look for sustained lyrical passages, arias, ensembles and the like. Another of the composer's purposes was to protest opera built around elaborate solo and concerted numbers. Don't look for this opera to make good, realistic sense. Prokofiev, at least here, entertains us rather with dramatic non sequiturs and characters that have little to do with sensible life. *The Love for Three Oranges* is the operatic equivalent of the theater of the absurd, and it is meant just for fun — and for making fun.

An excellent recording in the French language of the premiere was available on Virgin Classics (VCD 7 59566) but has been deleted. If you can locate a copy, it would make a good addition to the collection, but notice that there is a French language video available. The Russian language recording listed here, however, is equally good. In any case, Prokofiev apparently composed the opera to a Russian text and then assisted in its translation into French for performance in Chicago.

(1997, 1998) Philips 462913, with Evgeny Akimov, Konstantin Pluzhnikov, Larissa Schevchenko, Anna Netrebko, Fyodor Kuznetsov, Olga Korzhenskaya, Chorus and Orchestra of the Kirov, St. Petersburg, Valery Gergiev, Conductor. English language libretto. (The recording quality is very impressive, an important detail in an opera by a composer who was a master of orchestration. Gergiev leads a lively performance that places appropriate emphasis on the humor. There are few outstanding vocalists in the cast, but this is an ensemble opera and *bel canto* singing is hardly in order. The conspicuous exception is Anna Netrebko, who brings to the role of Ninetta a beautiful, well focused lyric soprano.)

The Love for Three Oranges is available in French with Gabriel Bacquier and Jean-Luc Viala on DVD from Image and on VHS from Kultur.

War and Peace (1944–1959)

It took fifteen years from the performance of the first scenes in 1944 until a relatively complete *War and Peace* (in Russian: *Voina i mir*) was presented at the Bolshoi Theatre in Moscow in 1959. The problem was apparently Communist officialdom, and the composer repeatedly revised and

reduced and added in the attempt to shape the score into an "acceptable" form.

Prokofiev's earlier operas sound to us much more "modern" than the works composed after his return to Russia in the 1930s, and the assumption is frequently made that he corrupted his natural style in order to make his music acceptable to the Communist authorities. The change is certainly marked from the angular declamation and hard-hitting harmony of *The Gambler* (1915–1917) to the soaring lyricism and diatonic harmonies of *War and Peace*. Change, however, is not necessarily the same thing as corruption. There's no aesthetic law to dictate that a composer may not excel in more than one type of music, and among all of Prokofiev's operas, *War and Peace* is the one that has demonstrated the greatest popular appeal.

The opera is based on a selection of scenes from Tolstoy's novel of the same name. Opera and novel are both large, sprawling works with a sweeping view of Russian history during the Napoleonic wars. Musically, the opera seems to owe a great deal to Tchaikovsky, but dramatically it has much in common with Mussorgsky's historical operas, *Boris Godunov* and *Khovanshchina*. In keeping with its vast proportions, approximately four hours in performance, *War and Peace* presents epic challenges to the opera house that performs it and the companies that record it. In addition to large orchestral and choral forces, there are over fifty solo roles to fill. The version recommended here comes from St. Petersburg's great Kirov Opera, where all of the necessary resources are, of course, available.

(1991) Philips 434097, with Alexander Gergalov, Yelena Prokina, Sergei Alexashkin, Svetlana Volkova, Gegam Grigorian, Olga Borodina, Nikolai Ohotnikov, Chorus and Orchestra of the Kirov Opera, Valery Gergiev, Conductor. English language libretto. (This version was recorded during a stage performance, and the sound is not always as well balanced as a studio recording might have produced. There is also some staging noise, but the recorded quality is entirely listenable. The extensive cast is good, and they sing with the keen dramatic involvement and immediacy of an actual performance. Gergiev and the combined forces of the Kirov are adequate guarantee of a fully authoritative and authentic version of the opera.)

War and Peace is available with Alexander Gergalov and Yelena Prokina on VHS from Phillips. The recording listed above appears to be from the same performance.

Giacomo Puccini (1858–1924)

La Bohème (1896)

It is difficult to imagine anyone not liking *Bohème*. It is, after all, the most lovable of operas, an enchanting concoction of good tunes, high spirits, sentimental romance, and a three-handkerchief finale. In 1900, on the occasion of its first performance at the Metropolitan Opera, however, the distinguished critic Henry Krehbiel commented in the *New York Tribune* that *Bohème* "is foul in subject, and fulminant but futile in its music."* If Krehbiel thought he could stem the *Bohème* floodtide with his musical and moral complaints, he was completely wrong. The opera was already well on its way to the worldwide popularity that it still claims.

Although the simple law of averages assures us that there must have been some bad performances of *Bohème* since its premiere in 1896, it seems to be an almost indestructible opera. It can be performed simply, with limited resources (as I recall seeing it in the 1960s), or it can be done with a cast of hundreds crowding the stage (as it is regularly now at the Metropolitan in Franco Zeffirelli's epic production). It is

one of the few operas that is not even damaged by the updating of some of the recent "concept" productions. With a competent cast, orchestra, and conductor, and a tenor and soprano who really believe in the opera and can provide at least pleasant voices, *Bohème* will succeed.

La Bohème has been recorded at least thirty times, and almost every version offers one or two performances worth hearing. Choose a favorite tenor and soprano, and chances are you will find them represented in one or even more of the recorded editions, although they may not end up together in the same recording. The three recommended versions offer excellent performances with outstanding casts, but almost any modern recording will provide a satisfying experience of the opera. If you decide to go beyond a single edition, consider adding the recording led by Arturo Toscanini (RCA 60288 and other historical labels). Toscanini conducted the premiere of *Bohème* in 1896, and he brings tremendous vitality and obvious love to the score. In fact, he loves it so much that he sings along at the great lyrical climaxes. For a first choice, you will want a version with better sound and a silent conductor.

(1956) EMI 56236, with Jussi Bjoerling, Victoria de los Angeles, Robert Merrill, John Reardon, Giorgio Tozzi, Fernando Corena, Lucine Amara, RCA Victor Orchestra and Chorus, Thomas Beecham, Conductor. English language libretto. (This recording is in good monophonic sound. Beecham conducts a superb cast with great sensitivity. Bjoerling sings the way most other tenors can only dream about, and De los Angeles is the perfect Mimì, with a vocal purity that suggests fully the gentleness of the character. Whether *Bohème* is a great work of art is an issue that listeners must decide for themselves, but Beecham and his singers perform the opera as if they believe firmly that it is.

*Henry Krehbiel, quoted in *Metroppolitan Opera Annals: A Chronicle of Artists and Performances*, ed. William H. Seltsam (New York: H. W. Wilson Co., 1947), p. 116.

Unless stereo sound is a must for you, this is the first choice for an operatic collection.)

(1972) Decca/London 421049, with Luciano Pavarotti, Mirella Freni, Rolando Panerai, Gianni Maffeo, Nicolai Ghiaurov, Elizabeth Harwood, Schöneberger Sänger-knaben, Chorus of the Deutschen Oper Berlin, Berlin Philharmonic, Herbert von Karajan, Conductor. English language libretto. (Von Karajan brings out many often overlooked details in the orchestral score, and the superb stereo recording makes certain that we hear them. This is one of the best of Pavarotti's many recordings, and Freni is his ideal partner. Rudolfo and Mimì are roles they often sang together on stage. The other members of the cast sing well and are fully in the scene dramatically. If stereo is a must, this recording is probably the best choice.)

(1998) Decca/London 466070, with Roberto Alagna, Angela Gheorghiu, Simon Keenlyside, Roberto de Candia, Ildebrando D'Arcangelo, Elisabetta Scano, Chorus of children from the La Scala Conservatory, Chorus and Orchestra of Teatro alla Scala Milan, Riccardo Chailly, Conductor. English language libretto. (Compared to Beecham and Von Karajan, Chailly keeps things moving, but there's no sense of undue rushing in the performance, rather of exuberance and youth. Alagna and Gheorghiu are not only husband and wife, they are also the current superstars of opera, and some listeners will want to hear them together in this most romantic of operas. They sing in a way that convinces us that their celebrity is fully deserved, and the rest of the cast is quite good.)

La Bohème is available with José Carreras and Teresa Stratas on DVD from Pioneer, and with Mirella Freni and Gianni Raimondi on VHS from Universal/Deutsche Grammophon.

Madama Butterfly (1904)

The premiere of *Madama Butterfly* at La Scala in Milan was a classic fiasco, probably the most famous in all of the history of opera. Laughter, hisses, and assorted verbal assaults almost drowned out the second act.

Puccini, always the practical man of the theater, withdrew the opera and took it back to his worktable. Three months later it reached the stage again, this time in Brescia. The hour and a half second act was recast as Acts II and III, a solo was added for Pinkerton, the tenor, in the last act, and some of the extraneous local-color material was excised from the first act. In its revised form, *Madama Butterfly* became as great a success as it had initially been a failure.

During World War II the Metropolitan Opera put *Butterfly* on the shelf because an opera in which an American naval officer deserted a highly sympathetic Japanese woman was hardly politically correct. Five months after the end of the War, however, *Butterfly* was back on the stage, in the person of the great Italian soprano Licia Albanese, and as popular as ever.

More than almost any other opera, *Butterfly* depends on its heroine, and it is a tremendously demanding role for the soprano, both vocally and dramatically. The other roles — Lt. Pinkerton, Suzuki, Sharpless — sing much less, and they will never make or break a performance of the opera. On stage, it is the soprano's show all the way, and opera houses often engage one real star — of the expensive variety that is — for the title role and then economize on the other singers. On recordings, however, we have a right to demand more than that, and in general the producers have met that demand, particularly with the role of Lt. Pinkerton.

It may seem a redundancy to recommend four different versions of *Madama Butterfly,* but there's a reason for this extravagance. Four great sopranos dominated this role in the second half of the twentieth century, and each of them made two studio recordings of the role. The editions listed here are all in good, modern stereo sound, and have uncommonly strong tenor support. Trying to choose one of the sopranos, however, can bring hardcore opera lovers almost to blows, and if I left out a favorite, I would stand in danger of life and limb. My hesitant recommendation is the Von Karajan recording with Mirella Freni, but that has more to do with the quality of the conducting, orchestra, and other cast members than it does with the soprano. Some listeners will be interested in hearing the opera in its original unsuccessful version. It is available on Vox Classics 7525. The performance is acceptable, but it will win no new converts to Puccini's opera as it was first heard.

(1958) Decca/London 452594, with Renata Tebaldi, Carlo Bergonzi, Fiorenza Cossotto, Enzo Sordello, Orchestra and Chorus of Accademia di Santa Cecilia, Rome, Tullio Serafin, Conductor. No English libretto, but there is a detailed synopsis keyed to the discs. (Serafin takes his time and lingers over details in the score, but the result is a keen underlining of the tragedy. Bergonzi is the excellent tenor, and there is strength in the entire cast. The star, of course, is Tebaldi. She doesn't suggest a fifteen-year-old Japanese girl, but she sings magnificently in a rich, creamy voice that is a joy to hear.)

(1959) EMI 63634, with Victoria de los Angeles, Jussi Bjoerling, Miriam Pirazzini, Mario Sereni, Orchestra and Chorus of Teatro dell'Opera, Rome, Gabriele Santini, Conductor. English language libretto. (Santini brings no special insight to the score, but his soprano, Victoria de los Angeles, catches the heart of the role from the very beginning and never lets go. She is the most subtle interpreter among these four sopranos, and her voice suggests youthfulness more than any of the others. Pirazzini as Suzuki is disappointingly insecure in tone, but Bjoerling is, as usual, a joy to hear.)

(1966) EMI 69654, with Renata Scotto, Carlo Bergonzi, Anna di Stasio, Rolando Panerai, Orchestra and Chorus of Teatro dell'Opera, Rome, John Barbirolli, Conductor. English language libretto. (Barbirolli knows this opera perfectly and conducts it with a master's touch. The supporting singers are all good, particularly Rolando Panerai, as an unusually sympathetic Sharpless. Scotto is the most dramatic Butterfly, keenly aware of every changing emotion in the opera. Hers is not the most beautiful voice, but she rises well to every climax. Her death scene is overwhelming.)

(1974) Decca/London 17577, with Mirella Freni, Luciano Pavarotti, Christa Ludwig, Robert Kerns, Vienna State Opera Chorus, Vienna Phlharmonic Orchestra, Herbert von Karajan, Conductor. English language libretto. (Freni combines some of De los Angeles' subtlety with a good measure of Scotto's passion, and she brings a beautiful Italian voice to the role. Pavarotti is at his best as Pinkerton, and Christa Ludwig is by far the best Suzuki on any of the recordings. The Vienna Philharmonic under Karajan plays the score magnificently.)

Madama Butterfly is available with Mirella Freni and Plácido Domingo on VHS from Universal/London and on DVD from Universal/Decca.

Manon Lescaut (1893)

Puccini's *Manon Lescaut,* his first big success, was the third operatic setting in thirty-seven years of the Abbé Prévosts' brief eighteenth century novel about Manon and Des Grieux. Except for the rare revival, the first, by Daniel-François-Esprit Auber, has disappeared from the stage, although it has been recorded more than once. The second, Massenet's *Manon,* had its premiere in 1884 and remains one of the most popular French operas. Less than ten years later, Puccini's version appeared.

All three of the operas have libretto problems. Apparently the Prévost novel refused to be shaped into neat dramatic form. Puccini, who had a keen sense of what worked in terms of drama, went through a whole series of librettists and consultants, and still ended up with a gaping void in the story between Acts I and II. What Prévost and Puccini's assorted collaborators did provide, however, was a hero with numerous opportunities for passionate song and a heroine with a complex, often contradictory but always fascinating personality. What's more, she had the good grace to suffer and die in the last act, and from *Manon Lescaut* on, Puccini proved that he was at his best composing music to fit those situations. Manon is Puccini's first successful picture of a suffering, dying woman in a musical portrait gallery that includes Mimi, Tosca, Madama Butterfly, Suor Angelica, and Liu.

In performance, the opera depends almost entirely on the quality of the singers in the roles of Manon and Des Grieux. There are operas, *Bohème* for example, that will survive merely competent performers. *Manon Lescaut* is not one of them. It must have a tenor whose voice projects the drama and will ride the large orchestral climaxes that Puccini provides, and a soprano who can send a beautiful piano tone into the auditorium and who, as the older critics used to say, has a measure of "tears in the voice." That's exactly what our three recommended recordings offer.

(1954) BMG/RCA 60573, with Licia Albanese, Jussi Bjoerling, Robert Merrill, Franco Calabrese, Mario Carlin, Enrico Campi, Anna Maria Rota, Rome Opera Orchestra and Chorus, Jonel Perlea, Conductor. English language libretto. (Jussi Bjoerling is the best recorded Des Grieux. His is, of course, one of the finest, most beautiful tenor voices of the twentieth century, and in this recording it is under complete control. Albanese may not suggest the fifteen-year-old girl of Prévost's novel, but she was the most outstanding Puccini stylist of her day. Her death scene in the last act is heartbreaking. There are other good editions, but this monophonic recording is an essential version of the opera.)

(1983) Deutsche Grammophon 13893, with Mirella Freni, Plácido Domingo, Renato

Bruson, Kurt Rydl, Robert Gambill, George Macpherson, John Fryatt, Brigitte Fassbaender, John Tomlinson, Chorus of the Royal Opera House, Covent Garden, Philharmonia Orchestra, Giuseppe Sinopoli, Conductor. English language libretto. (Domingo is, as usual, in good, ample voice, and he is always communicative and musical. Like Albanese, Freni is a mistress of Puccini style, and her voice is wonderfully soothing to the ear. The performance has not quite the spontaneity of the BMG/RCA version, but it is dramatically and musically satisfying. This recording is in excellent stereo sound. Freni also recorded the opera with Luciano Pavarotti in a performance on Philips 40200. I have not heard it, but it has also won high critical praise.)

(1992) Naxos 660019/20, with Miriam Gauci, Kaludi Kaludov, Vincente Sardinero, Marcel Rosca, Donald George, Henk Lauwers, Ludwig van Gifzegem, Lucienne Van Deyck, Jaak Gregoor Choir, BRT Philharmonic Chorus and Orchestra, Alexander Rahbari, Conductor. Italian language libretto only. (This budget priced issue is one of the best of the operas available on the Naxos label. Miriam Gauci sings a keenly felt, beautifully vocalized Manon. Kaludov has a strong, expressive voice, and he is clearly into the role, perhaps a trifle too energetically on occasion. If stereo is required and money is no object, choose the Deutsche Grammophon issue, but this is certainly a good alternative version.)

Manon Lescaut is available with Renata Scotto and Plácido Domingo on VHS from Paramount.

Tosca (1900)

Ever since the distinguished critic Joseph Kerman branded *Tosca* a "shabby little shocker,"* serious opera lovers have found it convenient either to conceal their love for Puccini's opera or at least to apologize for it. A "shocker" *Tosca* surely is. Whether or not it is "shabby" is a matter of

---

*Joseph Kerman, *Opera as Drama* (New York: Vintage Books, 1959), p. 254.

personal taste. But it is certainly not "little." The three main characters — Tosca, Cavara-dossi, and Scarpia — are surely larger-than-life figures. They are by no means your everyday "little people," the kind that we find, for example, in Puccini's *Bohème.* The performers may act their parts with great subtlety, but *Tosca* cries out for large vocal and dramatic gestures.

If we contrast Puccini's opera with a profound work of musical and dramatic art such as Verdi's *Otello,* as Kerman does, we will discover that *Tosca* is not precisely a masterpiece. With an opera like *Tosca,* the responses of the audience truly are the result of a special kind of emotional manipulation, but in this case the manipulation is done by a composer who knows what he's about. Puccini was a master musical magician, the Houdini of the opera house. We may realize that we're being tricked into responding, but the magic is so well done that we go ahead and enjoy it.

There have been many recordings of *Tosca* over the last seventy or so years. Sopranos of all types, and occasionally even mezzo-sopranos (who should have known better), have coveted the opportunity to sing the title role. A good performance, however, requires more than a good soprano with sound dramatic instincts. Cavaradossi provides a star turn for the tenor, and the opera falls apart if the singer portraying Scarpia cannot convince us through his vocal and histrionic gifts that this man truly is the suave, calculating villain that his deeds proclaim him to be. The two recordings suggested here provide powerful, committed performances for all three of the major roles.

(1953) EMI 66444, with Maria Callas, Giuseppe di Stefano, Tito Gobbi, Chorus and Orchestra of Teatro alla Scala, Milan, Victor de Sabata, Conductor. English language libretto. (This is one of all too rare recordings in which everything and everyone came together at precisely the right time. De Sabata conducted a passionate, red-blooded performance. Di Stefano had not yet pushed his voice out of focus, and he sang with conviction and wonderful beauty of tone. Callas was at her best, with the voice secure and the ability to convey meaning through vocal color at its prime. Gobbi had everything a great Scarpia should have, and his performance is fully as dramatic and persuasive as the great Callas herself. This is one of the handful of truly great recordings, and every collection should have a copy of it.)

(1972) BMG/RCA 105, with Leontyne Price, Plácido Domingo, Sherrill Milnes, John Alldis Choir, New Philharmonia Orchestra, Zubin Mehta, Conductor. English language libretto. (Mehta yields nothing to De Sabata in terms of dramatic conducting. At one or two points, he may take the drama a trifle too far, but it is undoubtedly exciting. This is a *Tosca* for generous, lush voices. The singing is always dramatic, perhaps occasionally a little bit over the top. Sherrill Milnes manages to sing beautifully and still sound convincingly cruel. Domingo sings quite well and generally with composure and discipline, but even he pushes drama at the expense of vocal quality in the "Vittoria" ensemble of Act II. Price's Tosca is a real prima donna, emotionally and vocally, but she carries it off remarkably well. Her voice, particularly at the top of the range, was one of the glories of the opera world in the 1960s and 1970s. The stereo sound has remarkable impact.)

Il Trittico (1918)

By 1918 Puccini was the most exciting composer in the world of opera, and the premiere of his latest work on December 14 was surely the proudest event in the history of the Metropolitan Opera House since its opening night in 1883. And it wasn't just the premiere of a single new work by Giacomo Puccini. No, there were three of them — three completely different, completely new one-act operas.

Puccini gathered his three works under a common title, *Il Trittico,* the Italian term for a triptych, the three-part painting or carving frequently seen in old altarpieces. The implication is probably that they are complementary works and should be seen and heard together. The plots and musical styles of the three operas, however, actually have little in common. *Il Tabarro* is a violent story of love, jealousy, and revenge set on a Seine River barge, and the music belongs to Puccini's own rather sophisticated brand of *verismo* tempered by the influence of Debussy. The second, *Suor Angelica*, is the tragic story of a young nun who takes her own life when she learns of the death of her child. Through the years *Suor Angelica* has been the least often performed. Musically the highly sentimental score is often considered the weakest of the three. It was, however, Puccini's favorite. *Gianni Schicchi*, the opera that concludes the triptych, is a rollicking comedy that reminds us of the music Verdi composed for *Falstaff*. *Il Tabarro* and *Gianni Schicchi* both continue to hold the stage, and from time to time an enterprising opera company will put the triptych back together again.

The recommended recordings present something of a problem. In order to have the best version of each of the operas, you will have to purchase at least two and perhaps all three, since the individual works are not available separately. The compromise, however, is not great because all of the performances, with one possible exception, are acceptable. The most recent version has much to recommend it, but on the whole the Sony recording offers the best casts for all three operas. If you can manage two recordings, choose the earlier EMI as a supplement. With the exception of the *Tabarro*, it is musically and dramatically satisfying.

(1955; 1957; 1958) EMI 64165, *Tabarro*, with Margaret Mas, Giacinto Prandelli, Tito Gobbi, Chorus and Orchestra of the Rome Opera, Vincenzo Bellezza, Conductor; *Suor Angelica*, with Victoria de los Angeles, Fedora Barbieri, Chorus and Orchestra of the Rome Opera, Tullio Serafin, Conductor; *Gianni Schicchi*, with Tito Gobbi, Victoria de los Angeles, Carlo del Monte, Rome Opera Orchestra, Gabriele Santini, Conductor. English language libretto. (*Tabarro* is the weakest of the three performances, and it is the only one that is not in stereo. Gobbi is masterful, as usual, but the other members of the cast let him down. In *Suor Angelica,* Victoria de los Angeles uses her beautiful lyric voice to excellent effect in the title role. Hers is surely the most eloquent Angelica in all of the performances. Barbieri is properly threatening and forbidding as her aunt. *Gianni Schicchi* is a delight. Gobbi is the most mercurial and colorful Schicchi, and De los Angeles a vocally perfect Lauretta.)

(1976–1977) Sony 35912, *Tabarro*, with Renata Scotto, Plácido Domingo, Ingvar Wixell, Ambrosian Opera Chorus, New Philharmonia Orchestra; *Suor Angelica*, with Renata Scotto, Marilyn Horne, Ambrosian Opera Chorus, Desborough School Choir, New Philharmonia Orchestra; *Gianni Schicchi*, with Tito Gobbi, Ileana Cotrubas, Plácido Domingo, London Symphony Orchestra, Lorin Maazel, Conductor for all three. Italian language libretto. (Here is the preferred *Tabarro* cast. Domingo and Scotto bring to their respective roles the best voices on any of the recordings. Wixell sings well, but he is not the equal in interpretation of Gobbi. In *Suor Angelica*, Scotto is vocally strong and keenly aware of the drama. More than any other singer of the role, she is attentive to the small details of interpretation, but her voice is not as naturally beautiful as De los Angeles'. Tito Gobbi repeats his excellent *Gianni Schicchi* with a voice just a little less fresh than in the earlier recording. Cotrubas suffers only if compared to De los Angeles, and Domingo is the best of Rinuccios. He lightens his voice effectively for this essentially lyric role.)

(1997) EMI 54587, *Tabarro*, with Maria Guleghina, Neil Shicoff, Carlo Guelfi, London Voices, London Symphony Orchestra; *Suor Angelica*, with Cristina Gallardo-Domâs, Bernadette Manca di Nissa, London Voices, Philharmonia Orchestra; *Gianni Schicchi*, with José Van Dam, Angela Gheorghiu, Roberto Alagna, London Symphony Orchestra, Antonio Pappano, Conductor for all three. English language libretto. (Guleghina is a passionate Giorgietta, perhaps not as fully idiomatic as Scotto, who apparently has Puccini's *verismo* blood flowing in her viens. Shicoff is strong of voice, second only to Domingo as Luigi. Guelfi is a sympathetic, suffering Michele, effectively vocalized. Gallardo-Domâs brings a beautiful lyric soprano to Angelica. Nissa is less satisfying as her aunt, too conspicuously angry for a role that calls for cold dignity. *Gianni Schicchi* fares particularly well in this version, with Van Dam almost the equal of Gobbi as an interpreter and probably his superior in purely vocal terms. Gheorghiu and Alagna are excellent as the young lovers. They also sing small roles in *Il Tabarro*.)

Il Trittico is available (*Il Tabaro*, with Piero Capuccilli and Sylvia Sass; *Suor Angelica*, with Rosalind Plowright and Dunja Vejzovich; *Gianni Schicchi*, with Juan Pons and Cecilia Gasdia) on VHS from Kultur.

Turandot (1926)

On the recommendation of Arturo Toscanini, the Italian composer Franco Alfano was assigned one of the most thankless jobs that any musician ever faced — to complete from Puccini's sketches the final duet and closing scene of *Turandot*. Thankless indeed! He certainly wasn't thanked on the evening of the world premiere when Toscanini, who was conducting, ended the performance after Liu's funeral procession, precisely the point at which Puccini had stopped composing before his death. It was a sentimental gesture, but I've often wondered how Alfano felt about it. Since that night, however, Alfano's conclusion, usually in somewhat truncated form, has brought *Turandot* to its conclusion.

Puccini had counted on Calaf and Turandot's closing duet to be the emotional climax of the opera. The princess of ice would melt in the arms of the unknown prince, and together they would hymn the power of love in music of transcendent beauty. As it is, we have Alfano's version. It is singable and serviceable, a fact for which we should be grateful, but it doesn't have the sure touch of Puccini's genius. One result is that the emotional climax of the opera comes too early, in the death of Liu, a scene on which Puccini lavished all of his remarkable gift to build sympathy for a suffering woman. The end of *Turandot* always seems anticlimactic. Otherwise, however, the opera is the summit of Puccini's artistic achievement and one of the few operas since 1920 to enter the standard repertoire of opera houses all over the world.

Turandot and Calaf are two of the great operatic roles for soprano and tenor, and they require voices large enough to project over the full orchestra, and over each other as well. There's always the danger that *Turandot* on stage will become a shouting match between the tenor and soprano, but recordings of the opera have generally been free of competitive vocal contests. After all, a twist of the knobs by the engineer can make a little tone into a large one or vice versa. The two recommended recordings represent two approaches to the title role, both of them valid, and in these versions, both of them carried out triumphantly.

(1959) BMG/RCA 62687, with Birgit Nilsson, Renata Tebaldi, Jussi Bjoerling, Giorgio Tozzi, Mario Sereni, Piero de Palma, Tommaso Frascati, Chorus and Orchestra of the Rome Opera, Erich Leinsdorf, Conductor. English language libretto. (Leinsdorf may miss some of the excitement in the score, but everything is neat and in order. Bjoerling sings Calaf more beautifully than any other tenor. His voice was not as large as Nilsson's, but it balances well in the recording, perhaps with some engineering assistance. Nilsson is a vocal force of nature with a voice that in its seemingly unlimited volume and absolute security perfectly portrays the ice princess. Tebaldi's Liu is also a vocal marvel, and her warm Italianate tone contrasts effectively with Nilsson's cool northern timbre. The stereo recording is very good.)

(1972) Decca/London 14274, with Joan Sutherland, Luciano Pavarotti, Montserrat Caballé, Nicolai Ghiaurov, Tom Krause, Pier Francesco Poli, Piero de Palma, Peter Pears, John Alldis Choir, Wandsworth School Boys' Choir, London Philharmonic Orchestra, Zubin Mehta, Conductor. English language libretto. (Sutherland seemed at the time a strange choice for Turandot, a role entirely different from her usual coloratura flights, and one that she did not sing on stage. As it turned out, her performance on disc was a triumph, ample in volume and more alive in diction than she had often been. From the very beginning, her Turandot is warmer in tone than Nilsson's, as if the ice has already begun to melt. Pavarotti is in glorious voice, and Caballé, an occasional Turandot herself, sings beautifully as Liu. Add Ghiaurov as Timur, and this recording is truly a vocal feast. Mehta is the good conductor of a superbly recorded version. This recording is the first choice for this opera.)

Turandot is available with Eva Marton and Michael Sylvester on DVD from Image, and with Marton and Plácido Domingo on VHS from Universal/Deutsche Grammophon.

Henry Purcell (1658/1659–1695)

Dido and Aeneas (1689?)

Henry Purcell's *Dido and Aeneas* is the greatest British opera before Benjamin Britten's *Peter Grimes*. It may, of course, be a greater opera than *Grimes*, but at that high level of achievement pinpoint evaluation is beside the point. They are both remarkable operas, and the only regret is that it took 250 years to get from one to the other.

We can't be absolutely certain when *Dido* was first presented to the public, but we know that "the young gentlewomen" of Josias Priest's boarding school performed the opera before December 1689. Whether Aeneas and the other parts for male singers were sung by the young ladies is an open

question, and there is certainly no way to recapture today precisely the sight and sound of that performance. We probably would not want to. *Dido and Aeneas,* although not unusually difficult from the vocal or instrumental standpoint, is not a work for amateurs. It requires mature interpreters, particularly for the role of Dido.

It was Purcell's only true opera. His four semi-operas were essentially spoken dramas with musical interludes, known as masques. In these works, the noble characters never sing, and the action is carried forward primarily through dialogue. *Dido,* however, is an opera all the way. The emotional and dramatic content is conveyed throughout in the music, and the heroine is one of the most rewarding operatic roles in the entire repertoire.

At least fourteen versions are currently available, and many of those recordings are praiseworthy and would enhance an operatic collection. The three that I have chosen to recommend give three different, well conceived and effectively carried out approaches to the opera.

(1961) Decca/London 466387, with Janet Baker, Patricia Clark, Raimund Herincx, Monica Sinclair, St. Anthony Singers, English Chamber Orchestra, Anthony Lewis, Conductor. English language libretto. (This is a solid, middle-of-the-road approach to the opera. A major challenge in the performance of operas of the Baroque period is to strike a balance between authenticity and accessibility, and Lewis has achieved that balance admirably here. Janet Baker is an eloquent Dido. Her singing in the final aria is the standard against which other performances must be judged. This is probably the best choice if you will have only one recording of *Dido and Aeneas*.)

(1985) Philips 16299, with Jessye Norman, Marie McLaughlin, Thomas Allen, Patricia Kern, unidentified chorus, English Chamber Orchestra, Raymond Leppard, Conductor. English language libretto. (Leppard conducts a lush, rich sounding performance that may have little to do with the Baroque tradition.

He has a remarkable cast, even in the smaller roles. Thomas Allen provides the best sung Aeneas on any of the recordings. Jessye Norman, the Dido, is vocally magnificent, and hers is one of the greatest voices.)

(1994) Sony 62993, with Emily van Evera, Janet Lax, Ben Parry, Haden Andrews, Taverner Choir and Players, Andrew Parrott, Conductor. (This performance seeks to recreate the style and sound of the Baroque period. The instrumental sound is spare, almost austere, and much of the singing is more concerned with dramatic expression than with vocal beauty. The key exceptions are Van Evera as Dido and Parry as Aeneas, both of whom sing quite beautifully. Van Evera's closing lament is sung simply and is more moving for that simplicity.)

Nicolai Rimsky-Korsakov (1844–1908)

The Golden Cockerel (1909)

The Golden Cockerel is probably better known under its French title, *Le Coq d'Or* (the original Russian is: *Zolstoy petushok*). The opera is based on an imitation folk story by Alexander Pushkin, which in turn was based on two passages in Washington Irving's *The Alhambra*. Rimsky and Vladimir Bel'sky, his librettist, however, found in Pushkin's poem an opportunity to comment satirically on contemporary issues. Russia was still suffering under their humiliating defeat in the Russo-Japanese war in 1905, and an opera that showed the foolish old King Dodon declaring his ignorance of the meaning of the word *law* and then being conquered in battle by the enemy struck too close to home for comfort. Rimsky refused to soften its effect or to tone down the implied attack on the tsarist regime in general, and the official censors denied permission for the performance of *The Golden Cockerel*. As a result, in Rimsky's lifetime the work was performed only in fragmen-

tary form in concerts, and the composer was never able to see it staged in full.

Musically, *The Golden Cockerel,* Rimsky-Korsakov's last opera, is more advanced in its harmony than most of his works, but the ban on its performance during his lifetime had nothing to do with its "modernism," rather with its political implications. In addition to political satire, however, the score pokes delightful fun at various musical conventions, including the elaborate coloratura of the operatic soprano and the overly colorful orchestration of some composers, among whom Rimsky himself was perhaps the most colorful of all.

As with *Sadko,* the one available recording of *The Golden Cockerel* is adequate and will serve as a useful stopgap until something better comes along. The absence of an English language libretto is particularly unfortunate in a work that depends for its full effect a great deal on verbal satire.

(1985) Capriccio 10760, with Nikolai Stoilov, Lyubomir Dyakovski, Elena Stoyanova, Yavora Stoilova, Evgenia Babacheva, Chorus and Orchestra of the Sofia National Opera, Dimiter Manolov, Conductor. No English libretto; a brief synopsis keyed to the music tracks. (Chorus and orchestra are impressive in this well recorded version. Many of the cast members are beset with varying degrees of vocal insecurity, but the performance survives on the basis of good characterization and the feel of real involvement in what's going on. Stoilov is wonderfully pompous as King Dodon. He has a voice that calls up a visual image of the character. Manolov, the conductor, keeps the action moving.)

Sadko (1898)

Outside Russia, where his works retain their popularity, Rimsky-Korsakov is probably the most underperformed of the great opera composers. That his operas are "underperformed" can be confirmed by a review of the repertoires of the major opera houses other than those in Russia and other

Slavic nations. That he is also a "great opera composer" can only be established on the basis of critical preference and personal taste. Familiarity with *Sadko*, however, will demonstrate Rimsky's capacity for popular appeal. It is a delightful work, musically satisfying, filled with beautiful melodies dressed in exciting, forward-looking harmonies, interesting rhythmical patterns, and incredibly imaginative orchestration.

Sadko is rooted in Russian folklore. The opera asks a question typical of much folk literature: "How did land-locked Novgorod, the ancient Russian city, get an outlet to the sea?" The answer is that Volkhova, the beautiful Sea Princess, who loves Sadko, melts into a mist and becomes the river that bears her name. It flows first into Lake Lagoda and thence, by way of the River Neva, into the Bay of Finland and the Baltic Sea. It isn't much of a plot, but the incidents on the way gave Rimsky the opportunity for a variety of wonderful music. The musical centerpiece of the opera is the scene in which three merchants — Viking, Indian, and Venetian — sing of their homelands. The great Russian opera companies claim that opportunity to bring out their best bass, tenor, and baritone for a brief star turn.

The recommended recording is not ideal, but it will fill the gap until something better comes along. We can always hope that Gergiev and his Kirov forces will bring us a new and improved version of *Sadko* to replace their 1993 recording. There is one other currently available edition of *Sadko* (Opera d'Oro 1246). It reproduces a 1964 staged performance from Moscow's Bolshoi Theatre. The recording quality is dismal, with an incredible amount of extraneous noise, but the performance is exciting and some of the singing far better than on the recommended recording. There is no libretto, only a sketchy synopsis with an incorrect and incomplete cast listing, a serious liability in an opera that will be unfamiliar to many listeners.

(1993) Philips 42138, with Vladimir Galusin, Marianna Tarassova, Sergei Alexashkin, Valentina Tsidipova, Larissa Diadkova, Bulat Minjelkiev, Alexander Gergalov, Gegam Grigorian, Chorus and Orchestra of the Kirov Opera, St. Petersburg, Valery Gergiev, Conductor. English language libretto. (There are some stage and audience noises in this "live" recording, although much less than in the earlier Russian version. Otherwise, the sound is good. Gergiev conducts a lively, convincing performance, but his singers let him down at several points. In the key role of Volkhova, Valentina Tsidipova makes a sweet sound not always completely secure. Vladimir Galusin as Sadko is loud most of the time, and Gegam Grigorian, who sings the song of the Indian Merchant, the most familiar music in the score, makes little of his opportunity.)

Sadko is available, with Vladimir Galusin and Marianna Tarassova, on VHS from Philips. The video probably derives from the same performance as the recording listed above.

Gioachino Rossini (1792–1868)

Il Barbiere di Siviglia (1816)

The first performance of *Il Barbiere di Siviglia* was a colossal fiasco. To begin with, Rossini was treading on sacred ground. Giovanni Paisiello, Rossini's senior by fifty years, was a highly respected composer, and his own *Barbiere* had been a favorite in Italy for thirty years. So did this presumptuous young upstart, a mere twenty-three years in age, think he could successfully tread in the footsteps of an acknowledged master? Many in the audience on that February night in 1816 came prepared to boo Rossini's opera off the stage. They almost managed, and they had the help of a series of disasters during the performance. The singer of Basilio stumbled, fell, and bloodied his nose before his big aria, and an errant cat wandered onto the stage more than once — to the distraction of the cast and the delight of the audience. The premiere was a disaster, but beginning with the second performance, *Il Barbiere* became a sensational success. It is the only Rossini opera that has never been absent from the standard repertoire.

There is every possible reason for the long-standing popularity of Rossini's *Barbiere*. It is based on a masterpiece of French literature, Pierre Augustin Beaumarchais' comedy *Le Barbier di Séville*, the first in a series of three plays that also provided the source for Mozart's *Le Nozze di Figaro*. It has a magnificent score, music that precisely mirrors the action and the characters, but that is also worth listening to outside the context of the opera. It provides rewarding roles for five singers, each of whom not only participates in bubbling ensembles but also has a wonderful solo aria or two to sing. And both the plot and the music are funny in the way a true *opera buffo* is meant to be funny, so that the audience laughs out loud. As pure operatic comedy, it is always at the top of the list.

Il Barbiere has been a favorite in recording studios since the earliest days, both in complete versions and in isolated selections. Two more or less complete versions predate the advent of electrical recording, and in 1929–30 it was one of the early complete operatic recordings of the electrical era. That version is available still (Grammofono 78722; Arkadia 78008). The performance reflects the bad old ways of doing things, but it does preserve the golden age Figaro of Riccardo Stracciari a bit too late in his career, and the young Salvatore Baccaloni as Bartolo just at the beginning of his. The three recordings listed here represent three different approaches to the opera, particularly in the casting of Rosina. Another good version, not quite so spectacular in terms of casting, is available at budget price on Naxos 660027.

(1957) EMI 56301, with Tito Gobbi, Maria Callas, Luigi Alva, Fritz Ollendorff, Nicola Zaccaria, Gabriella Carturan, Philharmonia Orchestra and Chorus, Alceo Galliera, Conductor. English language libretto. (Galliera conducts an appropriately lively performance of the score with the standard theatrical cuts of an earlier day. Gobbi doesn't have the most beautiful voice among the various Figaros, but he creates the most interesting character. Callas surprised even her admirers with her Rosina. The voice is distinctive as always, and she points words as meaningfully as in the most tragic of operas, but she captures the spirit of comedy remarkably well. Luigi Alva is an accomplished Almaviva, with a very light tenor voice. The other cast members are acceptable without any special brilliance.)

(1958) BMG/RCA 68552, with Robert Merrill, Roberta Peters, Cesare Valletti, Giorgio Tozzi, Fernando Corena, Margaret Roggero, Orchestra and Chorus of the Metropolitan Opera, Erich Leinsdorf, Conductor. English language libretto. (This recording reproduced in the studio what might have been heard on a good night at the Metropolitan Opera in the 1950s. For many years, *Il Barbiere* was appropriated by high sopranos with changes in the vocal line to suit their voices. Roberta Peters was one of the best of them. Cesare Valletti is an excellent Almaviva. For the first time in recorded versions of the opera, he is given Almaviva's extremely difficult final aria, "Cessa di più resistere," and he carries it off effectively. Merrill brings a big, luxurious voice to Figaro, and Tozzi and Corena both have significant vocal equipment. This is very much a performance fit for a truly big opera house, and some of the comedy is apparently aimed at the last row of the top gallery.)

(1992) Teldec or Elektra/Asylum 74885, with Håken Hagegård, Jennifer Larmore, Raúl Giménez, Samuel Ramey, Alessandro Corbelli, Barbara Frittoli, Chorus of the Grand Théâtre de Genève, Orchestre de Chambre de Lausanne, Jesus Lopez-Cobos, Conductor. English language libretto. (With Lopez-Cobos the action moves rapidly, and he has a cast that can keep up with him. Hagegård doesn't have the big voice of many Figaros, but he is fully in character and meets the vocal challenges effectively. Larmore convinces us that the original mezzo-soprano version is preferable to any soprano alterations. She is a relatively serious Rosina, but her voice is beautiful and she is technically accomplished. Giménez is an excellent Almaviva, the equal of Valletti but with a somewhat smaller voice. He, too, sings the difficult final aria quite well. This version is a good first choice among the many recordings of *Il Barbiere*.)

Il Barbiere di Siviglia is available with Maria Ewing and John Rawnsley on VHS from Warner Home Video, and with Jennifer Larmore and David Maris on DVD from Image.

La Cenerentola (1817)

Don't come to *Cenerentola* expecting a fairy tale. Perrault's heroine may have had the help of a fairy god mother to get to the ball, but Rossini's Cinderella depends entirely on human assistance — and she surely doesn't wear glass slippers. In fact, Rossini had no patience with the supernatural elements in the story, and what he and his librettist give us is a common sense, rational plot about a sadly mistreated young lady and how in the long run her goodness is rewarded. The subtitle of the opera sums up the story for us: *La Bontà in Trionfo*, "Goodness Triumphs!" Cinderella, whose name in the opera is Angelina, early proves herself sweet, thoughtful, and kind, but she also has a mind of her own, a down-to-earth desire for the better things in life, and a realistic understanding of what really matters. She's not quite a liberated woman yet, but she's on her way.

Rossini has sometimes been accused of laziness, but that's a difficult charge to substantiate. He was twenty-four years old and an experienced composer with nineteen operas behind him when he created *Cenerentola*. The task took him all of three weeks of what must have been concentrated work, but he did have a little help from another composer, Luca Agolini, and he borrowed the overture from one of his earlier works.

He was, of course, a practical man of the theater, but hardly lazy.

La Cenerentola is a happy opera, a *dramma giocoso* as originally labled, but it is not a comic opera in the traditional sense. We might well call it a comedy with heart. We encounter the typical *buffo* characters in Don Magnifico and Dandini, but Cenerentola herself, Don Ramiro, and Alidoro are meant to be taken seriously, as their music clearly tells us. One mark of Rossini's developing artistry is the skill with which he combines the comic and the serious elements without violating the sense of musical unity.

The opera was popular almost from the beginning, but later in the nineteenth century it passed out of the standard repertoire. In more recent years, a number of gifted mezzo-sopranos with the technical ability to sing Rossini's difficult music have reclaimed *Cenerentola* and other Rossini operas. The recommended recordings highlight two of these singers.

(1992) Decca/London 36902, with Cecilia Bartoli, William Matteuzzi, Alessandro Corbelli, Michele Pertusi, Enzo Dara, Orchestra and Chorus of Teatro Communale di Bologna, Riccardo Chailly, Conductor. English language libretto. (Sound quality and conducting enhance this recording of Cecilia Bartoli's Ceneretnola, and she is surrounded by cast members who understand Rossini style and can handle the composer's technical demands adeptly. Bartoli's interpretation brings out the strength and determination of the character, and she is brilliant in coloratura. The rondo finale is taken at breathtaking speed and every note is clearly articulated.)

(1994) Teldec or Elektra/Asylum 94553, with Jennifer Larmore, Raúl Giménez, Gino Quilico, Alastair Miles, Alessandro Corbelli, Orchestra and Chorus of the Royal Opera House, Covent Garden, Carlo Rizzi, Conductor. English language libretto. (Rizzi is the expert conductor. The cast is fully equal to Rossini's music, and Giménez is an ingratiating Don Ramiro with beautiful voice and excellent technique. Larmore demonstrates in this recording a more naturally beautiful voice than Bartoli. Hers is not as pointed and lively a characterization as Bartoli's, but she is equal to the technical challenges and makes a charming Angelina. The recorded quality is excellent. This recording is my first choice, but both versions are worthy representations of Rossini's score.)

Cenerentola is available with Cecilia Bartoli and Raúl Gimenez on VHS from Universal/London and with Ann Murray and Francisco Araiza on DVD from Image.

Guillaume Tell (1829)

Guillaume Tell was Rossini's last opera. He was thirty-seven years of age at the time of its premiere, and he had already produced thirty-nine operas. Rossini lived another thirty-nine busy years, during which he composed a great deal of music, religious and otherwise, and took an active interest in a number of operatic projects, but there were no more operas from his pen. For all the speculation of historians and biographers, no one really knows why.

What we do know is that this final opera was Rossini's most ambitious work. *Guillaume Tell* is a lengthy opera, almost four hours in performance without intermissions, and it is a large work in other ways as well. It deals with such big issues as liberty and the struggle to realize it in Switzerland, and the conflicts between personal affection and the call of loyalty to nation and family in a time of political turmoil. There are large-scale musical structures, including the often praised ensemble at the end of Act II, when citizens of three different Swiss cantons, each represented by its own choral group, swear to end Austrian domination. There are massive scenic demands, and Rossini calls not only for a full cast of soloists able to handle *bel canto* vocal style expertly, but also for large orchestral forces and a company of ballet dancers. There are scenes of intense drama and suspense, in one of which Tell truly does shoot an apple from the head of Jemmy, his son. In every sense, *Guillaume Tell* is *grand opéra*, one of the great works that define that distinctive nineteenth-century French musical form.

Guillaume Tell is well served in two modern stereo recordings, one in the original French and the other in Italian translation, the version in which — until recent years — the opera was most often performed outside of French speaking countries. Since both performances are worthy, the choice between them depends essentially on which language is preferred. If there is to be only one version in the collection, my personal preference is for the French edition, since it is the original.

(1972) EMI 69951, with Gabriel Bacquier, Montserrat Caballé, Mady Mesplé, Nicolai Gedda, Kolas Kovats, Gwynne Howell, Ambrosian Opera Chorus, Royal Philharmonic Orchestra, Lamberto Gardelli, Conductor. English language libretto. (Effectively recorded and conducted by Gardelli, this edition of the French version offers a good cast in a complete performance, with the addition of an extra aria for Jemmy that is not included in the printed scores. Outstanding in the cast are Montserrat Caballé and Nicolai Gedda. Gedda sings the role of Arnold, with its incredibly high tenor tessitura, in authentic French style and with real panache.)

(1978–1979) Decca/London 417154, with Sherrill Milnes, Mirella Freni, Della Jones, Luciano Pavarotti, Nicolai Ghiaurov, John Tomlisnon, Ambrosian Opera Chorus, National Philharmonic Orchestra, Riccardo Chailly, Conductor. English language libretto. (The Italian version is conducted in vigorous, lively fashion by Chailly. The vocal gifts of the cast are on the whole superior to the French language recording, although the effect is probably as much a matter of French vowels in contrast to the open, pure Italian vowels. Pavarotti cannot equal Gedda in matters of style, but he makes a ringing, heroic Arnold. Milnes is powerful and sensitive as Tell, and Freni sings engagingly and sympathetically as Matilde.)

Guillaume Tell is available with Giorgio Zancanaro and Cheryl Studer on DVD from Image and on VHS from Public Media.

L'Italiana in Algeri (1813)

Rossini's *L'Italiana in Algeri* is the proof that opera can be insane without being inane. Here is a score of tremendous musical sophistication and a plot that moves logically from one point to another, but the madcap antics of the characters give substance to the words of the first-act finale. Freely paraphrased, they go something like this: "My head's ringing like a bell — ding, ding! A hammer's pounding at my brain — bang, bang! I feel like a featherless crow — caw, caw! There's a cannon exploding in my head — boom, boom!" *L'Italiana* is that kind of opera.

It's also an opera that glories in the strength, wit and sheer brainpower of a woman. We may think of the nineteenth century as an age that put women "in their place" and kept them there. On the operatic stage, however, particularly in the comedies, women often are the stronger and more intelligent characters, and none of them can top Isabella in *L'Italiana*. She has a lover to whom she is devoted, but Lindoro is actually not a very bright fellow. Without Isabella, he'd be lost. She has an admirer, Taddeo, whom she wraps around her little finger without even lifting it. She is a captive of Mustafà, the Bey of Algiers, and she manages to make a complete fool of him. Just imagine this pompous, proud ruler of men making a fool of himself as a *Pappataci*, and all at her command. And, needless to say, she managess the release of all of the captive Italians with pitifully little help from anyone else.

For a successful performance, *L'Italiana* requires a heroine who can act with vitality and verve, and sing like a conquering angel. Rossini gives her ample opportunity to demonstrate her ability: three major arias, a delightful duet, and her own part in several larger ensembles. She is clearly the star of the opera, but she's not alone on the stage. The men in the cast have their own parts to play with solo arias of their own, including an exercise in coloratura for the bass who sings Mustafà and two challenging cavatinas for Lindoro. The recommended recordings provide first-rate vocalism in almost every role and good recording quality.

(1980) Erato or Elektra/Asylum 45404, with Marilyn Horne, Ernesto Palacio, Domenico Trimarchi, Samuel Ramey, Nicola Zaccaria, Kathleen Battle, Coro Filarmonico di Praga, I Solisti Veneti, Claudio Scimone, Conductor. Italian language libretto only and a brief synopsis of the opera. (Scimone provides a clear, transparent sound from the relatively small orchestral ensemble, and the effect is of a delightful chamber opera. The cast is good in depth, with Samuel Ramey an outstanding Mustafà, and Palacio a clear voiced, agile Lindoro. Rossini might have written the role of Isabella with Marilyn Horne in mind. Nothing in the difficult technical demands daunts her, and her voice has the distinctive ring of authority about it. It's clear from her opening aria that no mere man will get the best of her.)

(1987) Deutsche Grammophon 427331, with Agnes Baltsa, Frank Lopardo, Alessandro Corbelli, Enzo Dara, Ruggero Raimondi, Patrizia Pace, Concert Chorus of the Vienna State Opera, Vienna Philharmonic, Claudio Abbado, Conductor. English language libretto. (This is one of the best of Abbado's operatic recordings. On the whole, the cast is perhaps one half step below that of the Erato recording, although Frank Lopardo is a superior Lindoro, with a voice of more natural appeal than Palacio. Agnes Baltsa is an excellent Isabella, not quite as characterful or as brilliant in coloratura as Horne. But who is? This is a completely satisfying recording, but in spite of the absence of an English language libretto, I still prefer the Erato version. It is Marilyn Horne who makes the difference.)

L'Italiana in Algeri is available, with Doris Soffel and Robert Gambill, on DVD from Arthaus Music and on VHS from BMG/ RCA Victor.

Camille Saint-Saëns (1835–1921)

Samson et Dalila (1877)

Samson et Dalila had a difficult beginning. In 1867 Saint-Saëns began to consider composing a Biblical oratorio on the account of Samson in Judges 16. His librettist, Ferdinand Lemaire, however, suggested an opera instead, and Saint-Saëns started work on the score. When informal performances of portions of Act II produced little enthusiasm and a number of questions about the suitability of a Biblical subject for presentation on stage, the composer laid the project aside for a time. In 1875 the first act was given in concert performance, but Parisian and other French theaters weren't interested in staging the opera. It took Franz Liszt, who was always interested in new music, to schedule the initial performance at Weimar in 1877, but only in 1890 was *Samson et Dalila* seen in France. From then on, the objections disappeared and the opera went on to worldwide success.

Critical opinion has often accused *Samson et Dalila* of being more oratorio, as the composer originally intended, than opera. The libretto, however, provides convincingly motivated characters and a flow of interesting action more logical than many operas offer, and after the first fifteen minutes or so, the music becomes intensely dramatic. In fact, it is a beautifully constructed score. Saint-Saëns' inspiration produced a series of memorable and singable melodies, and he set them in a rich and varied orchestral framework. It's easy to understand why mezzo-sopranos and dramatic tenors con-

tinue to covet the leading roles, and audiences keep coming back for more.

With few exceptions, recordings of *Samson et Dalila* have been successful. For completely authentic style throughout, we would have to go back to 1946 and the first disc version, with a French cast under a French conductor, and the chorus and orchestra of the Paris Opéra. It is available on Naxos 8110063, but an opera as rich in orchestral sound as this one needs the advantage of modern stereo sound. The three recordings listed here serve Saint-Saëns' score well.

(1962) EMI 67602, with Jon Vickers, Rita Gorr, Ernest Blanc, Anton Diakov, René Duclos Chorus, Orchestra of the Théâtre de l'Opéra de Paris, Georges Prêtre, Conductor. English language libretto. (This recording has been reissued in good remastered stereo sound and preserves an idiomatic performance under Prêtre. Rita Gorr may not be the most seductive Dalila, but her voice is the real thing, a strong, even, decidedly French mezzo-soprano. Vickers is the most artistically expressive Samson on any of the recordings. His voice, however, is not inherently beautiful, and will be an acquired taste for many listeners.)

(1991) EMI 54470, with Plácido Domingo, Waltraud Meier, Alain Fondary, Jean-Philippe Courtis, Samuel Ramey, Chorus and Orchestra of l'Opéra-Bastille, Myung-Whun Chung, Conductor. English language libretto. (Chung paces the opera extremely well. Samson is an ideal role for the mature Domingo, and he brings to it the vocal amplitude and intensity of his excellent Otello. Compared to Rita Gorr, Waltraud Meier's Dalila is the complete seductress, almost flirtatious in her opening aria, and she brings a warm, caressing tone to her scene with Samson in Act II. This recording makes a good first choice for this opera.)

(1998) Erato or Elektra/Asylum 24756, with José Cura, Olga Borodina, Jean-Philippe Lafont, Egils Silins, Robert Lloyd, London Symphony Chorus and Orchestra, Colin Davis, Conductor. English language libretto. (Davis is a strong conductor in this extremely well recorded version of the opera. Olga Borodina characterizes less than some singers in her role, but she has the most naturally appealing and beautiful voice of any Dalila in these recordings. José Cura sings a sensitive Samson, ample in power but with the voice shaded appropriately in the more intimate moments. More than most of his recordings, this *Samson et Dalila* demonstrates why he has attracted such a large opera house following.)

Samson et Dalila is available, with Plácido Domingo and Shirley Verrett, on VHS and DVD from Kultur.

Arnold Schoenberg (1874–1951)

Moses und Aron (1951; 1954)

No one will pretend that *Moses und Aron* is easy going for most listeners. It isn't. The fact is that Schoenberg created an opera that challenges us on almost every count.

Musically, it adheres to his twelve-tone system, a complex form of musical structure outside the traditional tonal approach to composition. As Humphrey Searle commented in *Grove's Dictionary of Music and Musicians*, this system "has done much the same for music as the theory of relativity and modern atomic theories have done for physics."* We might expect music with the coldness and impersonality of scientific and mathematical theory, but Schoenberg's score is actually richly expressive and highly emotional. As with any artistic theory, the success or failure rests with the creator, and Schoenberg was not only an influential theorist, he was also a gifted and imaginative composer.

Schoenberg challenges us also with the dramatic presentation of his philosophical and theological views. The brothers, Moses and Aron (Schoenberg uses this spelling of his name rather than the usual *Aaron*) represent subtle differences in the understanding of the divine, and through them our attention is directed to one of the oldest and most difficult of theological issues. For Moses, in a radical application of the Biblical prohibition against images, God is completely *"unsichtbarer und unvorstellbarer,"* unperceivable and unimaginable, not only in graphic or plastic representation, but also through the imagery of language, and probably through music as well. Aron, on the other hand, senses the need of people to see God somehow demonstrated, made real in their own terms. It is significant that in the opera Aron sings but Moses only speaks. It is this conflict that forms the dramatic and philosophical center of *Moses und Aron*. In the opera itself, the tension is never resolved. Schoenberg wrote the libretto for a third act, actually in more than one form, but although he lived twenty years after completing Act II, he never composed the music for the final act. The opera as we have it ends with Act II, and with Moses' despair that even his own words have been fashioning an image of the God.

A recording is the ideal medium through which to approach this opera. Staging it effectively is a major problem for opera producers, and not just in how to realize Schoenberg's amazing description of the orgy around the golden calf. With a good recording, however, we can read the words as we listen and hear the score over again until we begin to appreciate how Schoenberg has translated philosophy into the language of music.

(1974) Sony 48456, with Gunter Reich, Richard Cassilly, Felicity Palmer, Gillian Knight, Orpheus Boys' Choir, BBC Singers and Symphony Orchestra, Pierre Boulez, Conductor. English language libretto.

Humphrey Searle, "Twelve-Note Music," in *Groves Dictionary of Music and Musicians* (fifth edition), Eric Blom, ed. (New York: St. Martin's Press, 1954), VII 620.

(Boulez conducts with conviction and brings this knotty opera to life. Cassily does not have a naturally appealing voice, and some critics complain that he is not completely accurate in his singing, but in the encounters with Moses he is convincing. Gunter Reich speaks his important lines with prophetic authority. I have not heard Boulez's later recording of the opera on Deutsche Grammophon 49174, but it has been well received by critics. Another highly praised recording, conducted by Georg Solti, is on Decca/London 414264, but it is available only as an import.)

Dmitry Shostakovich (1906–1975)

Lady Macbeth of the Mtsenek District (1934)

Shakespeare it isn't. Had it been, Stalin might not have left in a huff after the third act when he attended a Moscow performance in 1936. Until then, *Lady Macbeth of the Mtsenek District* had been extremely successful in Russia (as *Ledi Makbet Mtsenskovo vyezda*). After Stalin's early departure from the performance, however, an attack appeared in *Pravda* in short order, and the opera was quickly removed from the repertoires of Russian theaters. It reappeared as *Katerina Ismailova,* an extensively revised version of the original, in 1963.

This violent opera is, as the composer said, a "satire-tragedy," a cross between two idioms that may seem to have little in common. Much of the satire is directed at clerical, official, and even academic incompetence. We encounter a priest who launches into jolly dance music to comfort the bereaved, a pompous police sergeant and his cohorts who lament their underpaid lot in a jaunty little tune that might have come from Gilbert and Sullivan, and a socialist teacher who has discovered that frogs have souls, albeit very small ones that are not immortal. In the midst of the satire, however, we also find the grimmest of tragedy.

Katerina, a bored, dissatisfied wife, takes a lover, murders her father-in-law and husband, and finally, in despair because her beloved deserts her, takes his new lover with her as she plunges to her death in a river.

The satire and the tragedy are both in the music. The idiom, as one would expect, is modern, with often grating harmony and harsh, pounding rhythmical patterns. The music reflects the actions and the attitudes of the characters with virtually programmatic realism, so closely, as a matter of fact, that we may well wonder how Stalin managed to stay in the theater past the love scene in Act I. The score, however, is appealing and accessible even to the most musically conservative audiences, and there are passages of intense and beautiful lyricism, particularly for Katerina.

There is only one recording of the opera available. It presents Shostakovich's original score as it was completed in 1932 prior to the premiere.

(1978) EMI 49955, with Galina Vishnevskaya, Nicolai Gedda, Dimiter Petkov, Werner Krenn, Robert Tear, Aage Haugland, Birgit Finnila, Ambrosian Opera Chorus, London Philharmonic Orchestra, Mstislav Rostropovich, Conductor. English language libretto. (The performance under Rostropovich is superb. Vishnevskaya reminds us why she was the greatest star of opera in Russia before she and her husband, Rostropovich, defected. The voice is often beautiful and always dramatically communicative. The remainder of the international cast is excellent. Rostropovich and Vishnevskaya were personal friends of the composer, and the recording is dedicated to his memory.)

Lady Macbeth of the Mtsenek District is available on DVD and VHS from Image. The soundtrack of this video is derived from the recording listed above, but the actual singers do not appear in the video.

Bedřich Smetana (1824–1884)

The Bartered Bride (1866; 1870)

Before Janáček's operas entered the general repertoire, *The Bartered Bride* (or *The Sold Bride*, as the title is more accurately but less familiarly known; it is *Prodaná Nevěsta* in the Czech) was certainly the most popular Czech opera outside the composer's native land. While Smetana's other estimable stage works were for most opera lovers merely entries in musical dictionaries, *The Bartered Bride* was being performed in theaters all around the world. The situation hasn't changed a great deal, but through the medium of recordings all eight of Smetana's operas are now available.

The pleasures of *The Bartered Bride* have little to do with *what* happens and much more to do with *how* it happens. The plot is built of typical comic opera materials — a threatened romance, an unknown identity, and a comic character to stir up a little trouble (not unlike Dr. Dulcamara in Donizetti's *Don Pasquale*). From the beginning, we are certain that all will work out happily, that families will be properly reunited and Mařenka will be united with her beloved Jenik. Our interest is centered rather in the twisted path that leads to the conclusion, and the wonderful way Smetana brings it to life for us in the music.

The Bartered Bride is the essential Czech opera, the operatic representation of the nation. Although Smetana was generally opposed to the use of genuine folk tunes in his operas, he understood the Bohemian musical character, and composed his own folk tunes often set to typical Czech dance rhythms. The opera has frequently been performed in other languages by international casts, but it is so closely tied to the Czech people and their speech that it is always at its best done by native singers in their native tongue.

There have been several Czech recordings of *The Bartered Bride*. One of the earliest of them from 1933 has been reissued on Naxos 8110098. It is a lively performance, uneven vocally and obviously in dated sound. The most recent recording, recommended here, suffers from no such difficulties.

(1980-81) Supraphon 3511, with Gabriella Beňačova, Peter Dvorský, Richard Novak, Miroslav Kopp, Jana Jonášova, Czech Philharmonic Chorus and Orchestra, Zdeněk Košler, Conductor. English language libretto. (This performance is ideal in almost every aspect under a conductor who understands the opera perfectly. Beňačova has a voice of great sweetness, absolutely secure, and she is matched by her Jenik, Peter Dvorský. Miroslav Kopp sings a sympathetic Vašek, and manages to make the stuttering written into the score sound like an engaging part of the character's personality. Novák characterizes Kecal effectively, but the voice is not a model of security.)

Richard Strauss (1864–1949)

Ariadne auf Naxos (1912; 1916)

Ariadne auf Naxos started in 1912 as an added attraction for Hugo von Hoffmannsthal's version of Molière's *Le Bourgeois Gentilhomme*. The spoken play was dressed out with Strauss's delightful incidental music, and at its conclusion, Monsieur Jourdain, the *bourgeois gentilhomme* himself, would offer his guests as after dinner entiertainment Strauss's opera, a commedia dell'arte performance and a serious drama combined into one. The combination play and opera made for a long evening's program, over six hours, in part because the "brief" after dinner entertainment turned out to last 90 minutes. No doubt audience patience was severely tried.

Hoffmannsthal and Strauss then revised the work to produce the full-length opera that is usually performed today. Molière was omitted, and Monsieur Jourdain with him. In their place, we have a through-composed operatic prologue in which the announcement is made that the elevated poetic drama of Ariadne and the *commedia dell'arte* comedy must be performed simultaneously. What follows is a delightful combination of comic opera and *opera seria,* in which the comic characters try to brighten the outlook of Ariadne, who has been deserted by her beloved Theseus. The measure of Strauss's genius is the artistry with which he combines the comedy and the serious drama so that we can be amused by Zerbinetta and her colleagues and at the same time moved by Ariadne's grief.

In many ways, *Ariadne auf Naxos* is the connoisseur's choice among Strauss's operas, more delicate both musically and dramatically than his other works. It is virtually a chamber opera, lightly scored for an orchestra of only thirty-seven, although the vocal demands are extreme. Zerbinetta's big aria is one of most difficult in the repertoire of sopranos of coloratura persuasion, somewhat simplified in 1916 from the original 1912 form, but still calling for the full arsenal of vocal effects. Ariadne needs a soprano large of voice and temperament, and Bacchus must sing his relatively brief part with full youthful tone. The original 1912 version was available in a good performance on Virgin Classics 4511, with the play summarized in a spoken narration, but including Strauss's incidental music and, of course, the opera itself. This recording has been discontinued, but may still be available from some dealers. The more familiar 1916 version has been recorded infrequently, but often quite well. Both of the recommended recordings are of that final version.

(1954) EMI 67156, with Elisabeth Schwarzkopf, Rita Streich, Irmgard Seefried, Her-

mann Prey, Rudolf Schock, Philharmona Orchestra, Herbert von Karajan, Conductor. English language libretto. (This remastered monophonic recording is one of the classics of the phonograph, beautifully conducted and sung. Schwarzkopf, Streich, and Seefried have never been bettered in their respective roles. Seefried is the most eloquent of Composers in the Prologue. Schwarzkopf is radiant of voice and keenly aware of the words and their meaning. Streich, wonderfully sweet of voice, is in no way daunted by the vocal requirements of Zerbinetta. Unless stereo is an absolute necessity, this is the version of choice.)

(1988) Philips 422084, with Jessye Norman, Julia Varady, Edita Gruberova, Paul Frey, Olaf Bär, Gewandhaus Orchestra, Leipzig, Kurt Masur, Conductor. English language libretto. (The digital stereo sound brings out all the details of Masur's effective conducting. Bär brings a more beautiful voice to Bacchus than Schock, but he is a bit overwhelmed by his Ariadne, Jessye Norman. Norman is a vocal phenomenon, the voice is large and beautiful, although the text is not as dramatically pointed as it is by Schwarzkopf. Varady is an eloquent Composer, and Gruberova brings a warm, earthy voice and ample technique to Zerbinetta.)

Ariadne auf Naxos is available, with Jessye Norman and Kathleen Battle, on VHS from Universal/Deutsche Grammophon.

Elektra (1909)

Ernestine Schumann-Heink, the great contralto, sang Klytämnestra in the premiere of *Elektra*. It was not her favorite role. Her comment? "I will never sing the role again. It was frightful. We were a set of mad women.... There is nothing beyond *Elektra*."[*] She was at least partially right. The women in the opera, even gentle Chrysothemis, often seem to border on madness, and in some cases even cross the border, and the opera truly is "frightful." It was planned

---

[*]Quoted in the Earl of Harewood, *Kobbe's Complete Opera Book*, revised edition (New York and London: Putnam, 1954), p. 916.

that way from Sophocles' ancient original all the way to Hugo von Hoffmannsthal's play and libretto, and Strauss's opera based on it. How could the story of the murder of mother and stepfather set to music not be "frightful" and still be faithful to its source?

About one thing, however, Schumann-Heink was wrong. Opera has certainly gone a long way beyond *Elektra*, both in its music and its dramatic content. Listening to Strauss's opera today we may be more impressed with the traditional quality of the music than with its once decried "modernism." Parts of the score are decidedly unpleasant enough to fit the grim plot of the opera. Listen, for example, to the music that accompanies the execution of Klytmänestra and Aegisth. But there are also moments of true lyricism, the beautiful recognition scene of Elektra and Orest among them, and Strauss is brilliant in his use of the large orchestra, which becomes virtually another character in the drama. *Elektra* still has the power to shock audiences, but the shock is an artistic one, based on the musical and dramatic power of the opera.

It took the dawn of good, modern stereophonic recording to bring the full force of *Elektra* to disc. Our recommended recordings are both demonstration quality in sound. A version of the opera that I have not heard has met with critical approval and may be worth investigating. It is conducted by Giuseppe Sinopoli and can be found on Deutsche Grammophon 453429.

(1966–67) Decca/London 417345, with Birgit Nilsson, Marie Collier, Regina Resnik, Tom Krause, Gerhard Stolze, Vienna Philharmonic Orchestra, Georg Solti, Conductor. English language libretto. (Solti brings intense drama to the score, and he is conducting one of the world's greatest orchestras. Marie Collier as Chrysothemis and Gerhard Stolze as Aegisth are not on a par with the other members of this cast. Regina Resnik is a remarkably effective Klytämnestra. Birgit Nilsson encounters

nothing in Elektra's music beyond her ample vocal capabilities, and she is dramatically convincing.)

(1990) EMI 54067, with Eva Marton, Cheryl Studer, Marjana Lipovsek, Bernd Weikl, Hermann Winkler, Chorus and Orchestra of the Bavarian Radio, Wolfgang Sawallisch, Conductor. English language libretto. (Sawallisch is the excellent conductor on this recording, and he has a good cast to work with. Lipovsek as Klytämnestra and Studer as Chrysothemis are vocally assured and dramatically convincing, as are the men in the cast. Weikl is particularly strong as Orest. Eva Marton has neither the vocal power nor the security of Nilsson, but she communicates fully the passion and anguish of Elektra. Both recordings offer exciting versions of the opera, but this one is my preference.)

Elektra is available, with Birgit Nilsson and Leonie Rysanek, on DVD from Pioneer Video and on VHS from Paramount.

Der Rosenkavalier (1911)

Der Rosenkavalier was one of the few operas to make its way onto the silver screen as a silent film, albeit with an orchestral accompaniment arranged from the original score. It was not a successful financial venture, but the very fact that it happened at all points to one of the reasons for the monumental success of the opera. Quite simply, *Rosenkavalier* sets to music one of the best operatic libretti ever written. Hugo von Hoffmanstahl's text is filled with delightful period details from old Austria, and it presents a group of closely observed and believable human beings involved in experiences with which audiences can identify personally.

As an opera, however, it is the music that Strauss composed that makes it work. The opera has been criticized as overly sentimental, and I suspect that some commentators doubt the validity of a twentieth century work that still has some good tunes in it. In the long run, audiences have said that none of that really matters. Many people are sentimental, and even more of us like good tunes, particularly when they serve to bring to life a cast of wonderfully human characters.

Rosenkavalier, more than many other works, is very much a conductor's opera, and almost all of the several recordings are led by distinguished conductors of past and present. It is also an opera that rises or falls on the basis of the soprano engaged to sing the role of the Marschallin. She is not the title character, and she appears in only two of the three acts. When at the end of a staged performance the singers take their solo bows, it is traditionally Octavian, the title character, who receives the final bow. The Marschallin, however, is the heart of the opera, and great sopranos through the years have coveted the role, sometimes unwisely so.

There are several recordings of *Rosenkavalier*, and none of them is without at least some commendable features. The one abridged and three complete recordings recommended here have won general critical approval and are outstanding examples of what great recorded opera should be. Any one of them would grace the library opera shelves.

(1954) Decca 289 467 111-2, with Maria Reining, Ludwig Weber, Sena Jurinac, Hilde Gueden, Vienna State Opera Chorus, Vienna Philharmonic, Erich Kleiber, Conductor. (This recording is in monophonic sound, a drawback for a work that depends a great deal on clear orchestral and vocal textures. The conductor and cast are excellent on the whole, although Reining is not the most fully characterized Marschallin. Jurinac and Gueden, however, are among the best as Octavian and Sophie. Kleiber is the excellent conductor.)

(1956) EMI 56242 or 56113, with Elisabeth Schwarzkopf, Otto Edelmann, Christa Ludwig, Teresa Stich-Randall, Philharmonia Orchestra and Chorus, Herbert von Karajan, Conductor. (For many opera

lovers, this early stereo recording is the best available. Later in his career, Karajan tended to become overly fussy with orchestral details and often chose casts for which critics have felt it necessary to apologize. This, however, is early Karajan, strongly cast. Schwarzkopf was clearly the most famous Marschallin of the 1950s. Her performance has been subject recently to some negative critical reevaluation, but I find it deeply moving. Unlike the other complete recordings listed here, Karajan allows some cuts in the score. Christa Ludwig is the excellent Octavian.)

(1968–69) Decca 417 493-2, with Régine Crespin, Manfred Jungwirth, Yvonne Minton, Helen Donath, Vienna State Opera Chorus, Vienna Philharmonic, Georg Solti, Conductor. (Recently reissued with excellent remastered digital sound, this recording is probably the best recommendation for a library that will have only one *Rosenkavalier*. Crespin, like Schwarzkopf, presents a richly characterized Marschallin, and many listeners will find the voice more innately beautiful than other sopranos in the role. The rest of the cast is commendable, and there's the added luxury of having Luciano Pavarotti, the quintessential Italian tenor, in the role of the Italian Tenor.)

There is one historical recording from the early 1930s that preserves a performance of special importance. Even if your library has already a complete recording of the opera, you should consider adding this abridged version.

(1933) EMI CHS7 64487-2, also Pearl 9365, and on budget label Opera d'Oro 1221, with Lotte Lehmann, Richard Mayr, Maria Olczewska, Elisabeth Schumann, Vienna State Opera Orchestra and Chorus, Robert Heger, Conductor. (Lehmann was *the* Marschallin of the 1930s and early 1940s, and the other cast members were all famous in their roles. The sound is early but listenable monophonic, and this abridged recording includes approximately half of the opera.)

Der Rosenkavalier is available, with Eisabeth Scwarzkopf and Christa Ludwig, on

DVD from Sony Classics and on VHS from Kultur.

Salome (1905)

There's nothing as good as a little scandal to insure an immediate success. *Salome* provided the scandal, and the success followed. The censor refused permission for performances in Vienna, and at the Metropolitan Opera in New York the opera was withdrawn after one public performance. One of the New York critics referred to *Salome* as "this exudation from the diseased and polluted will and imagination of the authors."* In Great Britain, the producers were required to move the setting to Greece, omit all of the Biblical references, and leave John the Baptist's head (he was now renamed Mattaniah) safely in the cistern. In Germany, Emperor William II commented that *Salome* would do the composer "a lot of damage." Strauss's reaction? "The damage enabled me to build my villa in Garmisch."†

But was *Salome* only a *succès de scandale*? Time has surely proven otherwise. Now that there's no more scandal, the opera continues to attract enthusiastic audiences, and, we might add, to tempt ill equipped sopranos and occasional mezzo-sopranos to risk their vocal health in the title role.

The opera is based on Oscar Wilde's French play as translated from the original French into German by Hedwig Lachmann. The plot expands, quite considerably, the Biblical account of John the Baptist's death in Matthew 14, where Salome's name is never mentioned. In the opera, however, the emphasis is clearly on Salome and her obsessive desire, and the action moves inexorably toward the final scene, when she receives and embraces the severed head of the prophet.

Strauss made almost impossible demands on the singer in the role of Salome. What he asked for was a teenager with the voice of Isolde. Only a handful of candidates for the role have been able to meet that challenge, and surely none of them were actually in their teen years. The most impressive was Ljuba Weilitch, the legendary reigning Salome of the later 1940s and early 1950s. Unofficial issues of two of her complete Metropolitan Opera performances appear from time to time, and you may be able to locate the studio recording of the final scene on Sony 62866. The two recordings of *Salome* recommended here are equally effective and offer musically and dramatically satisfying performances of the opera in excellent stereo sound.

(1961) Decca/London 414414, with Birgit Nilsson, Grace Hoffman, Gerhard Stolze, Ebernard Wächter, Waldemar Kmentt, Vienna Philharmonic Orchestra, Georg Solti, Conductor. English language libretto. (Solti conducts an intense and passionate performance. Gerhard Stolze's Herod is generally over the top. Otherwise the cast offers good support for the superb Salome of Birgit Nilsson. She is dramatically involved, but the glory of her performance is the voice, absolutely secure and in complete control of every dynamic level, from hushed pianissimo to full fortissimo. The orchestra is uncommonly prominent in this recording, but Nilsson can handle it.)

(1990) Deutsche Graamophon 431810, with Cheryl Studer, Leonie Rysanek, Horst Hiestermann, Bryn Terfel, Clemens Bieber, Orchestra of the Deutschen Oper Berlin, Giuseppe Sinopoli, Conductor. English language libretto. (Sinopoli paces the opera effectively and the orchestral sound is impressive. Histermann is no improvement on Stolze as Herod, but the rest of the cast is good. Bryn Terfel is the outstanding Jochanaan, and Leonie Rysanek offers a

*Henry Krehbiel, in *The New York Tribune*, quoted in *Metropolitan Opera Annals: A Chronicle of Artists and Performances*, compiled by William H. Seltsam (New York: H. W. Wilson Company, 1947), p. 172.

†Quoted in Charles Osborne, *The Complete Operas of Richard Strauss* (North Pomfret, Vermont: Trafalgar Square Publishing, 1988), p. 42.

penetrating interpretation of Herodias. Cheryl Studer is an excellent Salome. Her youthful sound would have delighted Strauss. Even though she can't offer quite the voluminous Isolde voice of Nilsson, Studer's vocal equipment is entirely adequate for the role.)

Salome is available, with Maria Ewing and Michael Devlin, on DVD and VHS from Kultur. The performance may prove offensive to some viewers.

Igor Stravinsky (1882–1971)

The Rake's Progress (1951)

Musical works are inspired in many different ways, and we shouldn't be surprised that the idea for Stravinsky's opera originated in a trip to the Chicago Art Institute in 1947. There Stravinsky saw William Hogarth's series of eighteenth century prints on the subject of a young man's rise and fall, and the idea for the opera was born. At the suggestion of Aldous Huxley, Stravinsky asked the distinguished poet W. H. Auden to prepare the libretto, which task Auden readily accepted and carried out with the help of his colleague Chester Kallman. The result was *The Rake's Progress*, an opera that has earned a significant place in the contemporary repertoire.

What strikes the listener first about *The Rake's Progress* is the conscious, perhaps even self-conscious, use of earlier operatic traditions from a variety of earlier composers, particularly those of the eighteenth century. Formal arias, duets, and ensembles are linked with secco recitatives, accompanied with a harpsichord, and the language of the libretto reminds us of the poetry and drama of the neo-classical period in English literature. The more we know of the opera, however, the more we are aware that the composer and his librettists were twentieth-century artists who could not, even if they tried, escape their own time and place. The libretto abounds in moral ambiguities that are not solved by the neat proverb attached to the end of the Epilogue that the Devil finds work for idle hands, hearts, and minds. The music, as well, is tradition filtered through the artistic imagination of the same composer who many years earlier shocked Paris with *Le Sacre de Printemps*. Stravinsky changed his musical style more than once, but always he remained Stravinsky.

Stravinsky himself made two different studio recordings of *The Rake's Progress,* the first in conjunction with performances at the Metropolitan Opera in 1953. That version has not been reissued on compact disc, but his second recording, which I have not heard, was made in 1964 and is available on Sony 46299. I can vouch for the excellence of the version recommended here.

(1997) Deutsche Grammophon 459648, with Ian Bostridge, Deborah York, Bryn Terfel, Anne Sofie von Otter, Anne Howells, Martin Robson, Monteverdi Choir, London Symphony Orchestra, John Eliot Gardiner, Conductor. English language libretto. (Gardiner is an authority on the performance of eighteenth century and earlier music, and his approach is entirely appropriate for Stravinsky's opera. He is working with as good a cast as could possibly be assembled. Deborah York has the sensitivity and the clear lyrical soprano to do justice to Anne Trulove's music. Terfel is a magnificent Nick Shadow, ample of voice and at times terrifying. Ian Bostridge does not have a large voice, but he is a master of lieder and brings that important skill to bear on his interpretation of Tom Rakewell.)

The Rake's Progress is available with Jerry Hadley and Dawn Upshaw in an experimental production on DVD from Image, and with Leo Goeke and Felicity Lott in a more conventional production on VHS from VAI.

Peter Ilych Tchaikovsky (1840–1893)

Eugene Onegin (1879)

There have always been critics who lamented Tchaikovsky's operatic treatment of Pushkin's verse novel. After all, Pushkin is the greatest of the classic Russian writers, and *Eugene Onegin* (*Yevgeny Onyegin* in transliterated Russian) is generally considered his masterpiece. Any change or shift in emphasis is automatically subject to objection. The composer, however, treated Pushkin's poem with great respect, and the opera retains the major scenes and much of the language of Pushkin's original. The primary change was one of emphasis from the ironic contrast between the emptiness of opulent city life and the simple honesty of rural society to the emotional and psychological development of Pushkin's two main characters, Tatiana and Onegin.

In any case, Tchaikovsky's opera should be evaluated in its own terms and not on the basis of its faithfulness to its source. Viewed in that light, *Eugene Onegin* clearly deserves its popularity among the opera public in Russia and other parts of the world. Tchaikovsky was emotionally touched by the characters, particularly Tatiana, and he managed to find precisely the right music to define her youthful love, its unhappy outcome, and her growth into the mature woman of beautiful honesty, commitment, and even dignity. Onegin is the title character, and he too grows and develops, but Tatiana is certainly the center of interest. Her twelve minute "letter aria" is one of the great scenes in all of Russian opera, and in no other opera of any nation has the depth of feeling and impetuosity of youth been so clearly and so movingly portrayed.

There have been at least ten complete recordings of *Eugene Onegin* since the first complete version was made in 1936. Three good recordings are recommended here, but by far the best of them is the earliest, the Bolshoi version from the mid-fifties. The other two, however, are honest representations of the opera and will serve well if up-to-date stereo sound is a necessity in your collection.

(1956?) Opera d'Oro 1197, with Eugene Belov, Galina Vishnevskaya, Sergei Lemeshev, Ivan Petrov, Larissa Avdeyeva, Chorus and Orchestra of the Bolshoi Theatre, Moscow, Boris Khaikin, Conductor. No libretto; only a brief synopsis. (There are two reasons for skipping this recording — primarily dated, although not unpleasant, monophonic sound and the absence of a libretto. Otherwise, this is the recording of choice. Everything in the recording sounds appropriately Russian. Lemeshev, as Lenski, gives a lesson in Slavic vocal style that could be of benefit to tenors of all nations. Petrov sings Prince Gremin with the kind of controlled depth that we always listen for in the great Russian bassos. Vishnevskaya is magnificent, the voice secure and beautiful in a typical Slavic way, and the interpretation absolutely right. We can guess that this is exactly the way Tchaikovsky intended the opera to sound.)

(1974) Decca/London 417413, with Bernd Weikl, Teresa Kubiak, Stuart Burrows, Nicolai Ghiaurov, Julia Hamari, John Alldis Choir, Orchestra of the Royal Opera House, Covent Garden, Georg Solti, Conductor. English language libretto. (In this well recorded version, Solti is the sensitive conductor of a fine cast without a single Russian among them. I cannot comment on their skill in Russian pronunciation, but I do not get the feeling that they are singing the same language they would use if they were conversing among themselves. That caveat aside, there are a number of beautiful voices in this cast and the performance is emotionally convincing. I think particularly of Stuart Burrows, the Lensky, and Nicolai Ghiaurov as Prince Gremin. Kubiak portrays a more mature Tatiana from the beginning. She sings well and acts effectively with her voice. I prefer this recording to the Philips version by a narrow margin.)

(1992) Philips 38235, with Dmitri Hvorostovsky, Nuccia Focile, Neil Shicoff, Alexander Anisimov, Olga Borodina, St. Petersburg Chamber Choir, Orchestre de Paris, Semyon Bychkov, Conductor. English language libretto. (Here is a thoroughly acceptable performance competently conducted and quite well recorded. On the whole the cast is not as strong as the Decca/London line up. Nuccia Focile is lyrical and sweet toned, with a hint of insecurity from time to time. Neil Shicoff has an imposing voice, but would perhaps be more comfortable as Cavaradossi in *Tosca*. To my ears, he simply does not sound Russian. On the other hand, Hvorostovsky is the best Onegin on any of the recordings, both in vocal and dramatic terms, and he very definitely sounds Russian.)

Eugene Onegin is available, with Orla Boylan and Vladimir Glushchak, on DVD from Kultur, and with Galina Vishnevskaya and Yevgeni Kibkalo on VHS from Kultur. The vocalists provide the singing but other performers play the roles on the Kultur VHS version.

The Queen of Spades (1890)

Alexander Pushkin's story, on which Tchaikovsky's opera (in Russian: *Pikovaya dama*) is based, is matter-of-factly narrated almost like a news report, ironic, even comedic. The narrator comments at the end of the card game, which became the final tragic scene of the opera, that "Chekalinsky shuffled the cards afresh, and the game went on as usual," and in the few sentences that follow we are informed that Lisa "married a very amiable young man" and that Hermann "is now confined in room Number 17 of the Oboukhoff [mental] Hospital."*

By way of contrast, when we come to the end of the opera, Lisa has committed suicide by drowning herself in the Winter Canal in St. Petersburg, and Hermann has stabbed himself during that final game of cards and dies while a chorus prays for his

forgiveness. Pushkin's irony has disappeared, and there is absolutely nothing at all matter-of-fact about the opera. It contains some of the most convincingly dramatic music that Tchaikovsky ever penned, and the composer is constantly calling us to become emotionally involved in the feelings of Liza and Hermann. Of course, Tchaikovsky and his brother, who served as his librettist, were criticized for violating the tone of Pushkin's original, but for them the story was primarily a launching pad for one of the masterpieces of Russian tragic opera.

Tchaikovsky's music illuminates precisely the emotions of Hermann, his tormented anti-hero, and makes of Liza a remarkably sympathetic character. To these two is added the fascinating old Countess. It is she who possesses the secret of the three-card combination that Hermann believes will make him his fortune at the gaming table; and, even as the ghostly figure in the last act of the opera, her influence continues to control the destiny of the other characters. The scene of her death is one of the most effective in all of Russian opera, and Tchaikovsky is a master of musical effects throughout this score.

The Queen of Spades has not fared particularly well on disc over the years, but the recording from Gergiev and the Kirov Opera of St. Petersburg is an exciting version on all counts and certainly the first choice for the collection. The other recording listed here is an acceptable substitute if for any reason the Kirov version is unavailable.

(1988) Sony 45720, with Wieslaw Ochman, Stefka Evstatieva, Penka Dilova, Stefania Toczyska, Ivan Konsulov, Yuri Mazurok, Svetoslav Obretenov Bulgarian National Chorus, Gouslarche Boys' Chorus, Sofia Festival Orchestra, Emil Tchakarov, Conductor. English language libretto. (This performance is effectively

---

*Alexander Pushkin, "The Queen of Spades," in *The Queen of Spades and Other Stories*, trans. T. Keane (New York: Dover Publications, 1994), p. 24.

conducted and performed, and there are rewards in the casting. Ochman sings a very good Hermann with a lighter voice than usual, but he is sometimes overshadowed in vocal weight by his Liza, Stefka Evstatieva. Dilova overdoes the Countess, and her voice frequently evidences a wide tremolo. Yuri Mazurok, known from many earlier Russian recordings, has a star turn in Yeletsky's aria, but Chernov on the Kirov recording sings this beautiful aria more persuasively.)

(1992) Philips 38141, with Gegam Grigorian, Maria Gulegina, Olga Borodina, Irina Arkhipova, Nikolai Putilin, Vladimir Chernov, Kirov Opera Chorus and Orchestra, Valery Gergiev, Conductor. (This is one of the best of Gergiev's several opera recordings with the Kirov. He has a distinguished cast of the best current Russian singers. Gulegina makes a passionate Liza. Although she brings to the role more of the spinto voice than we often hear, she still manages to suggest youthfulness. Borodina is a magnificent Pauline. Her romance in the second scene of Act I is one of the highlights of this recording. The veteran Irina Arkhipova is an appropriately frightening Countess. Gegam Grigorian is the outstanding Hermann, not always as ingratiating to the ear as Ochman but always dramatically aware. Other roles are generally well taken.)

The Queen of Spades is available, with Tamara Milashkina and Vladimir Atlantov, on VHS from Kultur.

Giuseppe Verdi (1813–1901)

Aida (1871)

Contrary to a great deal of popular opinion, *Aida* was not performed during the celebrations for the opening of the Suez Canal, nor was it the work that inaugurated the new Cairo Opera House in 1869. That honor fell to Verdi's *Rigoletto*. *Aida*, however, was the great operatic event of 1871, and news of the success of its Christmas Eve premiere in Cairo was sent around the world. Its popularity has not waned in the years since.

For many people, *Aida* virtually defines *opera*. It is a large-scale work, the Italian equivalent of French *grand opéra*. In the course of its two and half hours, we have a series of wonderful arias and duets, ensembles great and small, a ballet, a grand triumphal parade (accompanied by opera's most famous march), a big chorus, a busy orchestra, and, if the producers can afford it, some spectacular stage settings. We also have real drama with a typical Verdian emphasis on the tensions that arise when human relationships encounter conflicting personal, family, or national demands. Aida, the Ethiopian princess enslaved by the Egyptians, is torn between faithfulness to her nation and family and loyalty to the man she loves. Her struggle is the subject of her great duet with Amonasro, her father and King of Ethiopia, and, if nowhere else in the score, here Aida comes to startling life for us. Radames, her Egyptian lover, is emotionally a far simpler character than Aida, but Verdi has provided his most psychologically convincing music for Amneris, the Egyptian Princess whose love for Radames runs headlong into her jealousy. She is the one great tragic character in *Aida*.

Verdi's opera needs five great singing actors. They must be able to vocalize beautifully and with technical assurance some of the composer's most difficult music, and at the same time convey the dramatic conflicts effectively and also with a sense of royal bearing. After all, the principals in this opera are two Kings, a General, a High Priest, and a pair of Princesses. There have been many interesting recordings of *Aida*, but in almost every case two or three excellent artists have shared the sonic stage with others considerably less gifted. The three editions listed here, however, keep the standard relatively high for all five of the leading roles, and in a few of the roles on these recordings that standard is about as high as it can go.

(1955) BMG/RCA 6652, with Zinka Milanov, Jussi Bjoerling, Fedora Barbieri, Leonard Warren, Boris Christoff, Plinio Clabassi, Chorus and Orchestra of the Rome Opera, Jonel Perlea. English language libretto. (Perlea is not the most exciting conductor, but he has one of the most outstanding casts ever assembled for any opera recording. The first voice we hear is Boris Christoff, and he immediately commands attention and respect, the way a high priest should. Then immediately we hear Bjoerling, and he brings to Radames the most beautiful tenor voice of his era. Barbieri is a passionate, strong Amneris, and Warren sings magnificently, if perhaps not with all of the dramatic tension his role warrants. Milanov is superb. This is surely the voice that Verdi dreamed of as he composed the music, able to ride over the ensembles and still float the purest pianos when called for in the Nile Scene. The absence of stereo is most damaging in the large ensembles, but this remains one of the all-time great recordings of *Aida*.)

(1962) Decca/London 17416, with Leontyne Price, Jon Vickers, Rita Gorr, Robert Merrill, Giorgio Tozzi, Plinio Clabassi, Orchestra and Chorus of the Rome Opera, Georg Solti, Conductor. English language libretto. (Solti is the dramatically aware conductor in this version. Price is another classic Aida, more vocally resplendent in this version than in a later recording. Vicker's Radames and Gorr's Amneris require a bit of adjustment for those attuned to more characteristically Italian voices in these roles. They, however, are both remarkable artists, and they provide the most penetrating interpretations of any singers in these roles. Tozzi and Merrill are both exemplary vocalists, and Merrill's confrontation with Price in the Nile Scene is a highlight of this recording. If I could have only one recording of *Aida,* this is the one I would choose.)

(1974) EMI 56246, with Montserrat Caballé, Plácido Domingo, Fiorenza Cossotto, Piero Cappuccilli, Nicolai Ghiaurov, Luigi Roni, Chorus of the Royal Opera House, Coven Garden, New Philharmonia Orchestra, Riccardo Muti, Conductor. English language libretto. (Muti conducts a highly disciplined performance, with occasionally rushed tempos. The casts in the other two recordings represent the best respectively of the 1950s and 1960s. This version offers the ideal cast of the 1970s. This is a much younger, fresher Domingo than we have heard in recent years. Montserrat Caballé is complete mistress of her beautiful voice, and she is far more dramatically aware here than in some of her other recordings. Ghiaurov is a strong Ramfis, but Cappuccilli, always appealing in tone and competent in interpretation, is actually out of his league with the others in this cast. Cossotto is a rich voiced, authoritative Amneris, not quite as impressive as Barbieri and Gorr. Take one or both of the other recordings first, but if you can have three, this one is a good choice.)

Aida is available, with Aprile Millo and Plácido Domingo, on DVD from Universal/ Deutsche Grammophon, and with Maria Chiara and Luciano Pavarotti on VHS from Kultur.

Un Ballo in Maschera (1859)

Verdi's *Un Ballo in Maschera* ("A Masked Ball") should have been an historical opera. At least that was Verdi's original intention before his encounter with the censors. His librettist came up with an Italian translation and revision of *Gustave III,* a French libretto that had been set to music in 1833 by Daniel-François Auber. *Gustave III* was based on an actual historical incident, the murder at a masked ball of King Gustave of Sweden in 1792, and although some details were changed, the conspirators who plotted the crime and Count Ankarstroem, who actually fired the shot from which Gustave died twelve days later, appeared as characters in the libretto. Naples would have none of it, and Verdi withdrew and took his opera to Rome. Here the censors were less demanding but still insisted that the setting be changed from Europe and that the King's rank be reduced. And that is how Verdi's historical opera was moved from eighteenth-century Sweden to Boston toward the end of the seventeenth century, and the unfortunate King of Sweden demoted to an entirely fictional Count of Warwick.

A less appropriate setting for *Un Ballo in Maschera* than Massachusetts in the seventeenth century is difficult to imagine. A masked ball? Frivolous aristocratic courtiers cavorting to dance tunes? A nighttime visit by the assembled group to a fortune teller who summons Satan to reveal the future and never gives a thought to the Salem witch scares of 1692? And I wonder where Cotton Mather was when the maskers sang to the pleasures of "love and dancing." It's easy to understand why since 1935 producers have often taken the setting back to Sweden and the tragic events of 1792.

Un Ballo in Maschera is one of Verdi's richest, most delightful scores. The somber subject matter is reflected accurately in much of the music, but of all Verdi's middle period operas, this is the one that offers the greatest variety. Oscar, the Count's page, a "trouser role" sung by a light, flexible soprano, would not be out of place in a French comic opera, and the Count himself is the most light-hearted of tenors except when he is declaring his love for his secretary's wife, Amelia, or dying with words of pardon on his lips. Even the conspirators have a sense of humor. It is this contrast between the weighty and the light that characterizes the score.

A number of good performances are available on disc, and the two suggested here are representative of a rich recorded heritage for this opera.

(1966) BMG/RCA 6645, with Leontyne Price, Carlo Bergonzi, Robert Merrill, Shirley Verrett, Reri Grist, Children's Chorus of Renata Cortiglioni, RCA Italiana Opera Chorus and Orchestra, Erich Leinsdorf, Conductor. English language libretto. (This is the kind of cast that might have been heard on an uncommonly good night at the Metropolitan Opera in the 1960s. Shirley Verrett sings the fortune teller Ulrica as if she really believes that Satan may rise up and speak. Merrill is a master of vocal art in this recording. Reri Grist is pert in interpretation and accurate in coloratura, although the voice as recorded seems small. Bergonzi sings with a clear understanding of Verdi style, the line always clear and the voice fully in focus. Leontyne Price sounds uncomfortable at the bottom of her range, but the voice rings out with true splendor in the higher register. The sound and conducting are both good.)

(1982–83) Decca/London 410210, with Margaret Price, Luciano Pavarotti, Renato Bruson, Christa Ludwig, Kathleen Battle, London Opera Chorus, Royal College of Music Junior Department Chorus, National Philharmonic Orchestra, Georg Solti, Conductor. English language libretto. (This well-recorded version features Solti's enthusiastic conducting and an outstanding cast. Pavarotti's forceful, fully alive performance often shows his voice to advantage, but he does not demonstrate the stylistic excellence of Bergonzi. Christa Ludwig is an unexpected but entirely satisfactory choice as Ulrica, and Bruson sings with a fine voice and skillful control of dynamics. Kathleen Battle sounds not at all like a boy, but the voice is ingratiating and the technique admirable. The star of this performance, however, is Margaret Price, with a rich, full voice and a sensitive interpretation. If it's the soprano who matters most to you, select this version; if it's the tenor, Bergonzi has the stylistic edge on Pavarotti.)

Un Ballo in Maschera is available, with Katia Ricciarelli and Luciano Pavarotti, on VHS from Paramount and on DVD from Pioneer.

Don Carlos (1867)

Don Carlos is based on Friedrich von Schiller's grand historical drama with a few additional suggestions from a French play by Eugène Cormon. It offered the kind of dramatic situation that the mature Verdi particularly liked — one in which personal and political interests come into conflict. The opera is set in the sixteenth century.

Spain and France seal their relationship through the politically arranged marriage of Emperor Philip II and Elisabeth de Valois, previously the fiancée of Don Carlos, Philip's son, who still loves her. Further complications arise when the Marquis of Posa, friend of both Philip and his son, strongly advocates freedom for Spanish controlled Flanders and enlists Carlos in his cause, a position opposed by the Catholic Church, represented in the opera by the powerful Grand Inquisitor.

Political and ecclesiastical conflicts may not seem to be the ideal material for operatic development, but Verdi refused to downplay the issues. He insisted on including two major political scenes, one in which the Marquis of Posa pleads his liberal cause with the Emperor, and a second in which the Grand Inquisitor pressures the Emperor to order the death of his son and the Marquis. They are among the highlights in this rich and complex opera, now considered one of Verdi's finest works. Added to the political complications, we also have Verdi's wonderful musical treatment of the frustrated love of Carlos and Elisabeth, and the equally frustrated jealousy of the Princess Eboli, who also loves Carlos.

Don Carlos was composed for performance at the Paris Opéra as a five-act French grand opera complete with a fifteen-minute ballet. Before it reached the stage, however, problems with length required serious cuts in the score. A shortened four-act version translated into Italian appeared in 1884, but two years later a further edition restored the deleted first act. Just how much of which versions will be included in any staged performance or recording of *Don Carlos* depends on the will of the conductor and the producer. The opera is also performed as often in Italian as in the original French. The versions recommended here reflect different decisions about what to include or exclude, and there are performances in both French and Italian. They

all include the five acts of the opera. The four-act version inevitably omits some important music and dramatic information.

(1971) EMI 67397, Italian translation with Plácido Domingo, Montserrat Caballé, Shirley Verrett, Sherrill Milnes, Ruggero Raimondi, Giovanni Foiani, Ambrosian Opera Chorus and Orchestra of the Royal Opera House, Covent Garden, Carlo Maria Giulini, Conductor. English language libretto. (This is probably the best conducted *Don Carlos* and presents the strongest cast of any of the recordings. Most of the singing is excellent, with particular high marks for Domingo, Milnes, and Caballé. Raimondi sings well as Philip II, but he is hardly a dramatic match for Foiani's threatening Inquisitor. The 1886 Italian translation is performed without cuts.)

(1983–84) Deutsche Grammophon 415316, original French with Plácido Domingo, Katia Ricciarelli, Lucia Valentini Terrani, Leo Nucci, Ruggero Raimondi, Nicolai Ghiaurov, Chorus and Orchestra of the Teatro alla Scala, Milan, Claudio Abbado, Conductor. English language libretto. (The first commercial recording in French was welcomed on its appearance, but even then there were complaints about the quality of the performance. On the whole, the vocalism is emotionally low-key by singers who, with the exception of Ghiaurov and Domingo, are underpowered for the powerful music they are called on to sing, but there are no real vocal disasters. The one advantage of this recording is its relative completeness. Included in an appendix are the complete ballet omitted from the other versions and approximately thirty minutes of music cut from the score before the initial performances in 1867.)

(1996) EMI 56152, original French with Roberto Alagna, Karita Mattila, Waltraud Meier, Thomas Hampson, José van Dam, Eric Hallvarson, Chorus of Théâtre de Châtelet, Orchestre de Paris, Antonio Pappano, conductor. English language libretto. (This performance was recorded live at the Théâtre de Châtelet. Pappano is the highly effective conductor. He picks and chooses from the material omitted from the Paris premiere, and there is no ballet. The cast is stronger on subtlety than vocal weight, but they are well balanced. Van Dam is the most effective of Philips, an outstanding performance that fully communicates the anguish of the emotionally torn Emperor. Alagna and Mattila sing beautifully and interpret effectively. Hampson does not have quite the voice we want to hear as Posa, but he makes up for it in artistic and dramatic sensitivity. This is my choice as the best *Don Carlos*.)

Don Carlos is available, with Mirella Freni and Plácido Domingo, on DVD from Pioneer and on VHS from Paramount.

Falstaff (1893)

In 1840 Verdi presented at Milan's La Scala his second opera and his first comedy, *Un Giorno di Regno*. Composed during a period of grave personal crisis in his life, it was a miserable failure and almost ended his career. It's no wonder that Verdi steered clear of the comic opera genre for the next fifty years. In 1889, however, Arrigo Boito, the librettist of *Otello*, suggested that Verdi consider an opera based on Shakespeare's *The Merry Wives of Windsor*, with supplementary material from *Henry IV, Parts I and II*. Verdi liked the idea, and work began on the opera that became *Falstaff*. It would be Verdi's final opera, his second comedy, and as great a success as *Un Giorno di Regno* had been a failure. *Falstaff* and its amorous, overstuffed title character have been delighting audiences ever since.

Falstaff is the most mercurial of operas. It moves with lightning speed from one musical idea to another, so rapidly that we hardly have time to grasp the beauty of one moment before something else amazing is happening in the score. Some listeners still complain that in *Falstaff* Verdi doesn't give us the beautiful full-scale arias, duets, and ensembles of his earlier operas. He doesn't, but he gives us something else instead. He gives us music that is completely responsive to situations and words.

In a sense, it's music that simply doesn't stop for us to catch up if we lose concentration for even a few seconds. Many comic operas beg to be taken seriously, not *Falstaff*. As the great final fugue announces, "Tutto nel mondo è burla... / The whole world is a joke!" If there is a message in the opera it is probably that we not take ourselves too seriously and that we be ready to admit it when our best laid plans go awry.

Falstaff has been remarkably successful on disc. I know of no recording of the opera that doesn't offer a satisfying performance. Two recordings, however, have attained the distinction of classics, and they are, of course, listed here. I have added to them one remarkably good contemporary version.

(1950) BMG/RCA 72372, with Giuseppe Valdengo, Herva Nelli, Nan Merriman, Cloe Elmo, Teresa Stich-Randall, Antonio Madasi, Frank Guarrera, Robert Shaw Chorale, NBC Symphony Orchestra, Arturo Toscanini, Conductor. English language libretto. (The cast members in this monophonic recording were hand picked for their roles and fill them quite well, although there is little outstanding vocalism. There is one significant exception: Cloe Elmo, who recorded much too little, is the ideal embodiment of Mistress Quickly. Toscanini, however, is the star, with a performance so full of life and youthfulness that it makes us wonder if he really was eighty-three years old at the time of this recording. Every collection should include this recording.)

(1956) EMI 67062, with Tito Gobbi, Elisabeth Schwarzkopf, Nan Merriman, Fedora Barbieri, Anna Moffo, Luigi Alva, Rolando Panerai, Philharmonia Chorus and Orchestra, Herbert von Karajan, Conductor. English language libretto. (This digitally remastered stereo recording belies its age. Karajan is a trifle slower than Toscanini but always completely in control of this effervescent performance. On the whole, he has better singers than Toscanini. The women are excellent, with an uncommonly personable performance as Alice Ford by Schwarzkopf and a characterful Mistress

Quickly from Fedora Barbieri. Gobbi never had a conventionally beautiful voice, but he was the great baritone vocal actor of his age. His Falstaff is brilliant. Among stereo recordings, this one is the first choice.)

(2001) Deutsche Grammophon 471194, with Bryn Terfel, Adrianne Pieczonka, Larissa Diadkova, Stella Doufexis, Dorothea Röschmann, Danil Shtoda, Thomas Hampson, Rundfunkchor Berlin, Berlin Philharmonic, Claudio Abbado, Conductor. English language libretto. (Abbado draws a wonderful performance from his excellent orchestra and his gifted cast. Bryn Terfel is a natural Falstaff in appearance, which doesn't help on a recording, but also with his multi-faceted voice that responds to every change of Falstaff's volatile character. The women have attractive, youthful voices, as does Danil Shtoda, who is Fenton. Hampson sings and acts Ford with conviction.)

Falstaff is available, with Renato Bruson and Katia Ricciarelli, on VHS from Kultur.

La Forza del Destino (1862; 1869)

Verdi composed *Forza del Destino* for the Imperial Theatre in St. Petersburg, Russia, where it had its premiere in 1862. Performances followed in Spain and Italy, as well as London and New York, but Verdi was not satisfied with the opera in its original form and produced a major revision in 1869. Among other changes, Verdi altered the ending by eliminating one of the three deaths in the final scene so that Padre Guardiano had at least one person left to console.

In bare outline, the plot, drawn from a Spanish play by the Duke of Rivas, is excessively grim as we follow the quest of Leonora for a place of refuge, her beloved Alvaro for spiritual peace, and her brother Carlo for vengeance. Anything Verdi could do to soften the blow was certainly an improvement. The score that he composed, however, has a great deal of variety in it, including some exciting military atmos-

phere, Fra Melitone, the first of Verdi's great comic characters, and Preziosilla, the gypsy girl who enlivens the music without adding appreciably to the plot. In other words, there is a great deal of dramatically extraneous matter in the opera, but musically it works extremely well, as the tragedy of the main characters is set in contrast with the comic and genre scenes.

La Forza del Destino is a long opera, and earlier recordings tended to make severe cuts in the score. That is true in the early Cetra recording, an exciting performance from Italy during World War II (available most conveniently on Opera D'Oro 9007) and the 1954 EMI/Angel version, which features the remarkable Leonora of Maria Callas (available on EMI 56363). More recent versions, including those recommended here, provide all or most of the music that Verdi composed. The Philips recording is of the original 1862 St. Petersburg version, and is considerably different at significant points from the more familiar revision. All versions listed here have effective recorded sound.

(1969) EMI 67124, with Martina Arroyo, Biancamaria Casoni, Carlo Bergonzi, Piero Cappuccilli, Ruggero Raimondi, Geraint Evans, Ambrosian Opera Chorus, Royal Philharmonic Orchestra, Lamberto Gardelli, Conductor. English language libretto. (Competently rather than brilliantly conducted, this performance offers some excellent vocalism in major roles. Carlo Bergonzi is certainly the most artistic interpreter of Alvaro, and Martina Arroyo, too rarely recorded, sings beautifully as Leonora. Other cast members are vocally pleasing and stylistically appropriate. Geraint Evans brings more voice than many to Melitone and a great deal of personality to boot. Casoni is lighter of voice than most Preziosilla's and a more cheerful gypsy than some in this excessively difficult role.)

(1976) BMG/RCA 39502, with Leontyne Price, Fiorenza Cossotto, Plácido Domingo, Sherrill Milnes, Bonaldo Giaiotti, Gabriel Bacquier, John Alldis Choir, London Symphony Orchestra, James Levine, Conductor. English language libretto. (Levine is the authoritative conductor. The cast is the cream of the 1970s crop. Domingo and Milnes are the best Alvaro/Carlo combination on any of the recordings. Cossotto is a remarkably good Preziosilla, the best since Ebe Stignani on the old Cetra recording. Leontyne Price's Leonora was one of the wonders of the age. The voice soars at the top and she manages to float beautiful pianissimos, but to be completely honest we have to recognize that the quality is not as fresh and free as it was in her 1964 recording [BMG/RCA 7971, but probably out of print]. Here, too, she was surrounded by an excellent all–American cast, and Robert Merrill sang the best Carlo on any of the recordings. If you can find that earlier edition, I recommend it above any of the others. If not, the available 1976 version is your best choice.)

(1995) Philips 446951, original 1862 version with Galina Gorchakova, Olga Borodina, Gegam Grigorian, Nikolai Putilin, Mikhail Kit, Georgy Zastavny, Chorus and Opera of the Kirov Opera, St. Petersburg, Valery Gergiev, Conductor. English language libretto. (Gergiev is the conductor of this highly dramatic version. The Russian singers bring superior vocal equipment to their roles, but only Gorchakova and Borodina sound truly comfortable and idiomatic. On the whole, the men sing the Italian text awkwardly, particularly Putilin as Carlo, and Grigorian, a strong-voiced tenor, has some of the typical Slavic cutting brightness on high notes. All of the singers, however, are into their roles dramatically, and they make for an exciting performance. If you can have more than one *Forza del Destino* in the collection, you may want to consider adding this recording of the original version.)

La Forza del Destino is available, with Leontyne Price and Giuseppe Giacomini, on VHS from Paramount, and on DVD from Pioneer Video.

Macbeth (1847; 1865)

Shakespeare was Verdi's favorite author, and one of the great regrets among opera lovers is that Verdi never composed the *King Lear* he often dreamed of and planned. We, however, can be grateful for the three outstanding Shakespeare operas that he did complete — his two final works, *Otello* and *Falstaff*, and also his earlier *Macbeth*. All three are masterpieces that greatly enrich the repertoire.

Verdi came to *Macbeth* early in his career. He had been before the public only eight years when *Macbeth*, his tenth opera, had its premiere in 1847. The evidence is that he took this work very seriously and exercised great care, both with the composition and with the preparation for the first performance at the Teatro della Pergola in Florence. According to David Kimbell, *Macbeth* was "the boldest, the most consistently inventive and the most idealistic opera he had yet written."* Eighteen years later, Verdi prepared a new edition of the opera for performance in Paris. He added a ballet and made a number of significant changes in the score, and it is in the revised version that *Macbeth* is usually performed today. By 1865 the mature Verdi was a considerably more experienced composer than he had been in 1847, and the new material composed for the revised *Macbeth* is musically more advanced than what he retained of the original. With justification, critics often point out the stylistic inconsistencies in the opera, but the differences do not obscure the dramatic rightness of Verdi's inspiration and the absolute sincerity and seriousness of his approach to his beloved Shakespeare.

Macbeth has had an interesting history on stage and on disc. It figured in the famous scandal when Rudolf Bing, General

---

*[David Kimbell], "Giuseppe Verdi," in *The New Penguin Opera Guide*, ed. Amanda Holden (London: Penguin Books, 2001), p. 985.

Manager of the Metropolitan Opera House, fired Maria Callas and substituted Leonie Rysanek for the title role in the opera. You can hear what the Metropolitan missed in the recording of Callas' magnificent Lady Macbeth on EMI 66447, a live performance from La Scala, Milan. It is poorly recorded and her colleagues are many levels beneath her. You can also experience the performance of her equally remarkable replacement in the recording on BMG/RCA 4516, with Leonie Rysanek and Leonard Warren, a good stereo recording with a strong cast. An acceptable performance of the original 1847 version of *Macbeth* is available on Dynamic 194, but it is of interest primarily to Verdi specialists. The two recommended versions, both from 1976, offer good stereo sound.

> (1976) EMI 67128, with Sherrill Milnes, Fiorenza Cossotto, Ruggero Raimondi, José Carreras, Ambrosian Opera Chorus, New Philharmonia Orchestra, Riccardo Muti, Conductor. English language libretto. (Muti is the conductor of this dramatic performance. He leads a cast of outstanding vocalists. Milnes sings Macbeth beautifully and acts convincingly. Cossotto is his accomplished Lady Macbeth. There are fine performances from Raimondi and Carreras, who has been praised for his good vocalism in the relatively brief role of Macduff .)

> (1976) Deutsche Grammophon 49732, with Piero Cappuccilli, Shirley Verrett, Nicolai Ghiaurov, Plácido Domingo, Chorus and Orchestra of the Teatro alla Scala, Milan, Claudio Abbado, Conductor. English language libretto. (Like the other recommended version, this performance boasts a superb cast of gifted vocalists. As Macbeth, Cappuccilli does not have all of Milne's beauty of voice, but he is a more intense interpreter of the role. Shirley Verrett is brilliant both vocally and dramatically. Abbado conducts with fire and conviction to produce what is the best recorded performance of *Macbeth*, clearly the first choice.)

Macbeth is available, with Renato Bruson and Mara Zampieri, on VHS from Kultur, and on DVD from Image.

Otello (1887)

For many music lovers, *Otello* is the greatest opera of all. Wagner fans, of course, will protest that *Die Meistersinger* or *The Ring* has surely earned first place, probably a few Mozartians will insist that *Le Nozze di Figaro* is more deserving, and no doubt someone will advance the cause of Bizet's *Carmen*. They are all wonderful operas, and any attempt to rank them neither detracts from nor adds to that greatness. *Otello,* however, truly does stand at the climax of the development of Italian opera since its very beginning almost three hundred years earlier. Here is the fulfillment of *dramma per musica*. What Verdi and Arrigo Boito, his superb librettist, accomplished in *Otello* is a perfect balance so that we are never drawn away from the music by the drama and never invited by the music to neglect the drama — for the simple reason that the drama is all in the music, never outside it.

In *Otello,* Verdi proves himself to be an enlightened musical traditionalist. If we approach *Otello* out of the background of opera in nineteenth century Italy, we will discover that we are still very much at home with the music, but we will also find that Verdi is moving forward, expanding the tradition and altering it to suit his dramatic purposes. There are indeed arias, duets, and ensembles, but they are constructed in new, freer forms than Verdi had ever used before. It is as if Verdi is saying to himself, "Whatever needs to be done in the music to communicate this tragic story, I will do it."

Both on stage and on disc, there are some special challenges in the performance of *Otello*. First is the title role itself, one of the most daunting assignments for dramatic tenors. Those who do not have the equipment to project over a large orchestra without losing vocal quality, and the dramatic ability to communicate effectively the character's complex and rapidly changing psychological states, need not apply. Then there is the villain of the piece, Iago, who must convey the basic evil of his nature subtly. A cartoon villain won't do. He must sing a little like an angel if he is to make his devilment convincing. Finally, *Otello*, more than many other Verdi scores, is also a conductor's opera. It requires a strong captain at the helm, one who can lead his forces to respect the ebb and flow of tempo and volume in Verdi's score. The three recommended recordings have one thing in common — conductors who know where they're headed in this opera and know how to get there.

(1947) BMG/RCA 60302 or perhaps also on 1969, with Ramón Vinay, Herva Nelli, Giuseppe Valdengo, Nan Merriman, Virginio Assandri, Leslie Chabay, Nicola Moscona, NBC Orchestra and Choruses, Arturo Toscanini, Conductor. English language libretto. (RCA has issued and reissued this broadcast performance under many catalogue numbers. If you have difficulty finding it on a BMG/RCA label, you can look for it on Arkadia 78055. The BMG/RCA issues, however, have remastered digital sound, and with this performance, that is a distinct advantage. Nineteen-year-old Toscanini played second cello in the orchestra at La Scala at the premiere of *Otello,* and he understands the opera as perhaps no other conductor ever has. He also has complete control over his orchestral and vocal forces, and the drama is communicated with overwhelming intensity. Vinay is a distinguished Otello, although his voice is not as naturally appealing as some tenors in this role. Valdengo is a genuine Verdi baritone with a beautiful voice always at the service of his powerful interpretation. Herva Nelli sings sweetly, but without great dramatic involvement. You will want also a modern stereo recording, but there are unique values in this performance, and it should be included in the collection.)

(1960) BMG/RCA 63180, with Jon Vickers, Leonie Rysanek, Tito Gobbi, Miriam

Pirazzini, Florindo Andreolli, Mario Carlin, Orchestra and Chorus of the Rome Opera, Tullio Serafin, Conductor. English language libretto. (This version is effectively recorded and staged for stereo, and it makes a big difference. Serafin conducts a slower performance than Toscanini by at least twenty minutes and has often been criticized for it, but the slower tempos pay dividends in the love duet and other more reflective passages. Vickers offers more psychological penetration than any other Otello. It is hard to imagine a more effective Iago than Tito Gobbi. We may wish for a more beautiful voice, but he does everything Verdi asks for vocally, and he is completely persuasive in both his duplicity and his evil. Leonie Rysanek is always an interesting, communicative artist, but the sound of the voice is too mature for a completely effective Desdemona.)

(1978) BMG/RCA 39501, with Plácido Domingo, Renata Scotto, Sherrill Milnes, Jean Kraft, Frank Little, Paul Crook, Ambrosian Chorus and Boys Chorus, National Philharmonic Orchestra, James Levine, Conductor. English language libretto. (Levine conducts an impassioned, exciting performance with an excellent cast. Plácido Domingo was the reigning Otello for many years, and he brings to the role a carefully studied dramatic performance and the most beautiful voice of any of the tenors on these recordings. Sherrill Milnes is not the actor that Gobbi is, but he is fully Domingo's vocal equal. Renata Scotto comes as near to perfection as it is possible to imagine as Desdemona. She colors her voice to suit the situation with the skill of a great artist. With excellent sound, this is the preferred choice for a stereo recording of *Otello*.)

Otello is available, with Plácido Domingo and Kiri Te Kanawa, on VHS from White Star and on DVD from Kultur.

Rigoletto (1851)

It is possible to present *Rigoletto* as if it were primarily a concert with stage settings and costumes. The music is wonderfully appealing in and of itself, and, with gifted singers, a performance can be satisfying on a purely vocal basis. *Rigoletto,* however, is considerably more than a staged concert. It is one of the most dramatically effective operas in the entire repertoire. The characters are human and believable, and given the built-in assumptions of romantic drama, if the audience has any imagination at all, the situations the characters face are convincing and emotionally moving. In short, *Rigoletto* should be taken seriously as drama, and the miracle of Verdi's music enables us to experience the drama over and over again. Therein is one of the secrets of a great opera: even though we know what's going to happen, the music enables us to experience it anew each time we hear it.

The libretto, one of the best in all of operadom, is based on Victor Hugo's *Le Roi s'Amuse,* which in turn was based on a very real king, François I of France. Verdi and Francesco Maria Piave, who wrote the libretto, had trouble with the pesky Italian censors. The censorial body found the story morally offensive and were, of course, disturbed by an opera in which a king, a real one at that, behaved like a cad and narrowly escaped an attempt on his life. The eventual solution was to change the king to a mere duke. The drama wasn't damaged in the least, and may even have been improved by the removal of the regal trappings and political implications of a royal court.

Rigoletto has had a long and honored history on records. Of the early versions, one, from 1930, allows us an opportunity to hear Riccardo Stracciari, a true "golden age" baritone, in one of his great roles. He is indeed impressive, although his colleagues don't live up to his example, and the sound is better than you might imagine for such an early recording. It is available on Arkadia 78023 and other labels that specialize in historical reissues. Each of the three listed here has some special distinction to justify its inclusion.

(1955) EMI 56327, with Tito Gobbi, Maria Callas, Giuseppe di Stefano, Nicola Zac-caria, Adriana Lazzarini, Chorus and Orchestra of Teatro alla Scala, Milano, Tullio Serafin, Conductor. English language libretto. (In this version, in good monophonic sound, Serafin shapes the most dramatically convincing of all the many recordings. Giuseppe di Stefano is youthful, not completely disciplined, but full of vitality as the philandering Duke of Mantua. Maria Callas lightens her voice appropriately for Gilda, but still phrases and colors words in total commitment to the changing situations. The voice is not always conventionally beautiful, but she uses it with complete mastery. Gobbi is the best Rigoletto on any recording. His duets with Callas are masterpieces of dramatic singing. There are a few traditional cuts in the performance. I recommend that you acquire this recording first, then add one of the stereo recordings later.)

(1961) Decca/London 14269, with Sherrill Milnes, Joan Sutherland, Luciano Pavarotti, Martti Talvela, Huguette Tourangeau, Ambrosian Opera Chorus, London Symphony Orchestra, Richard Bonynge, Conductor. English language libretto. (This is very much a singers' version of *Rigoletto,* but Bonynge does not shortchange the drama, and there is nothing bland about the beautiful vocalism in this performance. Milnes and Sutherland are not Gobbi and Callas, but Milnes sings with full, resonant baritone sound, and Sutherland is a vocal wonder. There is nothing she couldn't do with her voice, and on this recording she is more conscious of articulating words than she sometimes was. For musical characterization, however, we turn to Pavarotti, who knows exactly how to make the pleasure-loving Duke come to life.)

(1979) Deutsche Grammophon 457753, with Piero Cappuccilli, Ileana Cotrubas, Plácido Domingo, Nicolai Ghiaurov, Elena Obraztsova, Chorus of the Vienna State Opera, Vienna Philharmonic, Carlo Maria Giulini, Conductor. English language libretto. (Giulini is the distinguished conductor. My first impression was that he was slower than the other conductors. A check of the timing, however, shows little difference, and the overall effect of this performance is of intensity and dramatic aptness. Cappuccilli is an excellent Rigoletto, almost in the league with Gobbi, and he has the more pleasing voice. Cotrubas paints a picture of youth and innocence for Gilda. She isn't a vocal technician like Sutherland, but her voice is beautiful and perhaps more appropriate for the character. Domingo is not a born Duke, but he sings quite well, acts sensitively, and tempers the voice to match Cotrubas in their duet. Overall, I believe this is a more effective version of the opera than the Decca/London recording.)

Rigoletto is available, with Ingvar Wixell and Luciano Pavarotti, on VHS from Universal/London and on DVD from Universal/Deutsche Grammophon.

Simon Boccanegra (1857; 1881)

The *Simon Boccanegra* that is ordinarily performed today is considerably different from the opera that had its premiere in Venice in 1857. By 1881, Verdi had arrived at his full artistic maturity. *Otello*, the first of his two final masterpieces, was already in the planning stages, and with the somewhat reluctant assistance of his librettist, Arrigo Boito, the composer undertook what turned out to be a major revision of *Simon Boccanegra*, which had received only minimal success during its initial performances. The new version managed to clarify the somewhat confusing action of the original and to some extent brought a little light into what had been an excessively dark, somber tragedy. Verdi made changes, great and small, throughout the score, but the most significant was the new finale of Act I, the magnificent "Council Chamber" scene, in which Simon, the Doge of Genoa, appeals for unity and peace among the battling Italian factions. (For listeners who would like to compare the two versions, the 1857 *Boccanegra* is available in an acceptable live performance recording on Dynamic 268.)

In addition to the political implications of the plot, with the inspiring picture of Boccanegra's statesmanship, Verdi found in the opera another opportunity to address the relationship of father and daughter, a subject that had brought from him some of his most moving music. The recognition of Amelia by her father, Boccanegra, Act I, Scene 1 in the 1881 revision, is, next to the "Council Chamber" scene, probably the most admired portion of the opera.

For all the beauties in the score, however, *Simon Boccanegra* has never achieved the popularity of *Rigoletto, Traviata, Trovatore,* and *Aida*. It is a knottier opera, more austere than these works, with a dark seriousness in both the drama and the music. From time to time, however, audiences are invited to discover it anew when opera companies stage revivals, and it is available in good recorded performances designed to win new converts to Verdi's tragic, profound *Simon Boccanegra*.

> (1957) EMI 63513, with Tito Gobbi, Victoria de los Angeles, Giuseppe Campora, Boris Christoff, Walter Monachesi, Chorus and Orchestra of the Teatro dell'Opera, Rome, Gabriele Santini, Conductor. English language libretto. (Santini is no more than efficient as conductor, but the cast of this monophonic recording offers a number of rewards. Only tenor Campora disappoints as Gabriele. De los Angeles sings a beautiful, affecting Amelia. Christoff as Fiesco and Gobbi as Boccanegra are magnificent. It is difficult to imagine a better musical and dramatic pairing in these important roles. If you can have two recordings of *Simon Boccanegra,* this version is an ideal second choice.)

> (1977) Deutsche Grammophon 449752, with Piero Cappuccilli, Mirella Freni, José Carreras, Nicolai Ghiaurov, José van Dam, Chorus and Orchestra of Teatro alla Scala, Milan, Claudio Abbado, Conductor. English language libretto. (Well conducted and effectively reproduced in stereo sound, this version is one of the best recordings of a Verdi opera. Cappuccilli isn't Gobbi [who is?], but he's the best Boccanegra after Gobbi. There is impressive strength throughout the cast, and José van Dam almost steals the show in the smaller but extremely important role of Paolo. This recording makes the best possible case for *Simon Boccanegra.*)

Simon Boccanegra is available, with Sherrill Milnes and Anna Tomowa-Sintow, on VHS from Paramount, and on DVD from Pioneer Video.

La Traviata (1853)

Nothing demonstrates quite so vividly Verdi's basic approach to an opera as the contrast between the dramatic and emotional tone, the *tinta musicale* or "musical color," of *La Traviata* and *Il Trovatore*. The premieres of the two operas took place within two months of each other, and apparently while Verdi put the finishing touches on *Trovatore*, he was beginning work on *Traviata*. The *tinta musicale* of the scores, however, is completely different. The sound of *Trovatore* strikes the listener as precisely right for the thoroughly romanticized, larger-than-life characters of fifteenth century Spain. We sense that if they sang, this is the way they would sing. But the characters in *Traviata* are true to real life, and their private concerns and personal encounters with one another are believable in recognizable human terms. *Traviata* is the most realistic of Verdi's opera. For it, he composed the music of Paris in the 1850s, filtered, of course, through his own fertile artistic imagination.

Traviata had a rough beginning. Its source was enough to raise the eyebrows of the Venetian censors. The younger Alexandre Dumas' play *La Dame aux Camélias,* based on his short novel of the same name, told the tragic story of a Parisian courtesan. Verdi proposed retaining the contemporary setting and presenting the opera under the title *Amore e Morte* (Love and Death). The authorities vetoed both setting and title, and that is why the opera became *La Traviata*. At its premiere, and in performances for the next thirty years, the setting was shifted from the dangerous 1850s back to the perfectly safe early 1700s. The premiere was a fiasco, for reasons that scholars enjoy debating, but a second series of performances, also in Venice, little more than a year later proved successful.

The role of Violetta, the *Traviata* (the woman who strays) of the title, has long been a favorite of sopranos. The character is fully developed, from the pleasure-loving courtesan through the committed woman who sacrifices her joy and probably her life as well for the man she loves. Verdi's music for Violetta runs the full emotional gamut and demands a soprano who can master the coloratura of the first act and still project the depth and tragic suffering of the later scenes. That is the kind of soprano we find in the recommended recordings.

(1955) EMI 66450, with Maria Callas, Giuseppe di Stefano, Ettore Bastianini, Chorus and Orchestra of Teatro alla Scala, Milan, Carlo Maria Giulini, Conductor. English language libretto. (Every collection should have at least one version of Callas' Violetta. It was one of her signature roles, and many would say the greatest of them. Although the vocal quality is not flawless, the technique is admirable, and Callas plumbs every facet of Violetta's character. There are problems with the recordings. In this case, it is the poor sound from a live performance, but it offers the best all-around cast and the most accomplished conductor. The 1958 Lisbon recording [EMI 56330] has better sound and a good supporting cast, with Alfredo Kraus and Mario Sereni, but less effective conducting. The 1953 studio recording [Cetra 9; or Opera Homage 1842] offers a youthful Callas, but a spotty cast otherwise and a poor conductor. All of these versions are seriously cut.)

(1976–77) Deutsche Grammophon 415132, with Ileana Cotrubas, Plácido Domingo, Sherrill Milnes, Chorus and Orchestra of the Bavarian State Opera, Carlos Kleiber, Conductor. English language libretto. (Kleiber conducts effectively but tends to push the tempos. Cotrubas is an uncommonly sensitive Violetta. Her essentially lyric voice is not as conspicuously dramatic as Callas', but the emotional content of the role is fully communicated. Domingo and Milnes sing beautifully, and Domingo is thoroughly into his role dramatically.)

(1994) Decca/London 448119, with Angela Gheorghiu, Frank Lopardo, Leo Nucci, Chorus and Orchestra of the Royal Opera House, Covent Garden, Georg Solti, Conductor, English language libretto. (This is one of Solti's finest achievements as an operatic conductor. The occasional stage and audience sounds in this "live" recording are minimally distracting. Lopardo is the youthful, lyrical Alfredo, and Leo Nucci suggests the age of Giorgio Germont without distorting his vocal timbre. The headliner, however, is Angela Gheorghiu. Her voice is beautiful, and she manages the first-act coloratura with technical security. Her interpretation of the role is full of detail and highly responsive to the dramatic situation. Of the modern stereo recordings that I have heard, this one is my first choice.)

La Traviata is available, with Angela Gheorghiu and Frank Lopardo, on DVD from Universal/Decca, and with Tiziana Fabbricini and Roberto Alagna on VHS from Sony Classics.

Il Trovatore (1853)

Even before the Marx Brothers took it on in *A Night at the Opera*, comedians were having a field day with *Trovatore*. Perhaps there had been too many bad performances with overstuffed tenors and sopranos waving semaphore signals to one another while they shouted their high notes. Or maybe it was the plot, which appeared uncommonly confusing and illogical. After all, a mother who throws the wrong baby, her own in fact, into the flames may stretch the imaginations of even the most credulous. Sincere opera lovers have been known to cast critical stones at *Trovatore* and to suggest that we'd just as well let the story go and sit back and enjoy the beautiful singing.

A careful reading of the libretto, however, reveals that everything we need in order to understand what's going on is there in the words, and if the characters seem rather farfetched to us, it may help to remember that they are typical figures of romantic drama — a mysterious gypsy with

dark secrets in her past, and highborn members of the nobility. They behave exactly as they are supposed to behave, and Verdi discovered in them a series of tensions and conflicts that he could bring to musical life.

The musical structure of *Trovatore* maintains the basic traditions of nineteenth century Italian opera much more than *Rigoletto* and *La Traviata*, the works on either side of it in the Verdian chronology. Sticking with the conventions, however, in this case was a strength, not a weakness. It was Verdi's effective way of characterizing these passionate, single-minded people who lived in a world where high standards of pride and dignity prevailed. Only Azucena, the gypsy mother, falls outside the scheme, and musically she is more keenly characterized than the others.

Il Trovatore is very much a singer's opera, perhaps the last of the true *bel canto* works. Voice alone, however, will not produce a convincing performance, which requires emotional commitment. What *Trovatore* needs is a cast of vocalists who know how to use beautiful song in the service of the drama. The singers in the recommended recordings demonstrate that rare virtue.

(1952) BMG/RCA 6643, with Zinka Milanov, Fedora Barbieri, Jussi Bjoerling, Leonard Warren, Nicola Moscona, Robert Shaw Chorale, RCA Victor Orchestra, Renato Cellini, Conductor. English language libretto. (On this classic monophonic recording, although Cellini is a conventional conductor and offers no new insights into Verdi's score, he has an outstanding group of vocalists. Milanov's voice can sometimes sound unwieldy, but she has the true grand style, and when she floats magnificent pianissimos in the last act aria, we are treated to a sublime sound that no other singer in living memory has been able to duplicate. Warren sings beautifully as Count di Luna, and Barbieri plays the gypsy Azucena with real conviction. Bjoerling is the peerless Manrico. His tone caresses the ear at every volume level, and he phrases with sovereign grace. The performance uses the cuts standard at the time, including Leonora's cabaletta in the last act, one of the best that Verdi ever composed.)

(1956) EMI 56333, with Maria Callas, Fedora Barbieri, Giuseppe di Stefano, Rolando Panerai, Nicola Zaccaria, Chorus and Orchestra of the Teatro alla Scala, Milan, Herbert von Karajan, Conductor. English language libretto. (Karajan is the exciting conductor of this monophonic recording. On the whole, the cast is somewhat less conscious of *bel canto* virtues than those in the earlier recording, but they all have big, expressive voices. Di Stefano is an enthusiastic Manrico, sometimes unpleasant on the highest notes. Barbieri is not in as good vocal estate as earlier. Callas also has occasional high note problems, as she often did, but she suggests more than any other Leonora that the Spanish lady is a real human being. Callas sings the last act cabaletta with keen rhythmical precision.)

(1969) BMG/RCA 39504, with Leontyne Price, Fiorenza Cossotto, Plácido Domingo, Sherrill Milnes, Bonaldo Giaiotti, Ambrosian Opera Chorus, New Philharmonia Orchestra, Zubin Mehta, Conductor. English language libretto. (Mehta conducts a traditional performance with all the cuts opened. It is recorded in excellent stereo sound. The cast is in many ways vocally equal to that on the earlier RCA reording. Domingo's voice is captured at its youthful best, and Milnes sings a "Di Luna" filled with classical virtues. Cossotto is vivid in characterization and often brilliant in voice. After Milanov, Price is vocally the best Leonora we have had on any recordings. All of the singers, particularly Cossotto, sing with dramatic conviction without disturbing the flow of good vocal sound. This is my top recommendation for *Trovatore*.)

Il Trovatore is available, with Eva Marton and Luciano Pavarotti, on VHS and DVD from Universal/Deutsche Grammophon.

Richard Wagner (1813–1883)

Der Fliegende Holländer (1843)

Wagner himself felt that *Der Fliegende Holländer* marked the real beginning of his career as a composer. As the young composer struggled to find himself musically, his three previous operas were in a sense experiments, each of them illustrating a different approach to music for the stage. With *Holländer* the experiment continued, as it would throughout his life, but the direction he would take was now clear, and many of the themes that would occupy him were here at least in embryo. First, there is Wagner's ongoing dependence on the material of myth and legend. Then we encounter a theme that reappears in his later work, redemption through the love of a woman. There is also a new awareness of musical possibilities. Wagner is still composing identifiable arias, duets, and ensembles, but particularly in the music for the Dutchman and Senta, and often in the orchestral treatment, there is a newfound freedom to expand the traditions and break out of the formal boundaries. It is the earliest of his operas regularly performed at Bayreuth, the great Wagner shrine. Apparently even for Wagner's descendants, *Holländer* is the real beginning point for Richard Wagner.

The nature of the opera is proclaimed at the very beginning in the overture, the turbulent power of the sea, the mystery of the Dutchman, the redemption that will come through the sacrificial love of Senta. Over and over again in the opera, Wagner reminds us of the difference between the Norwegian seamen and villagers, whose music is conventional in melody and harmony, and the outsiders, the cursed Dutchman and the mystical, isolated Senta, both of whom are given freer forms of musical expression.

On stage, the opera is variously performed either as one continuous action without breaks or in three distinct acts. Either practice can be justified, since Wagner originally planned the opera as one long act but actually conducted it himself in the three-act form. On recordings, however, the issue is strictly beside the point. We can either sit still at the end of each act and let the recording continue, or we can stop the player and take any kind of intermission that strikes our fancy. Both of the recordings listed here provide exciting, convincing listening experiences, with or without intermission breaks.

(1991) Deutsche Grammophon 437778, with Bernd Weikl, Cheryl Studer, Plácido Domingo, Hans Sotin, Uta Priew, Peter Seiffert, Chorus and Orchestra of the Deutschen Oper Berlin, Giuseppe Sinopoli, Conductor. English language libretto. (Sinopoli's recording is beautifully and excitingly played, full of drama. The cast responds to this approach appropriately. Weikl brings a firm voice and keen intelligence to the Dutchman, and Studer sings well and presents a youthful, fully committed Senta. Sotin is appropriately dark hued as Daland. Domingo provides a strong voice for Erik, although he doesn't sound comfortable in his aria. Peter Seiffert sings the Steersman quite well. He graduates to Erik on the Naxos version. Unless economy is the major issue, this version should be your choice.)

(1992) Naxos 660025/26, with Alfred Muff, Ingrid Haubold, Peter Seiffert, Erich Knodt, Marga Schiml, Jörg Hering, Budapest Radio Chorus, ORF Symphony Orchestra, Vienna, Pinchas Steinberg, Conductor. German language libretto only; detailed synopsis keyed to the recording. (This well conducted and recorded budget recording would be competitive even at full price. The only familiar name in the cast is Peter Seiffert, who here sings a lyrical Erik and makes more of it than his famous counterpart on the other version. Otherwise, the voices are not as impressive as those on the Sinopoli version, although they are effective vocalists and dramatically involved. Ingrid Haubold is not as secure and assured as Studer, but she offers a fully committed

Senta. The absence of an English language libretto is a drawback.)

Lohengrin (1850)

People who don't know a grand opera from the "Grand Old" variety, and who can't separate coloratura from cauliflower, will ordinarily recognize a little something from *Lohengrin*. Many of them marched down the aisle to Wagner's famous "Bridal Chorus" at their weddings, a custom that dates back at least to 1858 and the wedding of Queen Victoria's daughter to Frederick Wilhelm of Prussia. Nowadays professional church musicians tend to discourage and in some cases prohibit the use of the familiar old "Here Comes the Bride," but old customs die slowly. It's a good tune, just one of many in *Lohengrin*. For many years it was the most popular of Wagner's operas, and it wasn't just the "Bridal Chorus" that attracted audiences.

The opera is built around a series of contrasts and the problems that arise because of them. The plot is firmly attached to historical events. We meet King Henry in the first scene. The year is 933, and he's calling the men of Brabant to action against the Hungarians. Historical reality, however, soon comes into contact with supernatural power when the mysterious Lohengrin appears drawn down the River Sveldt by a magical swan. Can Elsa's entirely realistic desire to know the facts coexist with Lohengrin's need for mystery and secrecy? The tragic answer is no. There's another contrast at work shaping the unhappy events in *Lohengrin*, the new Christian faith against the ancient pagan beliefs, represented by Ortrud and her husband, Telramund. That conflict too leads to tragic results.

Lohengrin was a transitional work for Wagner, an essential stepping stone from the relatively traditional *Tannhäuser*, which preceded it, and the more advanced operas *Tristan und Isolde* and *The Ring,* which were already on the horizon. In performance, it sometimes seems a trifle foursquare, but given a masterful conductor and a cast of fine singing actors, the ebb and flow of the music and the drama can bring the score to vibrant life. I believe that is what happens in the three recordings suggested here.

(1953) Teldec or Elektra/Asylum 93674, with Wolfgang Windgassen, Eleanor Steber, Astrid Varnay, Hermann Uhde, Josef Greindl, Chorus and Orchestra of the Bayreuth Festival, Joseph Keilberth, Conductor. English language libretto. (This digitally remastered monophonic recording was recorded at the Bayreuth Festival. Keilberth handles the music sensitively, even tenderly on occasion. Windgassen is not at his best as Lohengrin. The American soprano Eleanor Steber, however, sings a beautiful Elsa, gentle, lyrical, and emotionally involved. Astrid Varnay and Hermann Uhde are excellent as Ortrud and Telramund, with Varnay particularly adept at communicating the character's evil determination.)

(1962–63) EMI 67411, with Jess Thomas, Elisabeth Grümmer, Christa Ludwig, Dietrich Fischer-Dieskau, Gottlob Frick, Otto Wiener, Hans Braun, Chorus of the Vienna State Opera, Vienna Philharmonic, Rudolf Kempe, Conductor. English language libretto. (Kempe guides the opera with true understanding, and he has an excellent cast. Jess Thomas was at his best as Lohengrin, particularly good in communicating the tenderness of the character, and Elisabeth Grümmer is the ideal Elsa with her beautiful voice and keen dramatic awareness. Christa Ludwig and Dietrich Fischer-Dieskau equal the effectiveness of Varnay and Uhde in the earlier recording. All things considered, this is probably the best choice among the three recordings.)

(1985-86) Decca/London 21053, with Plácido Domingo, Jessye Norman, Eva Randová, Siegmund Nimsgern, Hans Sotin, Dietrich Fischer-Dieskau, Chorus of the Vienna State Opera, Vienna Philharmonic, Georg Solti, Conductor. English language libretto. (Solti's powerful conducting and the excellent digital recording quality make for an exciting performance. Randová and Nimsgern interpret well, but they are not as forceful as Varnay and Uhde or Ludwig and Fischer-Dieskau, who is impressive in the small role of the Herald in this recording. Elsa may have been the wrong role for Jessye Norman, as many critics have suggested, but the voice is amazing. The great joy of this set, however, is Domingo. I believe that Wagner would have delighted in the full, heroic voice used with the skill of a master of Italian vocal style. There's not even a hint of the "Bayreuth bark" in his singing.)

Lohengrin is available, with Plácido Domingo and Cheryl Studer, on DVD from Image, and on VHS from Kultur.

Die Meistersinger von Nürnberg (1868)

Two great nineteenth century operatic comedies stand above all the rest — Verdi's *Falstaff* and Wagner's *Meistersinger*. Aside from a baritone as the central character, they have little in common. *Falstaff* sparkles. *Meistersinger* glows. As a matter of fact, it is hardly a comedy at all in the traditional sense. Wagner makes us laugh only rarely, but he lets us smile over and again as we recognize the warm humanity of the characters and the music that portrays them.

Some of the critical speculation concerning the philosophical and personal underpinnings of *Meistersinger* seems to me to miss what the music makes obvious, that Wagner's first and greatest concern was to look with depth and sympathy into the human hearts of real people and to reveal what he found there in wonderful music. Admittedly, there is a heavy load of rather overbearing German nationalism in Hans Sachs' final tribute to "heil'ge deutsche Kunst... / holy German art"), but in that Wagner was no more than a reflection of his time and place in the years leading up to the Franco-Prussian War, and the anti–Semitism that is painfully obvious in his writings and a serious blot on his character makes no appearance in *Meistersinger*. In any case, the critic's responsibility is to judge the music, not the man who created it.

Die Meistersinger von Nürnberg is one of the happiest operas in the entire repertoire. There truly is no villain. Even Beckmesser, the nominal troublemaker and the one truly comic character in the opera, is more amusing than dangerous, and Hans Sachs is one of Wagner's finest creations, one whose music constantly reveals his wisdom, wit, and innate goodness. There are enough wonderful musical surprises in the score to assure the place of *Meistersinger* among the artistic masterpieces of the world. Listen, for example, to the way the famous overture blends into the chorale at the beginning of the first scene; Hans Sachs' two amazing soliloquies; the transcendent quintet at the end of Act II, Scene 1; and, of course, Walther's soaring "Prize Song" in the final scene.

The two recommended recordings offer excellent performances recorded in high quality digital stereo sound. Although my personal preference is for the Solti recording on Decca/London, that is entirely a matter of personal taste, and either version should satisfy the most discriminating listener.

(1993) EMI 55142, with Bernd Weikl, Cheryl Studer, Cornelia Kallisch, Ben Heppner, Deon van der Walt, Siegfried Lorenz, Kurt Moll, Chorus of the Bavarian State Opera, Bavarian State Orchestra, Wolfgang Sawallisch, Conductor. English language libretto. (Sawallisch knows *Meistersinger* and shows himself a master conductor in this recording. Weikl is a keen interpreter and his voice is the right weight for Hans Sachs. Studer is that rare phenomenon, an all-purpose soprano who can manage almost any role effectively, and Heppner, her Walther, sings with the kind of beauty that is all too rare in Wagnerian tenors. Lorenz is good as Beckmesser, and he sings with blessed freedom from vocal distortion for comic effect. I cannot imagine a better Pogner than Kurt Moll.)

(1995) Decca/London 452606, with José van Dam, Karita Mattila, Iris Vermillion, Ben Heppner, Herbert Lippert, Alan Opie, René Pape, Chicago Symphony Chorus and Orchestra, Georg Solti, Conductor. English language libretto. (Beautifully recorded and conducted during live Chicago concert performances, this recording sets high standards for any future version of *Meistersinger*. Mattila and Heppner make an unusually appealing pair of young lovers. Heppner is here as vocally resplendent as he is in the earlier recording. Like the Beckmesser on the EMI version, Alan Opie is a first-rate Beckmesser, who, if anything, has a more beautiful voice than Lorenz. The comedy, after all, is not so much in *how* Beckmesser sings, but in *what* he sings. Van Dam is not a natural Hans Sachs, but he interprets so well and his voice is so beautifully secure that he convinces us of his rightness in the role.)

Die Meistersinger is available, with Donald McIntyre and Helen Does, on VHS and DVD from Kultur.

Parsifal (1882)

In the not too distant past, *Parsifal* was considered more than an audience could handle without a meal break. In fact, it runs in performance about the same length as *Die Meistersinger, Siegfried,* or *Götterdämmerung,* and the survival rate in these admittedly long Wagner operas is amazingly high. To be completely honest, however, *Parsifal* often seems longer than these other works. For one thing, it has an inordinately extended first act, just a few minutes short of two hours, and for long stretches of magnificent music there is little variety. But then *Parsifal* is not your ordinary opera. In fact, it's not an opera at all, and Wagner was careful to make that clear by calling it a *Buhnenweihfestspiel,* a "stage consecration play." That title tells us a great deal about what Wagner intended in *Parsifal*. It would be reserved for special occasions at Bayreuth, where it would dedicate the stage of the festival theater to its high purpose, and the pace of a "stage consecration play" is no doubt bound to be slower than that of an ordinary opera.

Parsifal draws forth varied responses.

Christian commentators have been alternately offended or enlightened by what is perceived as the enactment on stage of the Holy Eucharist. There is a good reason why in New York for many years *Parsifal* was regularly performed on Good Friday. Others have seen in Wagner's work the glorification of human compassion in a dramatic representation of Schopenhauer's ethics, or perhaps a musical picture of the conflict of sensuality and spirituality. Some recent critics have discovered a hidden sermon relating to Wagner's notorious anti–Semitism, and no doubt a few commentators have found an unlikely anti-feminist tract concealed in Kundry.

Whatever the message — and that debate will no doubt continue — it's the music that speaks to us, and Wagner is at his mature best in *Parsifal*. The score takes us from the sensuous temptations of flower maidens to the religious awe of worship in the presence of the Holy Grail. If we are willing to go with the flow of the music, we may well discover that the message, whatever it is, is truly "too deep for words."

Parsifal has had a fortunate history on recordings. Other versions could certainly be recommended, but the two listed here are faithful and satisfying representations of Wagner's "stage consecration play."

(1962) Philips 464756, with Jess Thomas, Irene Dalis, George London, Martti Talvela, Hans Hotter, Gustav Neidlinger, Chorus and Orchestra of the Bayreuth Festival, Hans Knappertsbusch, Conductor. English language libretto. (This recording was made during stage performances at the Bayreuth Festival. Hans Knappertsbusch conducts in masterful style with profound knowledge of, and affection for, the score. As Parsifal, Jess Thomas sings and interprets well, and Irene Dalis is an effective, eloquently vocalized Kundry. Hotter and London bring their extraordinary insight to bear on Guernemanz and Amfortas. Neidlinger is a properly evil sounding Klingsor. The recorded sound is amazingly good for a live performance, and, of course, the

Bayreuth audience maintains a respectful, even worshipful, silence. Both of the recommended recordings are commendable, but Knappertsbusch's magisterial conducting gives this one the edge.)

(1989–90) Teldec or Elektra/Asylum 74448, with Siegfried Jerusalem, Waltraud Meier, José van Dam, John Tomlinson, Matthias Hölle, Günter von Kannen, Chorus of Deutschen Staatsoper Berlin, Berlin Philharmonic, Daniel Barenboim, Conductor. English language libretto. (Barenboim conducts an intense, deeply felt performance recorded in glorious sound. Meier's Kundry communicates fully the contrasting sides of Kundry's complex personality. Jerusalem is a vocally pleasing and fully communicative Parsifal. As Gurnemanz, Hölle is not able to equal Hotter's mastery, but as in many other roles, Van Dam, as Amfortas, demonstrates his mastery of secure, meaningful vocal acting.)

Parsifal is available, with Reiner Goldberg and Yvonne Minton, on DVD from Image and VHS from Kultur. The voices of the singers are dubbed in this filmed version of the opera.

Der Ring des Nibelungen (1876)

The *Ring* is the most monumental of all operatic works. It consists of four full-length musical dramas, a "Preliminary Evening" entitled *Das Rheingold* (1869) and three "days," as Wagner called them, to follow — *Die Walküre* (1870), *Siegfried* (1876), and *Götterdämmerung* (1876). A staged performance of the complete *Ring* occupies approximately fifteen hours, spread, of course, over a period of days. The artistic importance of Wagner's *Ring*, however, has more to do with the comprehensive scope of the composer's musical and dramatic vision than with its length. To plan this mammoth work, write his own libretto, and compose the music took Wagner twenty-six years, and although there are occasional stylistic discrepancies, the result is a single unified work, both dramatically and musically.

What is the subject of the *Ring*? The

plot is relatively complicated and frankly somewhat convoluted. It lent itself remarkably well to Anna Russell's hilarious satire, with which she delighted audiences for years. In essence, Wagner tells an extended story, largely drawn from Germanic and Nordic mythological sources, of how and why the reign of the ancient gods and goddesses ultimately collapsed. In the process, a number of issues are addressed, among them love, greed, the desire for power, the abuse of power, the force of law, and the failure of law. These issues are further complicated by the union of gods and mortals.

Audiences through the years, however, have realized that there must be something other than problems in the lives of ancient mythological figures to account for the success and continuing popularity of the *Ring*. For Wagner, there were certainly political issues involved. George Bernard Shaw, one of his most avid British fans, found in the *Ring* support for his own socialist views. Others delve into the mystery of Jungian psychology and emphasize Wagner's expression of the great common archetypal images. A work as rich and full as the *Ring* will always be the subject of new speculation.

For most listeners, however, Wagner's great work succeeds not because of its philosophical and psychological premises, but rather because even the gods and goddesses in the *Ring* behave like human beings. Perhaps that is why *Die Walküre,* the most human of the dramas, has always been the most popular. Of course, without Wagner's music it wouldn't matter one whit how anyone understands the *Ring*. In opera, it is always the composer who makes the difference.

The history of the *Ring* on recordings began with brief snippets from here and there in the four music dramas. That is not an approach that works well with the operas of Wagner's maturity because they are composed as total unified works, not as combinations of individual arias and ensembles.

After the dawn of electric recording in the mid–1920s, it became possible to record larger sections of the operas. The most impressive attempt was carried out by HMV between 1927 and 1932. The result was an abridged *Ring* that included approximately half of the music. These recordings are of great interest to collectors because they document performances of some of the greatest Wagnerian singers of the 1920s and 1930s. They are available in excellent compact disc transfers on Pearl GEMM 9137. Soon complete acts were recorded, and eventually it was possible to put together an entire *Die Walküre*. What opera lovers were hoping for, however, was a recording of the complete *Ring,* and the advent of the long-playing record made that prospect a distinct possibility. A "pirate" version, taken from a Bayreuth broadcast performance, was hardly adequate and was swiftly withdrawn, but in 1959 Decca/London released a stereo version of *Das Rheingold* and followed it over the next six years with the three remaining works. Since then there have been several additional commercial recordings, and some earlier live performances have also been made available on disc. The versions recommended here are two of the best, and they represent contrasting approaches to Wagner's score.

(1958–1965) Decca/London 455555, *Das Rheingold* with George London, Kirsten Flagstad, Claire Watson, Waldemar Kmentt, Eberhard Wächter, Set Svanholm, Paul Kuen, Jean Madeira, Gustave Neidlinger, Walter Kreppel, Kurt Böhme; *Die Walküre* with James King, Régine Crespin, Gottlob Frick, Hans Hotter, Birgit Nilsson, Christa Ludwig; *Siegfried* with Wolfgang Windgassen, Birgit Nilsson, Hans Hotter, Gerhard Stolze, Gustav Neidlinger, Kurt Böhme, Marga Höffgen, Joan Sutherland; *Götterdämmerung* with Wolfgang Windgassen, Birgit Nilsson, Gustav Neidlinger, Gottlob Frick, Claire Watson, Dietrich Fishcher-Dieskau, Christa Ludwig; Vienna State Opera Chorus, Vienna Philharmonic, Georg Solti, Conductor.

English language libretto. (Solti's version of the *Ring* has long been acknowledged as one of the greatest triumphs in the history of recorded sound. Solti's conducting throughout is highly dramatic and completely controlled, and, of course, the Vienna Philharmonic is a superb orchestra. In so far as it was feasible, the cast is consistent throughout the entire *Ring*. There are inevitable inconsistencies in performance over such an extended period, but these singers are probably the best that could possibly have been assembled at the time. Particularly distinguished are the performances of Hotter, in spite of some insecurity, in *Walküre* and *Siegfried*; Créspin's tender Sieglinde; Christa Ludwig as Fricka and later as Waltraute; Frick's sturdy Hagen; Neidlinger's irreplaceable Alberich; and, of course, Nilsson's classic Brünnhilde. Added bonuses are Flagstad's Fricka in *Rheingold* and Sutherland's Waldvogel in *Siegfried*. Every collection should include these outstanding discs.)

(1966–1970) Deutsche Grammophon 457780, *Das Rheingold* with Dietrich Fischer-Dieskau, Josephine Veasey, Simone Mangelsdorff, Donald Grobe, Robert Kerns, Gerhard Stolze, Erwin Wohlfahrt, Oralia Dominguez, Zoltan Kelemen, Martti Talvela, Karl Ridderbusch; *Die Walküre* with Jon Vickers, Gundula Janowitz, Martti Talvela, Thomas Stewart, Régine Crespin, Josephine Veasey; *Siegfried* with Jess Thomas, Helga Dernesch, Thomas Stewart, Gerhard Stolze, Zoltan Kelemen, Karl Ridderbusch, Oralia Dominguez, Catherine Gayer; *Götterdämmerung* with Helge Brilioth, Helga Dernesch, Zoltan Kelemen, Karl Ridderbusch, Gundula Janowitz, Thomas Stewart, Christa Ludwig; Chorus of the Deutschen Oper Berlin, Berlin Philhamonic, Herbert von Karajan, Conductor. English language libretto. (Although adequately dramatic, Karajan's conducting is slower, perhaps mellower than Solti's. His orchestra is the equal of the Vienna Philharmonic. Less attention is given to consistency in casting from opera to opera, and, as often with Karajan's recordings, there are some unusual choices of singers. There are tenor problems both with Brilioth in *Götterdämmerung* and Thomas in *Rheingold*, but Jon Vickers in *Walküre* is an effective, powerful

Siegmund. Dernesch, although she's a remarkably sensitive interpreter, is stretched by the higher reaches of Brünnhilde's role in the final two works. Créspin, a strange choice for the *Walküre* Brünnhilde, makes a surprisingly positive impression, and Gundula Janowitz is a first class Sieglinde. Many of the other roles are quite well taken. Whatever the weaknesses in casting, Karajan's conducting makes for a worthwhile performance, and the recording quality is excellent.)

Der Ring des Nibelungen is available, with Gwyneth Jones, Peter Hofmann, and Donald McIntyre (Patrice Chereau's controversial Bayreuth production), on DVD from Universal/Philips. The four operas are available, with Hildegard Behrens, Gary Lakes, and James Morris (the traditional Metropolitan Opera production), on VHS from Universal/Deutsche Grammophon.

Tannhäuser (1845; 1861)

Of the Wagner operas in the current standard repertoire, *Tannhäuser* is musically the most conventional and probably the least often performed. The famous "Pilgrim's Chorus" and Wolfram's "Song to the Evening Star" are frequently included in programs of popular classics, but the opera as a whole seems old-fashioned to many modern critics, particularly when seen beside Wagner's later works or even in comparison with the earlier *Der Fliegende Holländer*. The conflict of pure and carnal love, a theme in much of Wagner's work, is in *Tannhäuser* presented without ambiguity and with little subtlety, and much of the music in the early version (known conveniently, if not with complete accuracy, as the "Dresden" version) shows Wagner still struggling to reconcile the old-fashioned "numbers" approach to opera with the unified musical flow toward which he was moving. The later "Paris" version is a different matter, but the new music often seems uncomfortable in its earlier, more traditional setting.

The Paris performances of 1861 go down in history as one of the most notorious operatic failures. *Tannhäuser* was booed, hissed and otherwise cruelly mistreated by segments of the audience, ostensibly because they resented the absence of a ballet in the second act, but in reality probably as a form of political protest. Wagner withdrew *Tannhäuser* after only three performances, and we can only imagine how he felt when the expensive costumes for his opera were salvaged by the Paris Opéra for performances of Meyerbeer's *Robert le Diable.*

For all the problems with *Tannhäuser,* however, the opera contains music of great beauty, and in spite of the initial Parisian response and the negative opinion of some modern critics, it remains a favorite with many opera lovers. What a good performance requires is at least three great vocalists, and it doesn't hurt to have a fourth and fifth as well. Providing that cast would not be an overwhelming problem if it were not for the title role. Tenors who can sing a truly satisfying Tannhäuser are hard to find. It requires a heroic voice large enough to project over a sizeable orchestra and still maintain an appealing, steady tone and a smooth legato. The two recommended recordings of the "Paris" version meet that requirement with a fair measure of success.

(1960) EMI 163214, "Dresden" version with Hans Hopf, Elisabeth Grümmer, Marianne Schech, Dietrich Fischer-Dieskau, Gottlob Frick, Fritz Wunderlich, Chorus and Orchestra of the Berlin State Opera, Franz Konwitschny, Conductor. German language libretto only. (This is not a truly satisfactory version of the opera, and I include it only if there is a need for the "Dresden" version. It would pass muster if Hans Hopf could manage to sing *Tannhäuser,* but his performance is a disaster. Marianne Schech is no great bargain as Venus, but Grümmer, Fischer-Dieskau, and Frick are excellent, and Fritz Wunderlich in the smaller role of Walter von der Vogelweide is a special treat.)

(1970) Decca/London14581, "Paris" version with René Kollo, Helga Dernesch, Christa Ludwig, Victor Braun, Hans Sotin, Werner Hollweg, Chorus of the Vienna State Opera, Vienna Boys Choir, Vienna Philharmonic, Georg Solti, Conductor. English language libretto. (Solti conducts a strong performance and has one of the world's greatest orchestras at his command. Kollo is not the smoothest vocalist imaginable, but he has the notes and interprets intelligently. Dernesch is an intense, believable Elisabeth, and Sotin an excellent Landgraf. Braun is less impressive as Wolfram, but Christa Ludwig is the best Venus on any recording of the opera.)

(1989) Deutsche Grammophon 27625, "Paris" version with Plácido Domingo, Sheryl Studer, Agnes Baltsa, Andreas Schmidt, Matti Salminen, William Pell, Chorus of the Royal Opera House, Covent Garden, Philharmonia Orchestra, Giuseppe Sinopoli, Conductor. English language libretto. (Sinopoli conducts with authority and a good feel for shaping the music in this very lyrical opera. Studer is entirely successful as Elisabeth, and Baltsa, although not on the level of Christa Ludwig, is an effective Venus. Andreas Schmidt sings well as Wolfram. The crowning glory of the performance is Domingo, who sings with all of Kollo's conviction, but with a better voice, more beautiful and better able to handle the climaxes without any sense of strain. Both recordings of the "Paris" version are good, but this one is my preference.)

Tannhäuser is available, with Richard Cassilly and Eva Marton, on DVD from Pioneer Video, and on VHS from Paramount.

Tristan und Isolde (1865)

Tristan und Isolde is probably the most famous love story in all of opera and one of the strangest. It's the mythic account of a woman who intended to kill the wounded man who had slain her fiancé in battle, but as she raised the sword, their eyes met in one fateful glance and the weapon fell from her hands. It's also a story of guilt, betrayal, and death, perhaps more of death than anything else, because from the beginning

Isolde and Tristan realize that their love can only be fulfilled in dying. The opera ends with Isolde's great hymn to eternal union in death, the passage that is popularly known as the "Liebestod" (the "love death"), although Wagner preferred to think of it as Isolde's transfiguration. In that sense, the opera ends on a note of if not triumph, then at least of consolation and fulfillment.

The opera also ends firmly in the key of B major, but it goes almost everywhere else in the tonal spectrum to get there. This progressive harmonic structure, including the famous "Tristan chord" introduced in the Prelude, was not entirely new with Wagner, but its influence reached from *Tristan und Isolde* to much of the music that followed. Some historians would go so far as to claim that what we know as "modern" music actually began with this opera.

Tristan und Isolde has attracted the attention of great conductors since Hans von Bülow conducted the premiere in 1865. Many of them have committed the opera to disc. Three are represented in our recommended recordings. *Tristan*, however, cannot survive on the abilities of the conductor alone. It needs also a pair of operatic lovers who are richly endowed vocally and dramatically. The tenor role is particularly difficult and strenuous, and many a tenor has managed to begin the opera impressively only to come to disaster in the last act. Lauritz Melchior did not have that problem, and he possessed every other gift that a great Tristan needs. You can sample his voice and artistry in this role on Naxos 8110068, a 1936 broadcast performance from London's Covent Garden. Fritz Reiner conducts and Kirsten Flagstad is the Isolde.

(1952) EMI 56254, with Ludwig Suthaus, Kirsten Flagstad, Blanche Thebom, Dietrich Fischer-Dieskau, Josef Greindl, Chorus of the Royal Opera House, Covent Garden, Philharmonia Orchestra, Wilhelm Furtwängler, Conductor. English language libretto. (Furtwängler and Flagstad were clearly the justification for this famous recording. The rest of the cast merely pass muster, with the exception of the young Fischer-Dieskau, who makes a convincing, youthful Kurwenal. Furtwängler conducts a moving performance. It is the longest of the three recommended versions because he lingers over the music, but he lingers lovingly. Flagstad is magnificent. Her Isolde is regal but not cold, dignified but also passionate, and the voice is in good condition, even if she did let Elisabeth Schwarzkopf insert the high C's for her. The remastered monophonic sound is a great improvement over the initial issues of this recording.)

(1966) Deutsche Grammophon 449772, Wolfgang Windgassen, Birgit Nilsson, Christa Ludwig, Eberhard Waechter, Martti Talvela, Chorus and Orchestra of the Bayreuth Festival, Karl Böhm, Conductor. English language libretto. (Böhm keeps things moving in a performance that is dramatic and propulsive. The sound in this "live" recording is quite good and the occasional stage noises are not distracting. Windgassen's voice did not always record well, and on stage he tended to tire before the end of lengthy roles. This, however, is probably his best recorded performance. Nilsson is a vocal miracle. She's at her best perhaps when Isolde is angry, but the conclusion of the opera is sung with deep feeling. The remainder of the cast is strictly top drawer, and Christa Ludwig is the best Brangäne of all. For the first *Tristan* in the collection, this recording is an excellent choice.)

(1971–72) EMI 69319, with Jon Vickers, Helga Dernesch, Christa Ludwig, Walter Berry, Karl Ridderbusch, Chorus of the Deutschen Oper Berlin, Berlin Philharmonic, Herbert von Karajan, Conductor. English language libretto. (Reactions to this recording depend very much on one's response to Karajan's conducting and Vickers' idiosyncratic Tristan. Karajan lingers over the music, but not as much as Furtwängler. His performance revels in the plush sounds of Wagner's score — too much so for some listeners, but the recorded sound is excellent and the result is truly beautiful. Vickers offers the most troubled, agonizing Tristan of all, particularly effective in the last act. Dernesch is not without strain in higher passages, but she presents a warm, passionate Isolde. Ludwig repeats her superb Brangäne, and Berry and Ridderbusch are both effective in their roles.)

Tristan und Isolde is available, with Jon Frederric West and Waltraud Meier, on DVD from Image.

Carl Maria von Weber (1786–1826)

Der Freischütz (1821)

Der Freischütz was the flagship opera of German romanticism. Its influence reached to almost every other German composer in the remaining years of the nineteenth century, and it is difficult to imagine Richard Wagner and his operas without Weber before him. Here are elements that bore fruit in *Lohengrin* and *Tannhäuser*: the encounter of the natural world with the supernatural and the resulting conflict of the good powers with the evil. *Der Freischütz*, however, does not need the operas it influenced to justify itself. It is a delightful and powerful opera in its own right.

The libretto provided by Johann Kind is something of a shambles. It asks us to take seriously that a projected marriage depends on the outcome of a shooting match, and arrives ultimately at a "happy" ending in which the hero, Max, is placed under a one-year probation to prove himself worthy of the virtuous and beautiful Agathe. But if ever an opera demonstrated the validity of Joseph Kerman's famous dictum that in opera "the composer is the dramatist,"* *Freischütz* is the one. The characters come to life through the music. The earnest desire and youthful eagerness of Max, and the innocence, doubt and faith of Agathe — it is all in the musical score. Then there's the masterful Wolf's Glen scene,

which is frightening enough to inspire fear and trembling in the bravest man or woman in the audience. Weber brings it all to life for us.

Der Freischütz has inspired a number of good recordings. Three are listed here, and it is very difficult to choose among them. If pushed to do so, I'd recommend the Kleiber vesion on Deutsche Grammophon, but I wouldn't want to give up the other two.

(1959) EMI 69342, with Elisabeth Grümmer, Lisa Otto, Rudolf Schock, Karl Christian Kohn, Gottlob Frick, Hermann Prey, Chorus of the Deutschen Oper Berlin, Berlin Philharmonic, Joseph Keilberth, Conductor. German language libretto only, but a detailed synopsis in English. (Here is an excellent cast, probably the best ever assembled for a recording of *Freischütz*. Grümmer conquers every challenge in the difficult role of Agathe, and Lisa Otto is the sprightliest of Ännchens. Schock makes a powerful and enthusiastic Max. Keilberth understands the appropriate style and gives us an exciting Wolf's Glen scene. Earlier editions sometimes omitted the spoken dialogue, but it is included here, as it is on the other recommended recordings. Without an English language libretto, however, the dialogue won't make a great deal of difference to most listeners.)

(1973) Deutsche Grammophon 457736, with Gundula Janowitz, Edith Mathis, Peter Schreier, Theo Adam, Franz Crass, Bernd Weikl, Leipzig Radio Choir, Sstaatskapelle Dresden, Carlos Kleiber, Conductor. English language libretto. (Kleiber studied the manuscript sources in preparation for this recording, and the result is a carefully detailed performance that brings out the subtlety of Weber's orchestral writing. Janowitz is excellent, as are her counterparts in the other recordings. Peter Schreier is not the boldest Max on record, but he may well have the most beautifully controlled voice. As Caspar, Theo Adam is more threatening than vocally secure. The Wolf's Glen scene is as scary as it's meant

*Joseph Kerman, *Opera as Drama* (New York: Vintage Press, 1956), p. 29.

to be.)

(1995) Teldec or Elektra/Asylum 97758, with Luba Orgonasova, Christine Schäfer, Enrik Wottrich, Matti Salminen, Kurt Moll, Wolfgang Holzmair, Berlin Radio Choir, Berlin Philharmonic, Nikolaus Harnoncourt, Conductor. English language libretto. (The sound in this live concert recording is excellent, and the conductor leads an exciting performance, with a Wolf's Glen scene to make your hair stand on end. Orgonasova is right up there in the league with Grümmer and Janowitz as Agathe, a beautiful voice fully in tune with the character. Christine Schäfer sings beautifully, but hers is a very serious approach to the light-hearted Ännchen. Kurt Moll is a luxury as the hermit. Wottrich as Max is

BEYOND THE BASICS

Assuming that you now have your basic collection of opera recordings catalogued and shelved, where do you go from here? The truth is that you've just skimmed the surface. You may have the cream of the crop, but there's plenty of good, nutritious milk still to be tasted. The possibilities are virtually endless, but here are a few suggestions to help you move beyond the basics with additional operas for your library collection, including English-language versions of some of the classics, and a selection of vocal recitals from great singers of the past.

ADDITIONAL COMPLETE OPERAS

John Adams

Nixon in China (1987)

Nixon in China is one of a number of modern operas based on recent historical events, in this case, Nixon's visit to China in 1972. The style is eclectic, drawing on minimalism, which is more or less Adams' home base, and other more traditional forms of musical development. Listeners react to the repeated harmonic and rhythmic patterns with either ecstasy or yawning boredom.

(1987) Atlantic/Nonesuch 79177, with Trudy Ellen Craney, Sanford Sylvan, James Maddalena, Thomas Hammons, unidentified chorus, Orchestra of St. Luke's, Edo de Waart, Conductor. English language libretto.

Daniel-François Esprit Auber

Fra Diavolo (1830)

Fra Diavolo is a lighthearted French *opéra comique* with a notorious bandit who poses as a marquis and creates a great deal of highly melodic confusion for a pair of British travelers and the residents of a little Italian town. The recommended recording is no longer listed in American catalogues, but may be available as an import.

(1983–84) EMI 54810, with Nicolai Gedda, Rémi Corazza, Jane Berbié, Mady Mesplé, Thierry Dran, Ensemble Choral Jean Laforge, Orchestre Philharmonique de Monte-Carlo, Marc Soustrot, Conductor. English language libretto.

Samuel Barber

Vanessa (1958)

Vanessa has a libretto by Barber's fellow composer Gian-Carlo Menotti, and Barber clothed the poignant love story in accessible music of immediate appeal. Following its premiere at the Metropolitan Opera House, *Vanessa* pleased audiences, if not always the critics, in several productions.

(1958) BMG/RCA 7899, with Eleanor Steber, Nicolai Gedda, Rosalind Elias, Gorgio Tozzi, Regina Resnik Chorus and Orchestra of the Metropolitan Opera House, Dimitri Mitropoulos, Conductor. English language libretto.

Vincenzo Bellini

I Capuleti ed i Montecchi (1830)

I Capuleti has more to do with Matteo Bandello's sixteenth-century novella and a nineteenth-century play by Luigi Seola than with Shakespeare's *Romeo and Juliet*. The opera is a prime example of Bellini's *bel canto* style. The role of Roméo is sung by a mezzo-soprano. Attempts to reset it for tenor have not generally been successful.

(1985) EMI 64846, with Agnes Baltsa, Edita Gruberova, Gwynne Howell, Dano Raffanti, John Tomlinson, Orchestra and Chorus of the Royal Opera House, Covent Garden, Riccardo Muti, Conductor. English language libretto.

(1997) BMG/RCA 68899, with Vesselina Kasarova, Eva Mei, Umberto Chiummo, Ramón Vargas, Simone Alberghini, Chorus of the Bavarian Radio, Munich Radio Orchestra, Robert Abbado, Conductor. English language libretto. (This version includes in an appendix an alternate ending from Vaccai's 1825 opera, *Giulietta e Romeo*, and an alternate version of Romeo's Act I cavatina by Gioachino Rossini.)

Hector Berlioz

Béatrice et Bénédict (1862)

Freely adapted and considerably reduced from Shakespeare's *Much Ado About Nothing*, *Béatrice et Bénédict* is a cleverly orchestrated delight. The vocal writing is subtle and pointed in typical French style.

(1991) Erato 45773, with Susan Graham, Jean-Luc Viala, Sylvia McNair, Catherine Robbin, Gilles Cachemaille, Gabriel Bacquier, Chorus and Orchestra of Opéra de Lyon, John Nelson, Conductor. English language libretto. (This recording includes the spoken dialogue.)

(2000) LSO LIVE 04, with Enkelejda Shkosa, Kenneth Tarver, Susan Gritton, Sara Mingardo, David Wilson-Johnson, Laurent Naouri, London Symphony Chorus and Orchestra, Colin Davis, Conductor. English language libretto. (This recording does not include the dialogue.)

Leonard Bernstein

Candide (1956)

Candide underwent a number of revisions before it reached the form that we hear in the recommended recording of the final, 1989 version. Bernstein's setting of Voltaire's *Candide* is as much operetta as opera, but when it is performed as it is here by a cast of excellent operatic voices, it sounds very much like an opera.

(1989) Deutsche Grammophon 449656, with Jerry Hadley, June Anderson, Adolph Green, Christa Ludwig, Nicolai Gedda, London Symphony Chorus and Orchestra, Leonard Bernstein, Conductor. English language libretto.

Harrison Birtwistle

The Mask of Orpheus (1986)

Birtwiste's opera makes for a challenging listening experience. Electronically produced sounds are combined with orchestra and vocalists to produce strange, sometimes eerie aural effects. The plot, to the extent that it can be followed, takes us backwards and forwards in time and in and out of the human and mythic realms. The detailed 70 page libretto and production guide included with the recording imply that the full effect of Birtwistle's work requires visual as well as aural presentation. You may not like the opera, but Birtwistle is clearly one of the most significant contemporary composers for the stage.

(1996) NMC 50, with Jon Garrison, Peter Bronder, Jean Rigby, Anne-Marie Owens, Alan Opie, Omra Ebrahim, Marie Angel, BBC Singers, BBC Symphony Orchestra, Andrew Davis, Conductor. English language libretto and detailed notes.

Arrigo Boito

Mefistofele (1868)

Mefistofele is Boito's version of Goethe's *Faust*. Passages of sublime beauty alternate with some that tell us more about Boito's admittedly great intellect than about his musical inspiration. *Mefistofele*, however, makes a serious effort to deal with the more profound concerns of Goethe's original.

(1958) Decca/London 440054, with Cesare Siepi, Renata Tebaldi, Mario Del Monaco, Floriana Cavalli, Chorus and Orchestra of the Accademia di Santa Cecilia, Rome, Tullio Serafin, Conductor. English language libretto.

Mefistofele is available, with Samuel Ramey and Gabriela Beňačková, on DVD and VHS from Kultur.

Ferruccio Busoni

Doktor Faust (1925; 1985)

Busoni did not live to complete *Doktor Faust*, and the two dates refer to the versions first of Philipp Jarnach and later of Antony Beaumont. Busoni's version of the famous Faust story is intellectual in content and complex in musical structure, with adventurous harmony and frequent use of polyphony. It is unfortunately an opera more respected than performed.

(1997–98) Erato 25501, with Dietrich Henschel, Markus Hollop, Kim Begley, Torsten Kerl, Eva Jenis, Chorus and Orchestra of Opéra National de Lyon, Kent Nagano, Conductor. English language libretto. (This recording includes the Jarnach version and the further revision made by Beaumont.)

Alfredo Catalani

La Wally (1892)

Wally is hardly typical of late nineteenth-century Italian opera, with an approach more romantic and even gentler than the *verismo* works of the period. The tragic love story of Hagenbach and Wally contains the aria "Ebben? Ne andro lontan'," famous for its use in motion pictures and television commercials.

(1969) Decca/London 15417 or 460744, with Renata Tebaldi, Mario del Monaco, Piero Cappuccilli, Justino Diaz, Lydia Marimpietri, Coro Lirico di Torino, Orchestra National de L'Opéra de Monte-Carlo, Fausto Cleva, Conductor. English language libretto.

Francesco Cavalli

La Calisto (1651)

Cavalli's opera presents two mythological love stories — Jove and Calisto, Endymion and Diana. The music is a seventeenth-century delight, and the opera ends with Calisto, who has been turned into a bear by the jealous Juno, residing among the constellations in the night sky.

(1993) Harmonia Mundi 901515, with Maria Bayo, Marcello Lippi, Simon Keenlyside, Graham Pushee, Alessandra Mantovani, Gilles Ragon, Dominique Visse, Concerto Vocale, René Jacobs, Conductor. English language libretto.

Gustave Charpentier

Louise (1900)

Louise offers a romantic, decidedly French version of *verismo*. Charpentier was a gifted composer, and the story of Louise's rebellion against the conventional life of her parents' home brought from him music of lyrical beauty and dramatic intensity.

(1976) Sony 46429, with Ileana Cotrubas, Plácido Domingo, Gabriel Bacquier, Jane Berbié, Michel Sénéchal, Ambrosian Opera Chorus, New Phlharmonia Orchestra, Georges Prêtre. English language libretto.

This opera is available in an historic French film, with Grace Moore and Georges Thill, on VHS from the Bel Canto Society.

Marc-Antoine Charpentier

Médée (1693)

Along with Lully's *Armide*, *Médée* ranks as one of the two finest French operas of the seventeenth century. Charpentier's score is musically adventurous, dramatically convincing, and — particularly in the portrayal of the title character — psychologically penetrating.

(1984) Harmonia Mundi 2901139, with Jill Feldman, Jacques Bona, Agnès Mellon, Gilles Ragon, Philippe Cantor, Sophie Boulin, Chorus and Orchestra of Les Arts Florrisants, William Christie Conductor. English language libretto.

Francesco Cilea

Adriana Lecouvreur (1902)

Prima donna sopranos love this opera, and it has often been revived at their insistence. The sentimental, tuneful music adorns the story of an historical eighteenth-century French actress and her tragic romance.

(1961) Decca/London 430256, with Renata Tebaldi, Mario del Monaco, Giulietta Simionato, Giulio Fioravanti, Orchestra and Chorus of Accademia di Santa Cecilia, Rome, Franco Capuano, Conductor. English language libretto.

(1977) Sony 34588, with Renata Scotto, Plácido Domingo, Elena Obraztsova, Sherrill Milnes, Ambrosian Opera Chorus, Philharmonia Orchestra, James Levine Conductor. English language libretto.

This opera is available, with Mirella Freni and Peter Dvorsky, on VHS from Public Media, Inc., and on DVD from Image.

Léo Delibes

Lakmé (1883)

Here is an example of the late nineteenth-century fascination with orientalism *Lakmé* is generally treated as a coloratura showcase, but is actually a fair example of French lyricism. The story, like Puccini's later *Madama Butterfly*, portrays the tragic consequences of a romance between an oriental maiden and a western, in this case British, military officer.

(1967) Decca/London 25485, with Joan Sutherland, Alain Vanzo, Gabriel Bacquier, Jane Berbié, Chorus and Orchestra of Opéra de Monte-Carlo, Richard Bonynge, Conductor. English language libretto.

(1997) EMI 56569, with Natalie Dessay, Gregory Kunde, José van Dam, Delphine Haidan, Chorus and Orchestra of the Capitole de Toulouse, Michel Plasson, Conductor. English language libretto.

Lakmé is available, with Joan Sutherland and Henri Wilden, on VHS from Kultur.

Frederick Delius

A Village Romeo and Juliet (1907)

This opera contains what is probably the most famous of Delius' orchestral works, *The Walk to the Paradise Garden*. Delius' sensitive, moving score tells of the unhappy romance of Sali and Vreli, whose fathers are bitter enemies. The parallels with Shakespeare's play include a double suicide in the final scene.

(1948) EMI 64386, with Margaret Ritchie, René Soames, Dorothy Bond, Lorely Dyet, Gordon Clinton, unidentified chorus, Royal Philharmonic Orchestra, Thomas Beecham, Conductor. English language libretto.

Gaetano Donizetti

La Fille du Régiment (1840)

Donizetti composed a frothy French *opéra comique* that tells a story of confused identity and the eventual reward of true love. It is typical comic opera material, not unlike Gilbert and Sullivan, except that the music demonstrates a wonderful combination of Italian *bel canto* style and vivacious French élan.

(1967) Decca/London 14520, with Joan Sutherland, Luciano Pavarotti, Spiro Malas, Monica Sinclair, Chorus and Orchestra of the Royal Opera, Covent Garden, Richard Bonynge, Conductor. English language libretto.

The opera is available, with Joan Sutherland and Anson Austin, on VHS and DVD from Kultur.

Gaetano Donizetti

Lucrezia Borgia (1833)

Lucrezia Borgia is based on a Victor Hugo play that shows us Lucrezia as mistress both of poison and its antidotes. On the whole, she is presented with understanding, if not precisely sympathetically, in Donizetti's eloquent score.

(1966) BMG/RCA 6642, with Montserrat Caballé, Alfredo Kraus, Shirley Verrett, Ezio Flagello, RCA Italiana Opera Chorus and Orchestra, Jonel Perlea, Conductor.

Lucrezia Borgia is available, with Joan Sutherland and Alfredo Kraus, on VHS from Kultur.

Gaetano Donizetti

The "Three Queens"
[*Anna Bolena* (1830);
Maria Stuarda (1834);
Roberto Devereux (1837)]

These three operas are often grouped together as a matter of convenience, although they were originally simply three individual operas out of the more than sixty that Donizetti composed. Although they play fast and loose with British history, they are intensely dramatic and musically satisfying works.

Roberto Devereux (1969) Deutsche Grammophon 465964, with Beverly Sills, Robert Ilosfalvy, Peter Glossop, Beverly Wolff, Ambrosian Opera Chorus, Royal Philharmonic Orchestra, Charles Mackerras, Conductor. English language libretto.

Maria Stuarda (1971) Deutsche Grammophon 465961, with Beverly Sills, Eileen Farrell, Stuart Burrows, Louis Quilico, John Alldis Choir, London Philharmonic Orchestra, Aldo Ceccato, Conductor. English libretto.

Anna Bolena (1972) Deutsche Grammophon 465957, with Beverly Sills, Shirley Verrett, Stuart Burrows, Paul Plishka, John Alldis Choir, London Symphony Orchestra, Julius Rudel, Conductor.

The same recordings of the three operas are available as a single package on Deutsche Grammophon 465967.

Roberto Devereux is available, with Alexandrina Pendachanska and Giuseppe Sabbatini, on DVD from Image, and with Beverly Sills and John Alexander on VHS from VAI.

Maria Stuarda is available in a dubbed film, with the voices of Joan Sutherland and Luciano Pavarotti, on DVD and VHS from Image.

Anna Bolena is available, with Joan Sutherland and James Morris, on VHS and DVD from VAI.

Ferenc Erkel

Hunyadi László (1844)

Erkel, the first great Hungarian composer of operas, worked within the traditional forms but also included typical Hungarian elements in his music. *Hunyadi László* is a large scale historical drama based on the deeds of a great Hungarian military and national leader of the fifteenth century.

(1984) Hungaroton 12581, with Sylvia Sass, András Molnár, István Gáti, Dénes Gulyás, Hungarian Army Male Chorus, Chorus and Orchestra of the Hungarian State Opera, János Kovács, Conductor. English language libretto.

Manuel de Falla

La Vida Breve (1913)

La Vida Breve is a short, two-act opera. The story, reminiscent of Italian *verismo* operas, tells of Salud's betrayal by her lover, Paco. The music is intense and often violent, but there is a great deal of Spanish local color in the score.

(1993) EMI 67590, with Victoria de los Angeles, Carlo Cossutta, Inés Rivadeneyra, Orfeón Donostiarra, Orquesta Nacional de España, Rafael Frühbeck de Burgos, Conductor. English language libretto. (This recording also includes performances of El Sombrero de Tres Picos, El Amor Brujo, and Soneto a Córdoba and Psyché.)

Friedrich von Flotow

Martha (1847)

Martha has been out of favor in America for many years, but it remains a wonderfully happy combination of melodious arias, ensembles, and choruses. The most famous of the melodies is actually an Irish tune that we know as "The Last Rose of Summer," but there are many more of Flotow's own inspirations in the opera.

(1944) Berlin Classics 2163, with Erna Berger, Else Tegethoff, Peter Anders, Josef Greindl, Chorus of the Berlin State Opera, Staatskapelle Berlin, Johannes Schüller, Conductor. English language libretto.

A modern stereo recording, with Lucia Popp, Doris Soffel, Siegfried Jerusalem, and Karl Ridderbusch, the Bavarian Radio Chorus, and the Munich Radio Orchestra, conducted by Heinz Wallberg, may be available as an import on BMG/RCA 74321 32231. German libretto only.

Umberto Giordano

Fedora (1898)

Giordano set to music a story of political intrigue complicated by the desire for vengeance and, needless to say, intense romantic attachments. Musically it is a typical product of Italian *verismo* with a few good tunes, but not quite so many as Giordano's earlier *Andrea Chénier*.

(1986?) Sony 42181, with Eva Marton, José Carreras, Veronika Kincses, János Martin, Chorus and Orchestra of Hungarian Radio and Television, Giuseppe Patané, Conductor. English language libretto.

Philip Glass

Einstein on the Beach (1976)

This highly influential stage work brought together Glass's minimalist approach to composition and Robert Wilson's experimental developments in stage design and direction. The musical score is so shaped by the visual aspects of the performance that Wilson is certainly as much its creator as Glass himself. There is no plot, as such, and on the whole the sung music consists of either vocalized syllables or repeated numbers.

(1993) Nonesuch 79323, with the Philip Glass Ensemble, Michael Riesman, Conductor.

Christoph Willibald Gluck

Alceste (1767; 1776)

Alceste was the most thoroughgoing of Gluck's reform operas. In the original 1767 Italian version it is austere and monumental in effect. The revision for Paris in 1776 included significant changes and tended to make the opera more varied and listener friendly.

(1998) Naxos 8660066, Italian version with Teresa Ringholz, Justin Lavender, Jonas Degerfeldt, Miriam Treichl, Lars Martinsson, Drottingholm Theatre Chorus and Orchestra, Arnold Ostman, Conductor. English language libretto.

(1982) Orfeo 27823, French version with Jessye Norman, Nicolai Gedda, Tom Krause, Siegmund Nimsgern, Bernd Weikl, Chorus and Orchestra of the Bavarian Radio, Serge Baudo, Conductor. English language libretto.

The French version is available, with Anne Sofie von Otter and Paul Goves, on DVD from Image.

Charles Gounod

Mireille (1864)

Gounod made a number of revisions in *Mireille* after its first performances, one of which temporarily changed the death of the heroine into a sudden happy recovery. The version of this opera, based on Frédéric Mistral's Provençal poem, usually performed today restores the tragic conclusion.

(1979) EMI 749653, with Mirella Freni, Alain Vanzo, Jane Rhodes, Gabriel Bacquier, José van Dam, Chorus and Orchestra of the Capitole de Toulouse, Michel Plasson, Conductor. English language libretto.

Fromental Halévy

La Juive (1835)

La Juive is a mammoth, tragic *grand opéra*, one of the works that helped to define that distinctive French form. The story, set in fifteenth century Constance, revolves around the conflict of Jews and Christians. The role of Eléazar has been a favorite of many tenors, including Caruso, who sang it in his last public performance before his death.

(1989) Philips 420190, with José Carreras, Julia Varady, June Anderson, Dalmacio Gonzalez, Ferruccio Furlanetto, Ambrosian Opera Chorus, Philharmonia Orchestra, Antonio de Almeida, Conductor. English language libretto. (This recording uses standard cuts which reduce the opera from approximately four hours to three. It is not currently available, but it may be possible to secure a copy from a dealer who specializes in out-of-print recordings. Otherwise, a "live" version with Richard Tucker is listed on Myto 3222.)

George Frideric Handel

Alcina (1735)

Handel's *Alcina* was an early success in the modern revival of his operas. With a fantastic story drawn freely from Ariosto's *Orlando Furioso*, it offers opportunity for scenic spectacle, but also bravura roles for a cast of accomplished singers and music of great beauty.

(1999) Erato 80233, with Renée Fleming, Susan Graham, Natalie Dessay, Kathleen Kuhlmann, Timothy Robinson, Les Arts Florissants, William Christie, Conductor. English language libretto.

George Frideric Handel

Semele (1744)

Based on a libretto by William Congreve, *Semele* is a cross between an opera and a secular oratorio. It is composed to an English text. The story is one of many accounts from mythology of Jupiter's love for a mortal and Juno's resulting jealousy.

(1973) Vanguard SVC 82–83, with Sheila Armstrong, Felicity Palmer, Helen Watts, Robert Tear, Justino Diaz, Mark Deller, Amor Artis Chorale, English Chamber Orchestra, Johannes Somary, Conductor. English language libretto.

George Frideric Handel

Serse (1738)

Serse offers something of a turn on Handel's usual treatment of classical subjects. It is almost a comedy, and Serse (or Xerxes, as we usually know him) is treated lightly in the opera. More than anything else, *Serse* is remembered as the source for "Ombra mai fu," Handel's famous "Largo." It is sung by the title character in praise of the delightful shade provided by a plane tree.

(1997?) BMG/Conifer 51312, with Judith Malafronte, Jennifer Smith, David Thomas, Brian Asawa, Susan Dickley, Hanover Band, Nicholas McGegan, Conductor. English libretto provided.

Serse is available in an English language performance, with Lesley Garrett and Ann Murray, on DVD from Image.

Joseph Haydn

L'Anima del Filosofo, or Orfeo ed Euridice (1967)

This is an authentic work of Haydn, in spite of the premiere date. It was composed for performance in London in 1791, but it reached the stage only 176 years later in Florence, Italy. Haydn's take on this most popular of all operatic subjects neither dodges nor softens the tragic conclusion of the myth.

(1995–96) Oisseau-Lyre 452668, Cecilia Bartoli, Uwe Heilmann, Ildebrando D'Arcangelo, Andrea Silverstrelli, the Academy of Ancient Music, Christopher Hogwood, Conductor. English language libretto.

Paul Hindemith

Mathis der Maler (1938)

Hindemith's opera tells the story of Mathias Grünewald, a sixteenth-century German artist, in music of profound beauty. As Mathias confronts the pressures and ambiguities of the Peasants' Revolt of 1524, Hindemith delves into the complex relationship of, and conflict between, society and the artist. Mathis is Hindemith's finest opera and one of the most important operatic works of the last century.

(1977) EMI 55237, with Dietrich Fischer-Dieskau, James King, William Cochran, Rose Wagemann, Urszula Koszut, Chorus and Orchestra of the Bavarion Radio, Rafael Kubelik, Conductor. English language libretto. (This recording is currently unavailable in the U.S.A., but it may be found through dealers who specialize in out-of-print discs.)

Leoš Janáček

The Excursions of Mr. Brouček (1920)

Janáček's only comic opera (in Czech: *Výlety Pdně Broučkovy*) is a two-part satire in which a drunk landlord uses his imagination to transport himself into unlikely worlds. He first goes to the moon, where he encounters artistic esthetes, among whom Brouček emerges as a master of common sense; the second imaginary voyage takes him back in time to the fifteenth century and the Hussite wars, in which he proves himself a coward and is condemned to die. Of course, he wakes up in time to save his life.

(1980) Supraphon 2153, with Vilém Přibyl, Miroslav Švejda, Jana Jonášová, Richard Novák, Czech Philharmonic Chorus and Orchestra, František Jílek. English language libretto.

Leoš Janáček

From the House of the Dead (1930)

Adapted from a Dostoevsky novel, *From the House of the Dead* presents a grim account of prisoners in a Siberian work camp. Janáček, however, found in Dostoevsky's account moments of compassion and spiritual insight. Both dramatically and musically, this opera, the composer's last, is at once the most challenging and the most profound of his stage works.

(1980) Decca/London 430375, with Jiří Zaradníček, Ivo Žídek, Václav Žitek, Dalibor Jedlička, Chorus of the Vienna State Opera, Vienna Philharmonic, Charles Mackerras, Conductor. English language

libretto. This set also includes Youth, a composition for wind sextet, and Children's Rhymes, a work for chamber choir, tenor, and ten instruments.

Leoš Janáček

The Makropulos Case (1926)

An opera with a 337-year-old heroine might seem to have little going for it. In fact, however, Janáček offers a penetrating psycho/musical portrait of Emilia Marty, who emerges as a sympathetic character content at last to give up a life that has become empty and meaningless for her.

(1965–66) Supraphon 8351, with Libuše Prylová, Ivo Žídek, Rudolf Vonásek, Helena Tattermuschová, Přemsyl Kočí, Viktor Kočí, Prague National Chorus and Orchestra, Bohumil Gregor, Conductor. English language libretto.

Erich Wolfgang Korngold

Die Tote Stadt (1920)

Korngold was something of a *Wunderkind* at twenty-three when *Die Tote Stadt* propelled him into operatic celebrity. Much of this emotionally intense opera takes place during an extended dream sequence as a young man wrestles with grief over the death of his wife.

(1975) BMG/RCA 7767, with Carol Neblett, René Kollo, Hermann Prey, Benjamin Luxon, Chorus of the Bavarian Radio, Munich Radio Orchestra, Erich Leinsdorf, Conductor. English language libretto.

Ruggero Leoncavallo

La Bohème (1897)

This is the "other" Bohème. It has always stood in the shadow of Puccini's far more popular opera. Although Puccini's *Bohème* is the more attractive and appealing work, Leoncavallo's tuneful and highly dramatic score earns the right to an occasional revival on stage and on disc.

(1981) Orfeo 23822, with Lucia Popp, Alexandrina Milcheva, Franco Bonisolli, Bernd Weikl, Alan Titus, Chorus of the Bavarian Radio, Munich Radio Orchestra, Heinz Wallberg, Conductor. English language libretto.

Jean-Baptiste Lully

Armide (1686)

Armide is generally considered Lully's best opera. The plot, derived from Torquato Tasso's *Gerusalemme Liberata*, tells the story of the sorceress Armida's unhappy love for Rinaldo. In the opera, Lully demonstrates his mastery at setting French poetry to music.

(1992) Harmonia Mundi 901456, with Guillemette Laurens, Véronique Gens, Howard Krook, Gilles Ragon, Bernard Deletré, Collegium Vocale, La Chapelle Royale, Philippe Herreweghe, Conductor. English language libretto.

Pietro Mascagni

L'Amico Fritz (1891)

Mascagni followed the phenomenal success of *Cavalleria Rusticana* with this gentle pastoral comedy about a confirmed bachelor who, needless to say, ends up married to the soprano heroine. Other than *Cavalleria*, it is the only one of Mascagni's operas to hold a place in the repertoire.

(1968) EMI 47905, with Mirella Freni, Luciano Pavarotti, Laura Didier Gambardella, Vincenzo Sardinero, Chorus and Orchestra of the Royal Opera House, Covent Garden, Gianandrea Gavazzeni, Conductor. English language libretto.

Jules Massenet

Don Quichotte (1910)

Massenet's operatic version of the story of Cervantes' famous knight Don Quixote was one of the composer's last successes. The title role provides a magnificent vehicle for a bass. The death of Quixote is portrayed with great beauty and gentleness, but there is also some delectable comic music in the opera. Although *Don Quichotte*, along with *Hérodiade* and *Thaïs*, kept for many years only a tenuous hold on the operatic repertoire, they were never completely forgotten, and in recent years they have regained some of their popularity.

(1992) EMI 54767, with Jose van Dam, Alain Fondary, Teresa Berganza, Chorus and Orchestra of the Capitole de Toulouse, Michel Plasson, Conductor. English language libretto. (This recording may be available in the U.S.A. only as an import.)

Jules Massenet

Hérodiade (1881)

Based roughly on a story by Gustave Flaubert, *Hérodiade* tells the story of Salome, John the Baptist, Herod, and his wife Herodias. The manifestly absurd plot has almost nothing in common with either the Biblical account or with Richard Strauss' *Salome*, but there is a great deal of satisfying music in the score.

(1994) EMI 55378, with Cheryl Studer, Nadine Denize, Ben Heppner, Thomas Hampson, José van Dam, Chorus and Orchestra of the Capitole de Toulouse, Michel Plasson, Conductor. English language libretto.

Jules Massenet

Thaïs (1894)

Thaïs originated in a novel by Anatole France. The monk Athanaël goes to Alexandria to save the courtesan Thaïs but is soon enamored of her himself. She, however, turns to a life of faith and spiritual purity before her death. Massenet provided music that skillfully combines the themes of carnal love and spiritual ecstasy.

(1997–98) Decca/London 466766, with Renée Fleming, Thomas Hampson, Giuseppe Sabbatini, Stefano Palatchi, Chorus of the Opéra de Bordeaux, Orchestre National Bordeaux Aquitaine, Yves Abel, Conductor. English language libretto.

Gian Carlo Menotti

The Consul (1950)

The Consul presents a powerful story of life and death under an oppressive twentieth-century governmental authority. Menotti's opera made its way successfully from Broadway to the opera house stages because the story was — and no doubt still is — topical, and because the music is dramatically effective and approachable.

(1998) New Port Classics 85645, with Beverly O'Regan Thiele, Michael Chioldi, Joyce Castle, Emily Golden, John Cheek, Camerata New York Orchestra, Joel Revzen, Conductor. English language libretto.

Gian Carlo Menotti

The Medium (1946)

Like *The Consul, The Medium* began on Broadway as part of a Menotti double bill. The psychological disintegration of Madame Flora, the medium of the title, is portrayed in music of terrifying intensity.

(1996) Cedille 34, with Joyce Castle, Patrice Michaels Bedi, Diane Ragains, Peter van de Graaf, Ensemble of Chicago Opera Theater, Lawrence Rapchak, Conductor. English language libretto.

The Medium is available, with Marie Powers and Anna Maria Alberghetti, on VHS from VAI.

Giacomo Meyerbeer

L'Africaine (1865)

Meyerbeer's final opera had its premiere almost a year after his death. The hero is Vasco da Gama, although the opera has little enough to do with history, and the heroine is a princess of an uncertain land (probably Madagascar), who in the last scene dies tragically to some of Meyerbeer's finest music as da Gama sails away. Meyerbeer devoted years of careful composition to the score.

(1973) Gala 100605 or Opera d'Oro 1185, with Shirley Verrett, Plácido Domingo, Evelyn Mandac, Simon Estes, Norman Mittelmann, Chorus and Orchestra of the San Francisco Opera, Jean Perisson, Conductor. (This recording of a staged performance is cut, but it includes almost three hours of the opera and adds to that selections from another performance with Domingo and Montserrat Caballé.)

L'Africaine is available, with Verrett and Domingo, on DVD from Image and VHS from Kultur in a performance also from the San Francisco Opera, but not from the same performance as the compact discs listed above.

Giacomo Meyerbeer

Robert le Diable (1831)

Robert le Diable was the first of Meyerbeer's *grand opéras* for Paris. Its premiere was a sensational success and assured Meyerbeer's future. The plot, with its twist on the old legend of the person who sells his soul to Satan, is hardly believable. Meyerbeer, however, understood how to write for the voice and was a master of clever orchestration. A notable — and notorious — feature of the opera is a ballet by faithless nuns who have been raised from their graves to join the dance.

> (1985) Adonis 85003, with Alain Vanzo, Samuel Ramey, June Anderson, Michéle Lagrange, Walter Donati, Chorus and Orchestra of the Paris Opéra, Thomas Fulton, Conductor. No libretto; brief synopsis.

> (2000) Dynamic 368, with Warren Mok, Giorgio Surian, Patrizia Ciofi, Annalisa Raspagliosi, Alessandro Codeluppi, Bratislava Chamber Choir, Orchestra Internazionale d'Italia, Renato Palumbo, Conductor. English language libretto.

Claudio Monteverdi

Il Ritorno d'Ulisse in Patria (1640)

The plot is based, of course, on the concluding sections of Homer's *Odyssey*. When opera moved out of the palaces of the nobility and into the public theaters, Monteverdi adjusted his style to appeal to a more popular taste. As *Il Ritorno d'Ulisse* demonstrates, however, Monteverdi, the first great operatic composer, was artist enough to change without diluting the power of his music.

> (1992) Harmonia Mundi 901427, with Bernarda Fink, Christoph Prégardien, Christino Högman, Lorraine Hunt, Dominique Visse, Concerto Vocale, René Jacobs, Conductor. English language libretto.

The opera is available, with Thomas Allen and Kathleen Kuhlmann, on VHS from Kultur.

Wolfgang Amadeus Mozart

La Clemenza di Tito (1791)

At the conclusion of the opera, the Emperor Titus lives up to the title by forgiving those who had conspired against him

and swearing on his life to devote himself to the good of Rome. Mozart's score for *La Clemenza*, one of his final two operas, is relatively formal, in keeping with Metastasio's libretto, but also emotionally and musically satisfying.

> (1991–92) Oiseau-Lyre 444131, with Uwe Heilmann, Cecilia Bartoli, Della Jones, Barbara Bonney, Diana Montague, Gilles Cachemaille, Academy of Ancient Music Chorus and Orchestra, Christopher Hogwood, Conductor. English language libretto.

La Clemenza di Tito is available, with Philip Langridge and Ashley Putnam, on DVD from Image, and on VHS from Kultur.

Wolfgang Amadeus Mozart

Idomeneo (1781)

Although *Idomeneo* enjoyed only minimal success during Mozart's lifetime, it has very much come into its own in recent years. Mozart composed some of his finest music to illuminate the story of Idomeneo, his son Idamante, the two women who love him, and the vow that would require the father to sacrifice his son to the god Neptune.

> (1994) Deutsche Grammophon 47737, with Plácido Domingo, Cecilia Bartoli, Heidi Grant Murphy, Carol Vaness, Thomas Hampson, Frank Lopardo, Bryn Terfel, Chorus and Orchestra of the Metropolitan Opera, James Levine, Conductor. English language libretto.

Idomeneo is available, with Luciano Pavarotti and Ileana Cotrubas, on DVD from Parmaount.

Otto Nicolai

Die Lustigen Weiber von Windsor (1849)

When it was offered to him, Otto Nicolai rejected the libretto of *Nabucco*, which passed then to Verdi and became his first outstanding triumph. Eight years later, Nicolai scored his only lasting success with his version of Shakespeare's *Merry Wives of Windsor*. It's far from the equal of Verdi's *Falstaff*, based on the same source, but it is still a charming example of the German comic singspiel.

> (1976) Berlin Classics 2115, with Kurt Moll, Edith Mathis, Hanna Schwarz, Helen Donath, Bernd Weikl, Peter Schreier, Chorus of the Deutschen Staatsoper Berlin, Staatskapelle Berlin, Bernhard Klee, Conductor. German language libretto; English synopsis.

Christopher Pepusch, arranger

The Beggar's Opera (1728)

The Beggar's Opera is the most famous example of the British ballad opera. It has retained its popularity for more than two and a half centuries. The music, probably arranged by Pepusch, was drawn from popular ballads and the compositions of such popular composers as Handel and Purcell. John Gay's text is broadly satirical.

> (1991) Hyperion 66591, with Adrian Thompson, Bronwen Mills, Anne Dawson, Charles Daniels, Sarah Walker, the Broadside Band, Jeremy Barlow, Conductor, English language libretto.

The Beggar's Opera is available, with Roger Daltrey and Carol Hall, on DVD from Image, and on VHS from Kultur.

Giovanni Battista Pergolesi

La Serva Padrona (1733)

Intermezzi were short comic operas performed between the acts of more serious works. In the case of *La Serva Padrona*, it's the intermezzo that is remembered, not the *opera seria* with which it was associated. Pergolesi's comic masterpiece tells the story of a maid who marries the master and becomes the mistress of the house.

> (1989) Omega1016, with Julianne Baird, John Ostendorf, Philomel Baroque Chamber Orchestra, Rudolph Palmer, Conductor. English language libretto. (This recording also includes a Vivaldi flute concerto.)

Serva Padrona is available, with Patricia Biccire and Donato di Stefano, on VHS from Allegro Video.

Jacopo Peri

Euridice (1600)

Peri's *Euridice* is apparently the earliest opera that we have in complete form, and, as such, it certainly deserves a place in a collection of operatic recordings. Unfortunately, Peri did not share Monteverdi's genius, and his opera makes for something less than a musically exciting hour and forty minutes.

> (1992) Arts 47276, with Gian Paolo Fagotto, Gloria Banditelli, Mario Cecchetti, Giuseppe Zambon, Ensemble Arpeggio, Roberto de Caro, Conductor. English language libretto.

Hans Pfitzner

Palestrina (1917)

Pfitzner composed a long, problematic, sometimes tiresome, often brilliant opera that centers on the composition of Palestrina's great *Missa Papae Marcelli* in 1563. Palestrina is the kind of opera that leaves audiences not cheering, but meditating.

> (1973?) Deutsche Grammophon 427417, with Nicolai Gedda, Dietrich Fischer-Dieskau, Hermann Prey, Helen Donath, Brigitte Fassbaender, Karl Ridderbusch,

Bernd Weikl, Heribert Steinbach, Tolzen Knabenchor, Chorus and Orchestra of the Bavarian Radio, Rafael Kubelik, Conductor. English language libretto. (This recording is not currently available in the U.S.A., but you may be able to find it as an import or from a dealer in out-of-print discs. Another version that I have not heard is available on Orfeo 515993.)

Francis Poulenc

La Voix Humaine (1959)

Here is an opera with only one character, identified simply as "Elle." She suffers through wrong numbers, interrupted calls, and the growing awareness that the man she loves is no longer interested in her. Her personal tragedy is reflected moment by moment in Poulenc's sensitive score.

(1981) Phoenix 131, with Carole Farley, Adelaide Symphony Orchestra, José Serebrier, Conductor. English language libretto. (I have not heard the highly praised recording by Felicity Lott on Harmonia Mundi 901759.)

Sergei Prokofiev

Betrothal in a Monastery (1946)

Based on Richard Brinsley Sheridan's *The Duena*, Prokofiev's comic opera includes all the devices familiar from eighteenth century British comedy. Although sophisticated, the music is easy to listen to, with a full share of melody and more or less comfortable harmony.

(1997) Philips 462107, with Anna Netrebko, Larissa Diadkova, Nikolai Gassiev, Alexander Gergalov, Chorus and Orchestra of the Kirov, St. Petersburg, Valery Gergiev, Conductor. English language libretto.

Sergei Prokofiev

The Fiery Angel (1954)

The premiere date conceals the fact that the opera was composed almost thirty years earlier. Prokofiev's musical study of sexual psychosis and neurotic hallucination was far too strong for Russia — or for most of the rest of the world — until after World War II. It was not staged in Russia until 1983.

(1993) Philips 442078, with Galina Gorchakova, Sergei Leiferkus, Evgenia Perlasova-Verkovich, Mikhail Kit, Larissa Diadkova, Chorus and Orchestra of the Kirov, St. Petersburg, Valery Gergiev, Conductor. English language libretto.

The Fiery Angel is available, with the same cast listed above, on VHS from Philips.

Sergei Prokofiev

The Gambler (1929)

Prokofiev's operatic version of Dostoevsky's portrait of a man who becomes addicted to gambling is musically more advanced or "modern" than much of his later music. The musicians engaged for its proposed premiere in 1917 apparently found it too difficult to learn and perform. Of course, a revolution and Prokofiev's departure for the United States also intervened.

(1996) Philips 454559, with Vladimir Galuzin, Liubov Kazarnovskaya, Elena Obraztsova, Sergei Alexashkin, Nikolai Gassiev, Chorus and Orchestra of the Kirov, St. Petersburg, Valery Gergiev, Conductor. English language libretto.

Giacomo Puccini

La Fanciulla del West (1910)

The "Wild West," that is, complete with American Indians, a bandit, a sheriff, assorted miners, and a beautiful, pure-hearted saloon owner — and they all sing Puccini's music in Italian. Musically, in this score Puccini is reaching forward toward more complex harmonic patterns and musical structures.

> (1977) Deutsche Grammophon 19640, with Carol Neblett, Plácido Domingo, Sherrill Milnes, Francis Egerton, Robert Lloyd, Chorus and Orchestra of the Royal Opera House, Covent Garden, Zubin Mehta, Conductor. English language libretto.

> *Fanciulla* is available, with Plácido Domingo and Barbara Daniels, on VHS from Deutsche Grammophon.

Giacomo Puccini

La Rondine (1917)

Only in recent years has *Rondine* found a place in the operatic repertoire. Perhaps the public had come to expect large-scale emotional outbursts in Puccini's operas, and the music of *Rondine* is gentler, quieter, less excitable. The bittersweet story is similar to Verdi's *Traviata* without the death of the heroine.

> (1996) EMI 56338, with Angela Gheorghiu, Roberto Alagna, William Matteuzzi, Inva Mula, Alberto Rinaldi, London Voices, London Symphony Orchestra, Antonio Pappano, Conductor. English language libretto.

Jean-Philippe Rameau

Les Indes Galantes (1735–36)

Rameau's opera-ballet is virtually a tour of what would have been considered exotic destinations by Europeans in the eighteenth century. Delightful music accompanies four love stories, one each for the islands of the Indian Ocean, the Inca lands of Peru, a Persian palace, and the homeland of North American Indians.

> (1991) Harmonia Mundi 901367, with Claron McFadden, Sandrine Piau, Isabelle Poulenard, Noémi Rime, Miriam Ruggeri, Howard Crook, Jean-Paul Fouchécourt, Jérôme Corréas, Bernard Delétré, Nicolas Rivenq, Les Arts Florissants, William Christie, Conductor. English language libretto.

Maurice Ravel

L'Heure Espagnole (1911)

This mildly scandalous and utterly delightful comedy must have raised a few eyebrows when it was first performed at the Opéra Comique in Paris. For all of its Spanish setting and occasional rhythms, it is thoroughly, completely French.

> (1965) Deutsche Grammophon 449769, with Jan Berbié, Jean Giraudeau, Gabriel Bacquier, José van Dam, Michel Sénéchal, Orchestre National de la R.T.E., Lorin Maazel, Conductor. English language libretto. (This set also includes Ravel's "L'enfant et les Sortilèges," Rimsky-Korsakov's "Capricio Espagnol," and Stravinsky's "Le Chant du Rossignol.")

Nicolai Rimsky-Korsakov

The Legend of the Invisible City of Kitezh (1907)

Rimsky's penultimate opera demonstrates so clearly the influence of Wagner's music dramas that it has sometimes been called the "Russian *Parsifal*," a title that reflects both the music and the religious aura of the work. The contrast between the mystical Fevroniya and the all-too-human Grishka adds musical and dramatic variety to the opera.

> (1994) Philips 462225, with Galina Gorchakova, Yuri Marusin, Vladimiir Galuzin, Nicolai Putilin, Nicolai Ohotnikov, Chorus and Orchestra of the Kirov, St. Petersburg, Valery Gergiev, Conductor. English language libretto.

Nikolai Rimsky-Korsakov

The Tsar's Bride (1899)

Rimsky clothed this story of love and jealousy in and around the court of Ivan the Terrible with traditional *bel canto* arias, duets, and ensembles, including a full-scale "mad scene." The plot, however, might have served any one of the Italian composers of *verismo*.

(1998) Philips 462618, with Marina Shaguch, Olga Borodina, Evgeny Akimov, Dmitri Hvorostovsky, Sergei Alexashkin, Gennady Bezzubenkov, Orchestra and Chorus of the Kirov, St. Petersburg, Valery Gergiev, Conductor. English language libretto.

Gioachino Rossini

Armida (1817)

The story of the sorceress Armida and her love for Rinaldo has inspired a number of composers, including Lully, Handel, Haydn, Gluck, Salieri, and Dvořák. Rossini's version is heavy in its *bel canto* demands for the singers, particularly for Armida herself, and includes enough tenor roles to exhaust the rosters of the largest opera companies.

(1993) Sony 58968, with Renée Fleming, Gregory Kunde, Donald Kaasch, Ildebrando D'Arcangelo, Jeffrey Francis, Carlo Bosi, Jorio Zennaro, Orchestra and Chorus of Teatro Communale di Bologna, Daniele Gatti, Conductor. English language libretto.

Gioachino Rossini

Le Comte Ory (1828)

Le Comte Ory is a muddled comic tale replete with more mistaken identities and gender benders than most operas could survive. Half of the music Rossini adapted from an earlier opera, *Il Viaggio a Reims*. With everything against it, the wonder is that *Comte Ory* is one of the happiest of all Rossini's comic inventions.

(1956) EMI 64180, with Michel Roux, Jeanette Sinclair, Juan Oncina, Monica Sinclair, Ian Wallace, Cora Canne-Meijer, Sari Barabas, Glyndebourne Festival Orchestra and Chorus, Vittorio Gui. English language libretto.

Gioachino Rossini

Moïse et Pharaon (1827; 1829)

Rossini made substantial revisions in his 1818 opera *Mosè in Egitto* for performance in Paris. It is the revised version translated from French into Italian that is most often used in the rare contemporary performances, including the recording recommended here. The story is recognizably Biblical in the same sense that a Hollywood epic might be.

(1988) Orfeo d'Or 514992, with Ruggero Raimondi, Carol Vaness, Doris Soffel, Francisco Araiza, Eduardo Villa, Kurt Moll, Chorus of the Bavarian State Opera, Bavarian State Orchestra, Wolfgang Sawallisch, Conductor. (No libretto; there is a detailed synopsis keyed to the recording.)

Gioachino Rossini

Otello (1816)

Rossini's opera shows no more than a passing acquaintance with Shakespeare's great tragedy, and it should be judged purely on its own merits, which are considerable. In appendices, the recommended recording includes, among other occasional interpolations into the score, an alternate happy ending in which Otello is persuaded of Desdemona's innocence and everyone rejoices.

(1999) Opera Rara 18, with Bruce Ford, Elizabeth Futral, Ildebrando D'Arcangelo, William Matteuzzi, Juan José Lopera, Geoffrey Mitchell Choir, Philharmonia Orchestra, David Parry, Conductor. English language libretto.

Gioachino Rossini

Semiramide (1823)

Among Rossini's serious operas, *Semiramide*, derived from Voltaire's Babylonian tragedy, was one of the most popular in the nineteenth century. As a vehicle for an outstanding soprano and mezzo-soprano, it has received revivals in more recent years,

(1992) Deutsche Grammophon 37797, with Cheryl Studer, Jennifer Larmore, Frank Lopardo, Samuel Ramey, Ambrosian Opera Chorus, London Symphony Orchestra, Ion Marin, Conductor. English language libretto.

Semiramide is available, with June Anderson and Marilyn Horne, on DVD from Image, and on VHS from Kultur.

Gioachino Rossini

Tancredi (1813)

Like many other operas, *Tancredi* appears in multiple versions, the first with a happy ending, the second with the tragic death of Tancredi and the grief of his beloved Amenaide. The love story in the plot hinges on a question about the intended recipient of a secret letter that Amenaide wrote to Tancredi.

(1994) Naxos 660037, with Ewa Podles, Sumi Jo, Stanford Olsen, Pietro Spagnoli, Capella Brugensis, Collegium Instrumentale Brugense, Alberto Zedda, Conductor. Italian language libretto; a brief synopsis is included.)

Tancredi is available, with Maria Bayo and Raul Gimenez, on VHS from BMG/RCA.

Gioachino Rossini

Il Turco in Italia (1814)

Il Turco in Italia is a comical romp in which a straying wife is attracted to the Turkish Selim, and he to her. Of course, the confusion, replete with disguises, is finally cleared up and the couples properly united. Rossini's score is notable for its scintillating ensembles.

(1954) EMI 56313, with Maria Callas, Nicola Rossi-Lemeni, Nicolai Gedda, Mariano Stabile, Franco Calabrese, Jolanda Gardino, Orchestra and Chorus of Teatro alla Scala, Milan, Gianandrea Gavazzeni, Conductor. English language libretto. (This performance is cut. You may prefer the performance, which I have not heard, on Decca/London 458924, with Cecilia Bartoli, Ramon Vargas, Alessandro Corbelli, and Michele Pertusi.)

Bedřich Smetana

Dalibor (1868)

Dalibor has many similarities with Beethoven's *Fidelio*. A brave woman, Milada, disguised as a man, enters Dalibor's prison cell and plots for his escape. Unlike *Fidelio*, however, *Dalibor* ends in tragedy. Smetana's score reflects the influence of Wagner, and the music is intensely dramatic.

(1995) Supraphon 77–632, with Eva Urbanova, Leo Marian Vodička, Ivan Kusnjer, Jiří Kalendovský, Vratislav Kříz, Chorus and Orchestra of the Prague National Theatre, Zdeněk Košler, Conductor. English language libretto.

Gasparo Spontini

La Vestale (1807)

In ancient Rome, one of the Vestal virgins allows the flame on the altar to go out, and as a result, is condemned to death. A miraculous bolt of lightning saves her life. The role of Julia has attracted such great dramatic sopranos as Rosa Ponselle and Maria Callas.

> (1991) Orfeo 256922, with Rosalind Plowright, Gisella Pasino, Francisco Araiza, Pierre Lefébvre, Bavarian Radio Chorus, Munich Radio Orchestra, Gustav Kuhn, Conductor. English language libretto. (A "live" performance is sung in Italian by Maria Callas, Franco Corelli, and Ebe Stignani on Opera d'Oro 1227.)

Johann Strauss II

Die Fledermaus (1874)

Fledermaus is an operetta, but I have decided to include it among our full-fledged operas because it is regularly performed in the great opera houses by some of the world's outstanding singers. Strauss was notoriously careless in the choice of his librettos. Although *Fledermaus* fares better than most of the others, it is the music alone that keeps it alive.

> (1955) EMI 69531 or 67074, with Elisabeth Schwarzkopf, Nicolai Gedda, Rita Streich, Helmut Krebs, Karl Donch, Erich Kunz, Rudolf Christ, Philharmonia Orchestra and Chorus, Herbert von Karajan, Conductor. No libretto; detailed synopsis keyed to the discs.

Fledermaus is available, with Pamela Coburn and Eberhard Waechter, on DVD and VHS from Deutsche Grammophon.

Richard Strauss

Arabella (1933)

Arabella is not, as sometimes thought, simply *Rosenkavalier* advanced by a hundred years or so. It is, rather, a romantic comedy, with more romance than comedy, and it has its own musical aura. As often with Strauss, he gives his best music to his sopranos, and in this case he has two of them.

> (1957) Decca/London 460230, with Lisa della Casa, Hilde Gueden, George London, Anton Dermota, Otto Edelmann, Ira Malaniuk, Chorus of the Vienna State Opera, Vienna Philharmonic, Georg Solti, Conductor. English language libretto.

> (1981) Orfeo 169882, with Julia Varady, Helen Donath, Dietrich Fischer-Dieskau, Walter Berry, Adolf Dallapozza, Helga Schmidt, Chorus of the Bavarian State Opera, Bavarian State Orchestra, Wolfgang Sawallisch. English language libretto.

Arabella is available, with Kiri Te Kanawa and Wolfgang Brendel, on DVD and VHS from Deutsche Grammophon.

Richard Strauss

Capriccio (1942)

Capriccio is the work that proves the viability of an opera devoted to the problem that faces every operatic composer — the relationship of words and music. Strauss's last opera is beautifully composed for voice and orchestra. Much of the effect is of elegant and eloquent musically enhanced conversation, the kind appropriate to an eighteenth century drawing room.

> (1957–58) EMI 67391, with Elisabeth Schwarzkopf, Eberhard Waechter, Dietrich Fischer-Dieskau, Nicolai Gedda, Christa Ludwig, Hans Hotter, Philharmonia Orchestra, Wolfgang Sawallisch, Conductor. English language libretto.

Richard Strauss

Die Frau ohne Schatten (1919)

Once thought to be virtually impossible to cast and stage, *Die Frau ohne Schatten* is now one of Strauss's most popular and frequently performed operas. Hoffmanstahl's libretto is highly symbolic, but the characters, as they struggle to achieve their full humanity, are made believable and sympathetic through the music.

> (1996) Teldec 13156, with Deborah Voigt, Ben Heppner, Hanna Schwarz, Franz Grundheber, Sabine Hass, Chorus of the Saxon State Opera Dresden, and the Staatskapelle Dresden, Giuseppe Sinopoli, Conductor. English language libretto.

Karol Szymanowski

King Roger (1926)

King Roger is one of the few Polish operas to attract outside attention. In music of often transcendent beauty, Szymanowski lets us share the spiritual transformation of King Roger, who at last embraces light and life. The opera, however, remains a mystery that invites ever new symbolic interpretation.

> (1998) EMI 56823, with Thomas Hampson, Elzbieta Szmytka, Philip Langridge, Ryszard Minikiewicz, Chorus, Youth Chorus, and Symphony Orchestra of the City of Birmingham, Simon Rattle, Conductor. English language libretto.

Peter Ilych Tchaikovsky

Iolanthe (1892)

Composed as a one-act companion piece for the *Nutcracker* ballet, *Iolanthe* initially met with little favor. The story of the healing power of love, however, elicited from Tchaikovsky music of great beauty and gentleness. Largely through the medium of recordings, the opera has gained a measure of popularity in recent years.

> (1994) Philips 62796, with Galina Gorchakova, Sergei Alexashkin, Dmitri Hvorostovsky, Gegam Grigorian, Nikolai Putilin, Chorus and Orchestra of the Kirov, St. Petersburg, Valery Gergiev, Conductor. English language libretto.

Peter Ilych Tchaikovsky

Mazeppa (1884)

Tchaikovsky lavished some of his best music on *Mazeppa*, an opera almost unparalleled in its plot for unpleasant grimness. Set against the turbulent eighteenth century struggle of Ukrainian and Swedish forces against Tsar Peter the Great, Tchaikovsky provided his most satisfying music for the ill-matched lovers, Mazeppa and Maria. *Mazeppa* will probably never make its way into the international repertoire, but it certainly deserves a hearing.

> (1993) Deutsche Grammophon 439906, with Sergei Leiferkus, Galina Gorchakova, Anatly Kotscherga, Sergei Larin, Chorus of the Royal Opera, Stockholm, Gothenburg Symphony Orchestra, Neeme Järvi, Conductor. English language libretto.

Ambroise Thomas

Hamlet (1868)

No one would confuse Thomas' *Hamlet* with great art. It certainly is not that, although it contains enough audience-pleasing music to continue to earn an occasional revival. The recommended recording contains the original ending in which Hamlet, after killing Claudius, is proclaimed King; and, in an appendix, also the special ending composed for London in which Hamlet dies. The British apparently knew their Shakespeare too well to leave the theater with Hamlet still alive.

> (1993) EMI 54820, with Thomas Hampson, June Anderson, Samuel Ramey, Denyce Graves, Gregory Kunde, Ambrosian Opera Chorus, London Philharmonic, Antonio de Almeida, Conductor. English language libretto.

Ambroise Thomas

Mignon (1866)

Some composers, Thomas among them, are excessively adaptable when it comes to conclusions. The original version of *Mignon*, which is based in part of Goethe's *Wilhelm Meisters Lehrjahre*, ends with the happy union of Mignon and Wilhelm. For German audiences, however, Thomas sent her to her grave. Modern performances generally keep the happy ending, but either way it is Thomas' varied, tuneful music that makes the opera worth hearing.

(1977) Sony 34590, with Marilyn Horne, Ruth Welting, Frederica von Stade, Alain Vanzo, Nicola Zaccaria, Ambrosian Opera Chorus, Philharmonia Orchestra, Antonio de Almeida, Conductor. English language libretto.

Giuseppe Verdi

Attila (1846)

Verdi's operatic treatment of Attilla, the notorious "scourge of God," is anything other than subtle. The music is often loud and tempestuous. In his next opera, *Macbeth*, the composer began the process that would reach its climax in his great final operas. Even when Verdi's music is crude and hard-hitting, however, it is vital, and it always surges with passion.

(1989) EMI 49952, with Samuel Ramey, Cheryl Studer, Neil Shicoff, Giorgio Zancanaro, Orchestra and Chorus of Teatro alla Scala, Milan, Riccardo Muti, Conductor. English language libretto.

Attila is available, with Samuel Ramey and Cheryl Studer, on DVD from Image, and on VHS from Public Media.

Giuseppe Verdi

Ernani (1844)

Ernani, based on an extravagant Romantic tragedy by Victor Hugo, remains the most popular of Verdi's early period operas. The four major roles — one each for bass, baritone, tenor, and soprano, and each demanding full dramatic *bel canto* technique — assure a success for any opera company that can produce a cast equal to those demands.

(1967) BMG/RCA 6503, with Carlo Bergonzi, Leontyne Price, Mario Sereni, Ezio Flagello, RCA Italiana Opera Chorus and Orchestra, Thomas Schippers, Conductor. English language libretto.

(1982) EMI 47083, Plácido Domingo, Mirella Freni, Renato Bruson, Nicolai Ghiaurov, Chorus and Orchestra of Teatro alla Scala, Milan, Riccardo Muti, Conductor. English language libretto.

Ernani is available, with Luciano Pavarotti and Leona Mitchell, on DVD from Pioneer Video, and on VHS from Paramount.

Giuseppe Verdi

I Lombardi alla Prima Crociata (1843)

The action, set during the First Crusade, follows an unhappy love story and reaches its climax in the reconciliation of two estranged brothers. *I Lombardi*, Verdi's fourth opera, was one of his early successes, and it shows the young composer reaching out in the use of orchestra and harmony.

(1996) Decca/London 455287, with Richard Leech, June Anderson, Samuel Ramey, Patricia Racette, Luciano Pavarotti, Ildebrando' D'Arcangelo, Chorus and Orchestra of the Metropolitan Opera, James Levine, Conductor. English language libretto.

Lombardi is available, with José Carreras and Ghena Dimitrova, on VHS from Kultur.

Giuseppe Verdi

Luisa Miller (1849)

Based on a play by Friedrich Schiller, *Luisa Miller*, like many nineteenth century operas, presents another tragic love story. In this case, however, the drama is played out on a much more intimate, domestic level than previously, and *Luisa Miller* is an effective precursor of *La Traviata*, which appeared four years later.

(1975) Decca/London 417420, with Montserrat Caballé, Luciano Pavarotti, Sherrill Milnes, Bonaldo Giaiotti, Richard van Allan, London Opera Chorus, National Philharmonic Orchestra, Peter Maag, Conductor. English language libretto.

Luisa Miller is available, with June Anderson and Eduard Tumagian, on DVD and VHS from Kultur.

Giuseppe Verdi

Nabucodonosor (1842)

Nabucco, as the opera is usually known, was Verdi's third opera and his first great triumph. Verdi found ample inspiration in the account of Nebuchadnezzar, considerably expanded from the Biblical version, and the subject led him to compose an opera that is exciting, both musically and dramatically.

(1965) Decca/London 417407, with Tito Gobbi, Elena Suliotis, Nicolai Ghiaurov, Bruno Prevedi, Dora Carral, Chorus of the Vienna State Opera, Vienna Opera Orchestra, Lamberto Gardelli, Conductor. English language libretto

(1977–78), EMI 47488, Matteo Manuguerra, Renata Scotto, Nicolai Ghiaurov, Veriano Luchetti, Elena Obraztsova, Ambrosian Opera Chorus, Philharmonia Orchestra, Riccardo Muti, Conductor. English language libretto.

Nabucco is available, with Renato Bruson and Lauren Flanigan, on DVD from Image, and on VHS from Kultur.

Giuseppe Verdi

Stiffelio (1850)

An opera in which a Protestant minister forgives his erring wife after reading in the pulpit the account of Jesus' encounter with the woman caught in adultery must have seemed strange to nineteenth-century Italian audiences. In spite of an interesting, forward-looking score, *Stiffelio* was doomed to failure from the beginning. Verdi revised the opera in 1857 and gave it a new title — *Aroldo* — and an entirely different story. The original, however, is the more convincing opera.

(1979) Philips 422432, with José Carreras, Sylvia Sass, Matteo Manuguerra, Wladimiro Ganzarolli, ORF Symphony Orchestra and Chorus, Vienna, Lamberto Gardelli, Conductor. English language libretto.

Stiffelio is available, with José Carreras and Catherine Malfitano, on VHS from Kultur.

Giuseppe Verdi

Les Vêpres Siciliennes or *I Vespri Siciliani* (1855)

Verdi's French opera is almost always performed in its Italian translation. The background of the opera is historical, an incident that took place in Palermo in 1282, when the Italians massacred the French. There is a wealth of good music in the opera, somewhat diluted, however, by its excessive length.

(1973) BMG/RCA 63492, with Martina Arroyo, Plácido Domingo, Sherrill Milnes, Ruggero Raimondi, John Alldis Choir, New Philharmonia Orchestra, James Levine, Conductor. English language libretto.

Vespri Siciliani is available, with Chris Merritt and Cheryl Studer, on DVD from Image, and on VHS from Public Media.

Richard Wagner

Rienzi (1842)

Rienzi, the third of Wagner's operas, was one of his greatest successes during the early years of his career. It is a long opera based on an historical subject (the attempt of Rienzi to restore the grandeur of ancient Rome to fourteenth-century Italy). It is similar in style to the popular French *grand opéras* of the period, and although Wagner was soon to move in a new direction with *Der Fliegende Holländer*, there is much in *Rienzi* that hints of his future development.

(1974; 1976) EMI 67131, with René Kollo, Siv Wennberg, Janis Martin, Theo Adam, Peter Schreier, Günther Leib, Chorus of the Leipzig Radio, Chorus of the Dresden State Opera, Staatskapelle Dresden, Heinrich Hollreiser, Conductor. English language libretto.

Carl Maria von Weber

Oberon (1826)

Weber composed *Oberon* to an English libretto for performance in London. The plot, which combines elements of fairy tale with historical romance, stretches the limits of credibility almost to the breaking point, but the music of *Oberon* is Weber at his best.

(1970) Deutsche Grammophon 419038, with Birgit Nilsson, Plácido Domingo, Donald Grobe, Julia Hamari, Arleen Auger, Hermann Prey, Chorus and Orchestra of the Bavarian Radio, Rafael Kubelik, Conductor. English language libretto. (If you have difficulty finding this recording, look for the issue on BMG/RCA 68505 with Inga Nielsen and Peter Seiffert. I have not heard this recording.)

Kurt Weill

Aufstieg und Fall der Stadt Mahagonny (1930)

More conspicuously operatic than *The Three Penny Opera*, *Mahagonny* is a dark comedy that ends with the pessimistic opinion of the chorus, "Nothing can help us and you and anybody." More than Weill's other works, *Mahagonny* has found its way to the stages of the world's opera houses.

(1985) Sony 37874, with Lotte Lenya, Gisela Litz, Heinz Sauerbaum, Peter Markwort, Fritz Göllnitz, Horst Günter, North German Radio Chorus, unidentified orchestra, Wilhelm Brückner-Rüggeberg, Conductor. (I have not heard this recording, but it is the preferred version according to most critical opinion.)

Kurt Weill

Die Dreigroschenoper (1928)

Bertolt Brecht's acerbic text and Weill's ironic music combined to make what we generally know as *The Three Penny Opera* a major success, first in Germany (until it was outlawed by the Nazis) and then in much of the rest of the world. *The Three Penny Opera*, like its model in *The Beggar's Opera*, is an updated ballad opera combining spoken dialogue with songs of a more or less popular nature.

(1988) Decca/London 430075, with René Kollo, Ute Lemper, Milva, Helga Dernesch, RIAS Chamber Choir, RIAS Berlin Sinfonietta, John Mauceri, Conductor. English language libretto.

Riccardo Zandonai

Francesca da Rimini (1914)

Other than Puccini's operas, Zandonai's *Francesca* is one of the few twentieth-century Italian works to survive in the repertoire. Zandonai's richly evocative *fin de siècle* music is entirely appropriate for the play by Gabriele D'Annunzio from which it is derived.

(1994) Koch Schwann 313682, with Elena Filipova, Hana Minutillo, Philippe Rouillon, Frederic Kalt, Kenneth Riegel, Sofia Chamber Choir, Chorus of the Vienna Volksoper, Vienna Symphony, Fabio Luisi, Conductor. English language libretto.

Francesca is available, with Renata Scotto and Plácido Domingo, on DVD from Pioneer Video.

OPERA IN ENGLISH

Some operas, several of which have been included in our recommendations, are written to English texts, but many works originally in other languages have also been translated into English for performance. For some reason, British opera lovers have over the years been more receptive to opera translated into their native tongue than American listeners. It should come as no surprise, then, that the most extensive collection of recorded operas in English should originate in the United Kingdom. The Chandos label promises "opera that speaks your language," and backs up that promise with an ever growing catalogue of over twenty-five complete operas and a series of recital discs, all sung in English.

The Chandos "Opera in English" recordings are carefully prepared and performed by first-rate orchestras, conductors, and casts that include some of the best British and American vocalists, such famous artists as Jane Eaglen, Janet Baker, Thomas Hampson, and Kiri Te Kanawa among them. The translations used are literate, singable and on the whole free of stilted nineteenth-century English "librettoese." Complete texts are supplied with each recording. They are all presented in excellent stereo sound, some newly recorded and others reissued from earlier releases.

Before you jump to the conclusion that English language opera is the ideal way to build your library collection, however, you need to consider a few caveats. Many of the opera fans that use your collection will not be interested in performances in languages other than the original. It is certainly true that the overall tone of an opera depends not just on the composer's musical notes, but also on the sound of the language, and to hear the opera the way the creators intended it is to hear it in the original form. English simply cannot always reproduce the pure, open Italian vowels, the liquid flow of French elisions, or the crisp precision of German consonants. An added problem is the simple fact that sung words, even familiar ones, are not always easy to understand, and if we need to follow the libretto to know what's going on, we had probably just as well follow it through a performance in the original language. For all the excellences of the performances, consider also that the vocalists will almost always either have English as their native language or be able to speak it with natural facility, a fact that places limitations on the singers who can be engaged for the recordings. Would opera lovers really prefer to hear *Trovatore* in English rather than with Zinka Milanov and Jussi Bjoerling in Verdi's passionate Italian? I'm inclined to doubt it.

On the other hand, keep the Chandos English-language recordings in mind. They will make excellent second or third versions of many standard operas. I'm listing here some of the best of them for your consideration.

Gaetano Donizetti, *The Elixir of Love* (*L'Elisir d'Amore*), with Barry Banks, Mary Plazas, Andrew Shore, Ashley Holland, Geoffrey Mitchell Choir, Philharmonia Orchestra, David Parry Conductor. Chandos 3027.

Charles Gounod, *Faust*, with Paul Charles Clarke, Alastair Miles, Mary Plazas, Geoffrey Mitchell Choir, Philharmonia Orchestra, David Parry, Conductor. Chandos 3014.

George Frideric Handel, *Julius Caesar*, with Janet Baker, Valerie Masterson, John Tomlinson, English National Opera Orchestra and Chorus, Charles Mackerras, Conductor. Chandos 3019.

Leoš Janáček, *Osud* (*Fate*), with Helen Field, Phlip Langridge, Kathryn Harries, Orchestra and Chorus of Welsh National Opera, Charles Mackerras, Conductor. Chandos 3029.

Jules Massenet, *Werther*, with John Brecknock, Janet Baker, Patrick Wheatley, Harold Blackburn, Joy Roberts, English National Opera Orchestra and Chorus, Charles Mackerras, Conductor. Chandos 3033.

Giacomo Puccini, *Madam Butterfly*, with Cheryl Barker, Paul Charles Clarke, Gregory Yurisich, Jean Rigby, Geoffrey Mitchell Choir, Philharmonia Orchestra, Yves Abel, Conductor. Chandos 3070.

Giacomo Puccini, *Tosca*, with Jean Eaglen, Dennis O'Neill, Gregory Yurisich, Peter Kay Children's Choir, Geoffrey Mitchell Choir, Philharmonia Orchestra, David Parry, Conductor. Chandos 3000.

Giuseppe Verdi, *Rigoletto*, with John Rawnsley, Helen Field, Arthur Davies, John Tomlinson, English National Opera Orchestra and Chorus, Mark Elder, Conductor. Chandos 3030.

Richard Wagner, *The Ring Cycle* (*Der Ring des Nibelungen*), with Rita Hunter,

Alberto Remedios, Norman Bailey, Margaret Curphey, Ann Howard, Anne Collins, Aage Haugland, etc., English National Opera Chorus and Orchestra, Reginald Goodall, Conductor. Chandos 3065. (This remarkable recording was acknowledged as a major achievement for Reginald Goodall and the other artists involved when it first appeared on Angel/EMI. The entire set is on sixteen compact discs (Chandos 3065), but the four operas are also available separately on Chandos 3054, 3038, 3045, and 3060.

OPERATIC RECITALS

All of the great and nearly great singers, and a good number of the not so great singers, have recorded individual arias, duets, and other ensembles from various operas. Choose your singers and enter the names in the search box of almost any of the on-line dealers and you will quickly have a list of any recordings they have made. Almost all of the outstanding contemporary singers are heard on one and often several operatic recital discs. Many of them appear frequently in our recommended recordings of complete operas, and they will usually be heard at their best in complete roles. In any case, trying to keep up with the latest recital recordings of the important singers of today would take a large chunk of both budget and staff time.

You can provide a helpful addendum to your collection of complete operas, however, by providing library patrons recordings of great singers of the distant or recent past. Many of these artists had little or no opportunity to commit their choice complete operatic roles to disc, and even if they did, the recordings often came too late in their careers to represent them at their best. Others, of course, went to the studios before complete recordings were truly viable. If they are to be remembered at all, it will be through their recordings of individual operatic arias and ensembles. Opera fans enjoy making comparisons of the present with the past, more often than not to the detriment of the present. (It seems that the "golden age" is always a generation or two behind the present.) They will delight in the opportunity to weigh Pavarotti against the standard of Caruso, and compare the relative merits of Deborah Voigt and Kirsten Flagstad. What's more, these earlier recordings have historical significance and offer valuable and interesting lessons in the changing art of song over the years.

Our list includes recordings by sixty-one singers. It could easily have been twice that number, but I have made some more or less arbitrary choices based on my perception of the relative importance of the artists in the history of opera over the last one hundred years, the appeal that they exerted on the audiences of their day, and, of course, their vocal and artistic qualifications. The earlier recordings (roughly those before 1926) were made by the old acoustical process and will often be hard going for listeners not attuned to the ancient sound. After that date, the electrical recording greatly improved the sound quality, but none of the discs on this list represent the art of modern digital recording. All of them, however, represent the art of singing at its best.

I have included at least one recital recording for each singer on the list, and I have tried to choose recordings that will be easily available from the dealers. There are many other smaller, independent labels that include historical recordings in their catalogues, but they are often difficult to locate. Nimbus Records, one of the most valuable sources of many important historical vocal recordings, unfortunately ceased operation in 2002, but some of their vocal discs may still be available in dealer stocks. The name of each singer is followed by the label and number of the disc(s) and in some cases, a brief comment concerning the importance of the artist.

An asterisk before a name indicates a singer of great significance, one who should certainly be represented in a comprehensive opera collection.

Licia Albanese, BMG/RCA 60384 and MET 229

Pasquale Amato, Preiser 89064

*__Marian Anderson__, Pearl 9318 and 9405 (Anderson's fame rested primarily on her recital and concert performances, but she was the first African-America singer to appear in a leading role at the Metropolitan Opera.)

Mattia Battistini, Preiser 89045, or Preiser 89304, a three-disc set (Battistini was a superstar baritone from the early years of sound recording.)

Jussi Bjoerling, EMI 66306 (Bjoerling recorded some complete operas, but many of his roles are represented only in off-the-air recordings and in the individual arias in studio recordings. This set is a four-disc album at a reduced price.)

Alessandro Bonci, Bongiovanni 1062, a two-disc set (He was one of Caruso's contemporaries, but with a lighter, more lyrical voice.)

Lucrezia Bori, Pearl 9246 (One of the Metropolitan Opera's great lyric sopranos of the 1920s and 1930s. Her family name was Borgia. She changed it for obvious reasons.)

*__Enrico Caruso__, RCA 60495, a twelve-disc set of his complete recordings; Pearl 9046, 9047, and 9048 offer good selections. (Caruso influenced every tenor who came after him and almost singlehandedly established the success of operatic recording.)

*__Feodor Chaliapin__, Preiser 89030 and 89087 (Chaliapin was the most famous and most influential of the Russian bassos, with a personality as large and colorful as his voice.)

Giuseppe de Luca, Preiser 89036 and 89073

Fernando de Lucia, Preiser 9071, a three-disc set (Fernando de Lucia represents a freer nineteenth century vocal style than we are accustomed to. He was one of the great tenors of the early years of this century.)

Emmy Destinn, Supraphon 112136, a twelve-disc set of her complete recordings; Pearl 9172 includes a good selection. (During the early years of the twentieth century, Destinn was frequently thought to have the most beautiful soprano voice on the opera stage.)

Geraldine Farrar, Pearl 9420 (Caruso's frequent soprano partner at the Metropolitan, Farrar was the first diva to become a film star — during the silent film era, at that.)

Eileen Farrell, Testament 1073 (Farrell had a large, beautiful voice, but recorded few of her operatic roles. The Testament disc includes several outstanding arias.)

*****Kirsten Flagstad**, Preiser 89141 (Flagstad was the most famous Wagnerian soprano from the 1930s through the mid–1950s. This disc includes outstanding performances recorded at the height of her career.)

Amelita Galli-Curci, RCA 61413

*****Beniamino Gigli**, Pearl 9033 or RCA 7811. (In the years following Caruso's death, Gigli was considered by many opera fans to be the great tenor's true successor.)

Hans Hotter, Preiser 90200 (Hotter's career extended into the early stereo years, but these earlier recordings show him at his best.)

Marcel Journet, Pearl 21 (This great French bass's career lasted into the early period of electrical recording, when he sang in one of the recordings of *Faust* included in our earlier recommendations.)

Dorothy Kirsten, MET 217 (Kirsten was an outstanding American lyric soprano of relatively recent years, but she made no complete commercial recordings of her roles.)

Ivan Kozlovsky, Myto 92155 and 92568 (One of the best Russian tenors, Kozlovsky made many recordings of complete operas, but they have limited distribution in the United States.)

Giacomo Lauri-Volpi, Pearl 9010

Lilli Lehmann, Symposium 1207, a two-disc set (Lilli Lehmann was one of great soprano stars at the end of the nineteenth century and one of the few singers on disc who took part in the first Wagner festival at Bayreuth in 1876.)

Lotte Lehmann, Preiser 89189

Frida Leider, Preiser 89004

*****John McCormack**, Pearl 9335 or Nimbus 7820 (McCormack was a beloved tenor — less for his operatic career than for his concert appearances. If you can locate a copy, the Nimbus issue gives a good portrait of his singing in opera.)

Giovanni Martinelli, Pearl 9351 (Martinelli took over many of the Caruso roles at the Metropolitan after his colleague's death. The listed disc includes arias, also scenes from *La Forza del Destino*, where Martinelli is joined by Rosa Ponselle, Giuseppe de Luca, and Ezio Pinza.)

*****Nelly Melba**, Larrikin 221 and Nimbus 7890 (Both of these recordings may be difficult to find, but Melba was the most famous soprano at the beginning of the twentieth century. Unfortunately, her voice did not take particularly well to old recording apparatus.)

*Lauritz Melchior, Preiser 89068 and 89086 (For many critics, Melchior was the greatest heldentenor of the twentieth or any other century.)

Zinka Milanov, BMG/RCA 60074 (This disc may be difficult to locate, but Milanov recorded many of her roles past her vocal prime, and the RCA recording shows her at her impressive best.)

Grace Moore, Pearl 9116 (Grace Moore sang at the Metropolitan Opera, but attracted her public as much through her appearances in films as she did on the opera stage.)

Claudia Muzio, Pearl 9143 and Phonographe 5065

*Ezio Pinza, BMG/RCA 61245 and Sony 45693 (The earlier recordings on the RCA are better than the later ones on Sony. Pinza was the Metropolitan's outstanding bass during the 1930s and 1940s. He left the Met to star on Broadway in *South Pacific*.)

Pol Plançon, Pearl 9497 (Plançon was a great French bass with the kind of technique usually heard only in "coloratura" sopranos.)

Lily Pons, RCA 61411 and Sony 45694 (As with Pinza, the earlier RCA recordings are the better choice.)

*Rosa Ponselle, Pearl 9210 and Nimbus 1777 (If you can find it, the three-disc Nimbus set gives a fuller appreciation of Ponselle's remarkable soprano voice, one of the most beautiful of the twentieth century.)

Mark Reizen, Preiser 89059 (Reizen was one of the great Russian basses, with the characteristic dark, deep sound.)

Elisabeth Rethberg, Preiser 89051 and Pearl 9199

Titta Ruffo, Pearl 9088 (Among baritones, Ruffo was the great vocal phenomenon, often imitated by lesser singers but never emulated.)

Bidu Sayao, Sony 62355

Tito Schipa, Pearl 9017; Preiser 89160 and 89171

Friedrich Schorr, Preiser 89052 (Schorr was the most outstanding German baritone between the two World Wars, particularly in the Wagner roles.)

*Ernestine Schumann-Heink, Delos 5503, a two-disc set (Schumann-Heink became a kind of mother figure in the United States through her radio broadcasts in the 1930s. She was also one of the supreme contralto artists in the history of opera.)

Meta Seinemeyer, Preiser 89402 (Seinemeyer sang only briefly in the United States and is little known here, but hers was one of the finest voices of the period after World War I.)

Marcella Sembrich, Vocal Archives 1139 (Sembrich's recordings are often disappointing, but she was the great star of the first season at the Metropolitan Opera in 1883.)

Leopold Simoneau, Polygram/DG 457752 (A wonderful Canadian tenor, Simoneau was never given the attention he deserved from the recording companies.)

Eleanor Steber, VAIA 1072

Risë Stevens, MET 114 (Stevens was the reigning Carmen at the Metropolitan Opera during the 1940s and 1950s.)

Ebe Stignani, Preiser 89014 (Stignani was the greatest Italian mezzo soprano from roughly 1935 to 1950.)

Riccardo Stracciari, Pearl 9178

Conchita Supervia, Preiser 89023 (Not only an outstanding Carmen, Supervia was also a mezzo soprano leader in the revival of Rossini's operas.)

Ferrucio Tagliavini, Preiser 89163

Francesco Tamagno, Pearl Opal 9846 (A trumpet-voiced tenor, Tamagno was Verdi's first Otello.)

Richard Tauber, Preiser 89144; Pearl Flapper 7042 (Tauber sang everything well, from Mozart to the lightest popular numbers. The Preiser disc has excellent operatic arias; the Pearl Flapper is devoted to operetta.)

*****Luisa Tetrazzini**, Romophone 81025, a two-disc set. (Tetrazzini defines the meaning of coloratura soprano.)

Georges Thill, Preiser 89168 (One of the finest of French tenors, he sang the operas of his native land, as well as Wagner and the Italian works.)

*****Lawrence Tibbett**, Delos 5500, a two-disc set (Tibbett is generally recognized as the finest baritone America has ever produced.)

Helen Traubel, Preiser 89120 (Traubel sang all of the major Wagner soprano roles at the Metropolitan Opera, but her remarkable voice is not well represented on compact discs. The Preiser issue also includes selections from Frida Leider, Nanny Larsen-Toden, and Kirsten Flagstad.)

Richard Tucker, Sony 62357 (This disc includes only the music of Verdi.)

Leonard Warren, Preiser 89145 (Warren is represented on several complete opera sets, but these generally earlier recordings show his voice at his prime.)

Fritz Wunderlich, EMI 62993, two-disc budget priced set.

PART II

Rounding Out
and Maintaining an
Opera Collection

three

OPERA AND THE PRINTED WORD

The collection will include a large and diverse selection of operatic audio and perhaps video recordings, but libraries are still places for books. Sooner or later, patrons who have come to enjoy the recordings will want to learn more than the album liner notes tell them about the history of opera, the composers and their works, and the artists who perform them. What follows is more or less the "basic minimum"—volumes that the well-stocked library should consider providing to answer the research questions and satisfy the curiosity of opera lovers.

In some cases I have suggested books that I have neither read nor seen, on the basis of critical reports or the known reliability of the authors. I have also tried to include primarily works that will be interesting and helpful for readers without specialized or advanced musical training. Unfortunately, many of the best printed sources are currently out of print. Works that are currently unavailable from the publishers, however, can often be purchased from dealers that handle used and out of print books.

I've added to this chapter a brief section concerning opera resources on the web. A growing number of libraries now provide on-line computer service for their patrons, and there's a great deal of information on various web sites — along with some misinformation — about opera and almost everything else. A web page on the computer screen is not precisely the same thing as a book, but it's up there to be seen, it's printed, and people are certainly going to use it. Let's encourage them to use it to learn about opera.

DICTIONARIES OF OPERA

The standard reference work in the field of opera is ***The New Grove Dictionary of Opera*** (Stanley Sadie, ed., 4 vols. [Grove's Dictionaries of Music, Inc., 1992]).

The New Grove Dictionary will answer almost any question on the subject that library patrons and staff can dream up, and frequently you'll have a carefully chosen illustration to go along with the answer. It is well worth the investment (list price: $850 hard bound or $275 in sturdy soft covers) as a major addition to the library reference shelves. The four volumes provide almost 5,000 pages of operatic information.

Detailed articles on all the major composers include biographical and critical discussions, bibliographies of related printed materials, and a list of all operatic works, with significant information on performances, manuscripts, and printed editions. There are briefer biographical notices of less important composers, along with articles on librettists, singers, impresarios, producers, scholars, and others significant in the study of opera. Included are entries on opera companies and the history of opera in various nations and major cities. All significant operatic terms are fully defined, and detailed synopses cover all standard operas and many that are rarely performed. For example, you can read not only about Puccini's *Bohème* but also about Leoncavallo's opera of the same name, and then move ahead a couple of entries and discover Vive's *Bohemios,* a Spanish zarzuela similar in some ways to the more famous Puccini and Leoncavallo versions. Separate articles deal with literary, legendary, and historical sources for the opera plots.

Appendices identify the names of major characters in 850 operas and the first lines of hundreds of arias and ensembles. Just imagine the curious patron who has heard one of Fiordiligi's arias and wants to know the opera in which this character with such an imposingly musical name appears. With the aid of the appropriate index, you would quickly find her origin in Mozart's *Così Fan Tutte.* On the other hand, if the patron knew only the opening words of the aria "Come scoglio," the index of first lines would soon identify both Fiordiligi as the

singer, *Così* as the source, and Mozart as the composer. I guarantee that your library patron would be impressed.

There is also a ten-page list of contributors, and the quality of the preceding four volumes assures that almost every significant contemporary operatic scholar and critic will be included. Students of opera will run into many familiar names — Julian Budden, J. B. Steane, Barry Millington, Martin Bernheimer, Desmond Shawe-Taylor, and that's just the beginning.

A separate volume, **The New Grove Book of Operas**, published by St. Martin's Press (1997), includes 800 pages of articles on individual operas drawn from the four-volume work. It makes an excellent choice for the circulating collection, but it will not serve as an adequate substitute for someone interested in even moderately advanced operatic research. *The New Grove Dictionary of Opera* in its full form is the one indispensable reference resource in the field. There are many shorter dictionaries and guides, but there is only one *Grove Dictionary.*

The New Penguin Opera Guide, edited by Amanda Holden (Penguin Books, 2001), is a cross between a dictionary of opera and a collection of operatic synopses. You may already have in your collection the 1993 *Viking Opera Guide.* (It was also published in an abridged edition as *The Penguin Opera Guide* in 1995 and 1997.) *The New Penguin Opera Guide* brings the *Viking Guide* up to date with entries for significant operas and their composers active in the twenty-first century.

This hefty single volume of over 1100 pages includes brief introductions to 850 composers and their works. The research has been done carefully, and the critical opinions appear to be well balanced, precisely what we would expect from the group of distinguished musical commentators whose names and credentials are identified in an appendix. Also included are indices of librettists and opera titles. The composer entries are arranged alphabetically, but their operas are presented chronologically by the dates of their premieres, not alphabetically by title. I have noticed a similar arrangement in some other recent opera reference works, and it seems to me to hamper rather than help the novice looking for information on a specific opera. The index of titles solves the problem, but also adds an extra step to the process.

The New Penguin Guide is effectively but not lavishly illustrated, and the print is apparently designed for the ophthalmologically gifted. This volume, however, is a mine of interesting, valuable operatic information. You might want to have one or more copies available for circulation and reserve *The New Grove Dictionary* for in-house reference use.

There are a number of other worthwhile opera dictionaries. *Baker's Dictionary of Opera,* edited by Laura Diane Kuhn (Gale Group, 1999), a large volume of over 1,000 pages, adds six or seven years of operatic activity to the coverage of *The New Grove Dictionary.* Similar in scope, although not as recent, is the excellent *Oxford Dictionary of Opera,* edited by John Warrack and Ewan West (Oxford University Press, 1992). It is also available in condensed form as *The Concise Oxford Dictionary of Opera* (Oxford University Press, 1996). Charles Osborne's popular *Dictionary of Opera* is published in an up-to-date revised edition (Welcome Rain Publishers, 1999). Any of these volumes will be valuable additions to the collection, but the basic recommendation remains the *The New Grove Dictionary of Opera,* a work that satisfies the needs of both the new opera fan and the musical scholar.

HISTORIES OF OPERA

Opera has now entered its fifth century, and the story of how what began with Peri's *Dafne* led to Birtwistle's *Mask of Orpheus* is interesting and exciting. That story is also important in the broader picture of the world's cultural history. Musicians, historians, writers, and curious people in general should be able to come to the library and find answers to their questions about where opera came from and how it grew and developed. Here are some suggested titles that will help meet that need.

Donald Jay Grout's ***A Short History of Opera*** has been revised and updated by Hermine W. Williams (Columbia Univesity Press, 1990). Grout's volume has long been one of the standard English language works and is often used as a textbook in university and conservatory courses. At 900 pages, it isn't precisely "short," but it is sound in scholarship and comprehensive in coverage. I wouldn't recommend it for the beginning opera lover who wants just a little background information on opera in general, but Grout and Williams' book will form a good solid foundation for a small collection of resources on the history of opera.

Three brief histories may have greater popular appeal, not only for their brevity but also for their copious and attractive illustrations. ***The Oxford Illustrated History of Opera*** (Oxford University Press, 1994) is a gem that should adorn any collection. The editor, Roger Parker, has assembled a group of outstanding musicologists, including William Ashbrook and Roger Millington, to write twelve chapters, nine of which cover opera from the seventeenth century to the present, and a final three that discuss historical perspectives on staging, singers and "Opera as a Social Occasion." *The Oxford Illustrated History* is lavishly illustrated with carefully chosen photographs, paintings, and drawings, many reproduced in color. There is also an excellent annotated bibliography and a detailed chronology. A quality soft back edition published in 2001 is available.

Much shorter is Leslie Orrey's *Opera: A Concise History*, available now in a revised edition edited by Rodney Milnes (Thames and Hudson, 1987). Carefully researched and engagingly written, this slender volume, like the *Oxford History*, is enhanced by an excellent selection of 253 illustrations, including some in color.

Michael Raeburn's *The Chronicle of Opera* (Thames and Hudson, 1998) presents the history of opera in year-by-year chronological form. His book, however, is far more than a list of dates, names, and titles. Brief descriptions point out the significance of the entries. Sidebars at the beginning of each section remind us of important historical events for the historical period, and short one or two paragraph essays on interesting operatic subjects are inserted frequently in the text. *The Chronicle of Opera* looks like a typical illustrated "coffee table" book, with its large format and many colorful illustrations, but it is actually an interesting, accurate, and wonderfully entertaining history of opera. Raeburn has included a glossary of important terms, a time line of opera history, a separate list of important opera premieres, brief biographies of one hundred great singers, and a discography of recordings of many of the operas mentioned in the book.

Although our subject is opera and not operetta, often the line that separates the two is remarkably thin. Great singers were crossing that boundary long before our current crop of cross-over classical artists warbling the latest popular ditties; and even the Metropolitan Opera, a fortress of operatic respectability, stages *Fledermaus* and *The Merry Widow* from time to time. A reliable and entertaining history of the subject is available in Richard Traubner's *Operetta: A Theatrical History* (Doubleday and Company, 1983, available now only in soft cover from Oxford University Press, 1989).

But the history of opera actually needs to be heard, not just read. Naxos has issued in its AudioBooks format Richard Fawkes' *The History of Opera* (NA 417612). Narration is read by Robert Powell, and musical examples are provided throughout, primarily from Naxos recordings. The history is not presented in great detail, but almost six hours on four compact discs offers a good, if limited, survey of the field.

PLOT SYNOPSES

Surely the most frequently published — and purchased — operatic books are collections of plot synopses. Many modern recordings of complete operas include in the printed liner material not only introductory articles of varying value and brief accounts of the stories, but also word-for-word libretti in both the original language and English translation. Volumes of plot summaries, however, have a continuing importance for those who want to brush up on the story before attending a live performance or enjoying a televised or broadcast performance. The best examples of this genre place titles or first lines of individual selections from the operas in their proper place in the plot summary so that the listener will know the context in which an isolated aria or ensemble is performed.

Many opera lovers of my advanced age cut their operatic teeth on *The Victor* [Victrola company became Victor] *Book of the Opera*. First published in 1912, it went through many editions and countless printings, all of them now long out of print. Each volume combined synopses of opera plots with the ever-expanding catalogue listings of Victor operatic recordings. Until the final editions, the writing style was emotional, flowery, often eloquent, and the illustrations were magnificent evocations of an earlier age of operatic stage and costume design. It there's a copy of one of the editions of the *Victor Book* tucked away on your library shelves, hold on to it. (I was distressed to discover recently in my hometown library that the copy I read over and over again as a child has gone the way of worn-out books, to either the garbage bin or the Friends of the Library book sale.) Perhaps you'll discover the sixth edition from 1921, with what is surely one of the most beautiful bindings ever dreamed up for an opera volume. It's worth its weight in the gold stamping on the cover.

The *Victor Book* had one great rival, Gustave Kobbé's **Complete Opera Book**, first published in 1919, shortly after the death of its author. It, too, went through a number of editions, edited from 1954 by the Earl of Harewood, later with the assistance of Antony Peattie. Unlike its rival, however, Kobbé's book is still in print, now enjoying its eleventh edition as **The New Kobbé's Opera Book** (G. P. Putnam's Sons, 2000). It is a massive, oversized tome of over a thousand pages that includes plot summaries of almost 500 operas, including some of the most recent works. The synopses are clear and easy to follow, and the authors have managed to make sense even out of some of the virtually "plotless" contemporary operas. Major musical selections are keyed into the plot summaries at the proper points. The book is arranged alphabetically by composer, a distinct advantage over the earlier editions, which grouped operas by historical period and nationality. Unfortunately, the operas are then presented chronologically by the premiere dates. *Kobbé's Opera Book,* however, is the most comprehensive, up-to-date summary of opera plots currently available.

The two volumes of John W. Freeman's **The Metropolitan Opera Stories of the Great Operas** (W. W. Norton, 1984 and 1997) provide detailed synopses of 275 operas, with standard opera fare in the first volume and less familiar works in the second. The two-volume format is easier to handle than the giant *Kobbé's Opera Book,* but also necessitates frequent switching from volume to volume. Individual musical selections are indicated in the body of each article. In addition to the synopses, there are brief biographical sketches and small photographs of the composers. The composers appear alphabetically in each volume, but once again the operas are arranged chronologically by the dates of first performances.

Although now out of print, Mark Lubbock's **The Complete Book of Light Opera** (Appleton-Century-Crofts, 1962, with an American section by David Ewen) is well worth searching out via the used book dealers. Light operas, operettas, and musical plays are frequently neglected by other reference sources. Selections from them, however, are frequently included on concert programs and recordings with little or no indication of their dramatic context. Lubbock's book fills the gap adequately for operas and musicals prior to 1961.

There are two excellent series of guides to individual operas, the **Cambridge Opera Handbooks** (Cambridge University Press, various dates) and the **English National Opera Guides** (Calder Publications, various dates). The Cambridge series currently includes twenty-three titles. Each volume is edited by a different scholar or critic, and provides a detailed, full-length introduction to the work. The English National Opera Guides are briefer introductions, but they print the libretto in both English and the original language. Many of the English National Opera Guides are either out of print or difficult to obtain, but individual suppliers may still have stock on hand.

SINGERS, ON AND OFF THE RECORD

The story of opera is also the story of the singers who perform the various roles, and opera lovers are traditionally curious about these artists, their careers and even their personal lives. Witness: the incredible number of books about Maria Callas, many of them concerned less with her artistry than with her personal relationships with family, husband, and lovers. Biographies and autobiographies, often the "as told to" variety, of the most famous stars appear regularly. With occasional exceptions, they are of no more than passing interest and minimal quality. Too often they record questionable accounts of wildly successful performances and whispered references to back-stage opera gossip. Generally speaking, the value of these works as reliable historical records is decidedly limited.

Singing is an ephemeral art. Until roughly one hundred years ago, a vocal performance, once the last notes had been sung, had continuing life only in the often faulty memories of those who heard it. Attempts to reconstruct the history of singing prior to the invention of recorded sound depend on those memories, to the extent that they were written down and preserved. To those memories, historical scholars add a careful study of the music that was actually performed. Even with that material, however, the results are controversial. Contemporary critical reviews of modern operatic performances prove without question that two listeners who hear the same performance do not necessarily hear it the same way, and vocal music in printed or manuscript form, particularly from earlier periods, often tells us very little about what was actually sung in the opera house or how it was sung.

What is probably the most successful and approachable book on the subject is Henry Pleasants' *The Great Singers: From the Dawn of Opera to Our Own Time* (Simon and Schuster, originally published in 1966; most recently in paperback in 1985). Although currently out of print, Pleasants' book is important reading for those interested in the history of opera and will reward the effort to find a used copy. The value is enhanced by a judicious selection of illustrations, an excellent glossary of important vocal terminology, and an interesting bibliography of books about singers and singing.

The advent of sound recording at the end of the nineteenth century enabled us at last to *hear* the history of singing. The earliest recordings were primitive to say the least, and it takes patience and a measure of aural adjustment to siphon out the scratchy surface noise and the tinny orchestral sound before we can begin to grasp the true vocal quality of the artists. Some singers fared better than others with the recording horn, and in many cases we can be certain that audiences in the opera houses heard something that we miss on the old discs and cylinders. In time, however, particularly with the advent of electric recording in the mid 1920s, the sound quality improved. (Some would say it improved too much, so that we can never be certain now that we hear the true sound of a singer's voice rather than an electronically altered and sometimes augmented version of it.) Some complete operas were recorded on the old 78 RPM discs, but manipulating twenty or thirty of those heavy discs on and off the turntable was awkward to say the least. Eventually, with the long-playing record and the compact disc it became practical to hear on recordings one after another of the great and not-so-great singers, often in complete performances of their roles. Not only is it now possible to have the history of singing since 1900 in sound, but also, through the recording of hundreds of complete operas, the history of opera itself since its beginning.

The singing of an earlier age is documented first of all in a large number of reissues on compact discs of recorded material. Among the labels that specialize in such reissues are Pearl, Preiser, Marston, Arkadia, Romophone, and Minerva, and the major labels frequently make available discs drawn from their vocal archives. Some of the best of these discs are listed in Chapter Two. What can be learned of the history of singing from early recordings is admirably set forth in J. B. Steane's ***The Grand Tradition: Seventy Years of Singing on Record*** (Charles Scribner's Sons, 1974; reprinted with editorial changes, Timber Press, 1993). This is another out-of-print volume that is important enough to warrant a used book search. Steane is masterful in describing vocal sound in words, and he has apparently listened to almost everything there is to be heard. His critical standards for great singing are high, based as they are on the greatest historical examples of the art of song. He applies those standards assiduously but also graciously, and not without hope for the future as he surveys the prospects in 1970. *The Grand Tradition* is a book that opera lovers will read with pleasure, and from which they will emerge with a deeper appreciation for opera, for the artists who perform it, and for the tradition on which they build.

Two important volumes trace the history of singing on record from the earliest days through 1925, the date which marks the demise of the old acoustical recording process. ***The Record of Singing to 1914*** (Charles Scribner's Sons, 1977; Gerald Duckworth, 1993) and ***The Record of Singing, Volume Two: 1914 to 1925*** (Gerald Duckworth, 1979 and 1993; Northeastern University Press, 1990), both by Michael Scott, were written to accompany the first two volumes of a recorded history of singing issued by Angel/EMI records. Each singer represented is discussed in a biographical and critical essay, and comments are not limited to the selections included in the recordings. As with Steane, Scott has adopted demanding critical standards and, if anything, is even more exacting in applying them. The two volumes present a wealth of information and include almost every important singer active from 1900 to 1925. There are numerous photographs, many of them quite rare. The record sets for which these two volumes were written have not been reissued in compact disc format and are long out of print in their long-playing form. Volumes 3 (1926-1936) and 4 (1939 to the end of the "78" era), for which no books were written, have been made available on compact disc (Vol. 3, Testament SBT 0132; Vol. 4, EMI 69741).

Collectors of operatic recordings cherish the three volumes of **Opera on Record** (Vol. 1, Hutchinson and Company, 1979; Vol. 2, Beaufort Books, 1983; Vol. 3, Longwood Press, 1984). Like many of the volumes mentioned in this section, they are difficult to locate, but vocal collectors will be grateful for your effort. Alan Blyth, the editor, assembled a notable group of critics and scholars to review the history on sound recordings of almost two hundred operas and operettas. Not only the complete opera recordings, but many individual arias, duets, and ensembles are included in the comments. Although the quality of the essays inevitably varies from one writer to another, on the whole the comments on individual operas are informative, interesting, and helpful. The discographies at the end of each chapter are not always completely accurate, but most readers won't notice, and the ones who do will delight in correcting them.

The Metropolitan Opera Guide to Recorded Opera, edited by Paul Gruber (W.W. Norton, 1993), reviews the commercially issued complete recordings of 150 different operas. In the process, much of the history of operatic performance is covered by the twenty writers assigned to the individual operas. Some of the critical comments seem to me unduly harsh, and a few of the authors appear to have stylistic preferences strong enough to interfere with balanced judgment. As a result, some opera lovers will find their favorite recordings relegated to the trash bin. Such, however, is the nature of things in operatic criticism, and opera fans who can't handle a little disagreement without losing their cool had better go back to the Bobbsey Twins. *The Metropolitan Opera Guide* is both stimulating and entertaining.

Two further volumes deserve a special recommendation. Paul Jackson's critical and historical surveys of Metropolitan Opera broadcasts are among the recent masterpieces of writing about opera. ***Saturday Afternoons at the Old Met: The Metropolitan Opera Broadcasts, 1931–1950*** (Amadeus Press, 1992) and ***Sign-Off for the Old Met: The Metropolitan Opera Broadcasts, 1950–1966*** (Amadeus Press, 1997) are based on extensive research and careful, critical listening to hundreds of off-the-air recordings of broadcast material. Many of the world's most important singers were performing at the Metropolitan Opera during the period covered, and Jackson's books make a significant contribution to the general history of operatic singing during the central years of the last century. Since he is also a writer of clarity, charm, and acute critical perception, Jackson's two large volumes will be a delight to readers interested in opera. There are many interesting illustrations, and appendices in each book list all of the operas broadcast, with their casts.

COMPOSERS AND THEIR MUSIC

Although opera depends on performance to bring it to life, there is still one important element that comes before the singers, the orchestra, the dancers, the designers, the stage directors, and even the all-powerful conductor. That is the composer. Readers with a serious interest in opera will often be eager for a fuller, deeper view than even the most detailed guides and dictionaries can provide into the lives of the actual creators. Whether what they discover of the life stories will enhance their understanding and appreciation of the operas is no doubt the great unanswerable question of all biographies of creative artists. Accurate, carefully researched biographies of the composers, however, can not only satisfy a measure of curiosity. They can also offer interesting, perceptive, and therefore helpful critical comment on the operas themselves.

Choosing which biographies of which composers to add to the opera collection is inevitably based on more or less arbitrary decisions. The best I can offer is my personal list of thirty composers whose works constitute a major portion of the current standard operatic repertoire. For each of them, I have suggested one or more biographical and critical studies that will be of interest and value to the reader with a slightly more than average interest in opera. Unfortunately, musical biographies tend to go out of print in a hurry, often to reappear, albeit briefly, in paper covers. Many of them, however, are available from used book dealers and those stores that specialize in remainders. The bibliographies included with the various entries in *The New Grove Dictionary of Opera, The New Penguin Opera Guide,* or similar dictionaries will lead to biographical studies of additional composers and other, more specialized studies of operatic subjects.

Ludwig van Beethoven. Barry Cooper's ***Beethoven*** in the "Master Musician Series" (Oxford University Press, 2001) is a reliable, relatively brief approach to the composer, who composed only one opera, *Fidelio,* but that one a surpassing masterpiece. *The Beethoven Companion,* edited by Thomas K. Scherman and Louis Biancolli (Doubleday and Co., 1972), a large volume containing discussions of every one of Beethoven's contributions, is out of print, but it is worth finding as a significant addition to your collection of music reference materials in general.

Vincenzo Bellini. John Rosselli's *The Life of Bellini* is available from Cambridge University Press, 1997. Herbert Weinstock's earlier biography, *Vincenzo Bellini: His Life and Operas* (Alfred A. Knopf, 1971), currently out of print, includes a full biography and detailed introductions to each of the composer's operas.

Alban Berg. I have not personally reviewed these books about Berg and his music, but from the reports I have seen they deserve to be mentioned. Mosco Carner's *Alban Berg* (Holmes and Meier, 1980, revised edition) is the work of a recognized musical scholar and author. *The Cambridge Companion to Berg,* edited by Anthony Pope, is a recent guide to the composer's work. Be warned, however, that analyses of Berg's music tend to be too technical for the reader without advanced musical training.

Harrison Birtwistle. I have not seen Jonathan Cross's *Harrison Birtwistle: Man, Mind, Music* (Cornell University Press, 2000), but apparently it offers the general music lover an opportunity to understand more fully the advanced compositional techniques that Birtwistle uses in his operas. Those who encounter Birtwistle's operas for the first time will probably be looking for some help.

Georges Bizet. Greenwood Press reprinted two studies of Bizet in 1971 and 1977 respectively, Martin Cooper's *Georges Bizet* and Mina Curtis' *Bizet and His World*. They are both out of print, but used copies are often available from the appropriate dealers. There is need for a new, up-to-date biographical and critical study of Bizet and his operas.

Alexander Borodin. Gerald Abraham's *Borodin: The Composer and His Music* (AMS Press, 1974) is an early work by one of the most important writers on Russian music in general, and opera in particular.

Benjamin Britten. The excellent "Twentieth Century Composers" series includes Michael Oliver's *Benjamin Britten* (Phaidon Press, 1996).

Gaetano Donizetti. Look for a copy of William Ashbrook's *Donizetti and His Operas* (Cambridge University Press, 1982). It is currently out of print, but it is virtually indispensable for a study of Donizetti's astounding output of over sixty operas.

Anton Dvořák, Alec Robertson's *Dvořák,* originally published in 1943, was reprinted by J.M. Dent in 1973, but it is currently out of print. It is a good brief introduction to the composer's life and works, with a short chapter devoted to his operas. Michael Beckerman edited *Dvořák and His World* (Lightning Source, 1993), a collection of essays on various aspects of his life and works, including his American period.

George Gershwin. Gershwin's life story has been the subject of a great deal of controversy in the years since his early death. Rodney Greenberg's *George Gershwin* (Phaidon, 1998), part of the "Twentieth Century Composers" series, offers a carefully considered, well balanced account of his life and music.

Christoph Willibald von Gluck. I have not seen a copy of Ernest Newman's *Gluck and the Opera* (AMS Press, 1976), but Newman was a sometimes controversial, but always interesting and perceptive scholar and critic, and I imagine that his comments on Gluck's operas would be well worth reading.

Charles Gounod. You may have some difficulty located Stephen Huebner's ***The Operas of Gounod*** (Oxford University Press, 1992), but it is the most comprehensive study of Gounod's operas in the English language. Also out of print but worth searching out is James Harding's ***Gounod*** (Stein and Day, 1973).

George Frideric Handel. For a detailed study of the composer's life and career, look for a copy of Paul Henry Lang's ***Handel*** (W. W. Norton, 1966 in hardback, 1977 in paper cover; both out of print). You will find a great deal of helpful information on Handel in Donald Burrows' ***Cambridge Companion to Handel*** (Cambridge University Press, 1997).

Leoš Janáček. John Tyrrell's ***Janáček's Operas*** (Princeton University Press, 1992) is the book to have on the great Czech operatic composer. It is currently out of print, but keep your eyes open for it. As a relatively recent publication, it might well turn up soon in paper cover.

Pietro Mascagni. Published during the summer of 2002, Alan Mallach's ***Pietro Mascagni and His Operas*** (Northwest University Press) should satisfy the longstanding need for a biographical and critical study of an important Italian composer. We will continue to wait for a useful work on Ruggero Leoncavallo, whose *Pagliacci* is so often paired with Mascagni's *Cavalleria Rusticana*.

Jules Massenet. The only work on Massenet currently in print that I have found is Denar Irvine's ***Massenet: A Chronicle of His Life and Times*** (Amadeus Press, 1994). I have not seen it, but from descriptions it appears to be a relatively full account of his life and works. You may be able to find a copy of James Harding's out-of-print ***Massenet*** (St. Martin's Press, 1970). It offers a well written biography and account of the composer's several operas.

Wolfgang Amadeus Mozart. Peter Gay's ***Mozart*** (Viking Press, 1999) is a brief, well written biography in the "Penguin Lives" series. It is good as far as it goes, but it obviously doesn't go far enough to deal adequately with the life and music of Mozart. Maynard Solomon's highly praised biography ***Mozart*** (Harper Brothers 1995, hardback, 1996, paperback) is out of print but will reward a successful search for a copy. William Mann's ***The Operas of Mozart***, the most complete and helpful discussion of the composer's operatic works, is not only out of print, it is also a collector's item and frequently commands a price of several hundred dollars. For most budget-strapped collections, the 1988 paperback reissue of Charles Osborne's ***The Complete Operas of Mozart*** (Da Capo Press, 1988) will have to serve until Mann's excellent work is again available.

Modest Mussorgsky. I have seen neither of these books, but both seem to offer sound, useful information about Mussorgsky and his career as composer. Caryl Emerson's ***The Life of Mussorgsky*** (Cambridge University Press, 1999) is a recent addition to the excellent "Musical Lives" series. ***Mussorgsky Remembered***, edited by Alexandra Orlova (Indiana University Press, 1991), is a collection of reminiscences by Mussorgsky's contemporaries.

Jacques Offenbach. If you can locate a copy, James Harding's ***Jacques Offenbach: A Biography*** (Riverrun Press, 1981) will satisfy most readers' interest in the life of the German musical wizard who became the leading composer of nineteenth century French operetta.

Sergei Prokofiev. ***The Music of Sergei Prokofiev***, by Neil Minturn (Yale University Press, 1997), one volume in the

"Composers of the Twentieth Century" series, promises a useful, relatively brief introduction to the composer.

Giacomo Puccini. Another addition to the valuable "Composers of the Twentieth Century" series is Armand Wilson's *Giacomo Puccini* (Phaedon Press, 1997). William Ashbrook's *The Operas of Puccini* (Cornell University Press, 1985) is out of print but well worth seeking out. Included are detailed introductions and analyses of each of Puccini's operas.

Nicolai Rimsky-Korsakov. We need a good English-language study of Rimsky-Korsakov, whose operas are coming more and more to the attention of Western listeners. While we wait, however, you can look for a copy of his autobiography, *My Life*, one of the best composer self-examinations. It was published by Horizon House in 1983 in an edition now out of print, but it has been often reprinted over the years and second-hand copies are generally not difficult to locate.

Gioachino Rossini. Herbert Weinstock's careful, detailed biography *Rossini* (last available from Limelight in 1987) is unavailable at the present time. Richard Osborne's *Rossini* in the "Master Musicians" series was published by Oxford University Press in 2002.

Bedřich Smetana. I have found no currently available studies of the life and works of Smetana. If you can locate a copy, however, Brian Large's *Smetana* (Praeger Publishers, 1970) will provide a full picture of the composer's life and a thorough introduction to his eight completed operas.

Richard Strauss. An insightful short biography is Bryan Gilliam's *The Life of Richard Strauss* (Cambridge University Press, 1999), a volume in the "Musical Lives" series. Somewhat more detailed is Michael Kennedy's equally recommendable *Richard Strauss* (Oxford University Press, 2001), a revised and expanded version of his 1976 biography. One of the most useful books for opera lovers, *The Complete Operas of Richard Strauss*, by Charles Osborne (Trafalgar Square Publishing, 1988), is currently out of print but may be available from used book dealers.

Igor Stravinsky. Stephen Walsh's *The New Grove Stravinsky* (Grove, 2002) is a very brief account based on the authoritative material in *Grove's Dictionary of Music and Musicians*. You may also want to check out Eric Walter White's *Stravinsky: A Critical Survey* (Dover, 1997).

Peter Ilych Tchaikovsky. Edward Harden's *Tchaikovsky* (Oxford University Press, 2000) in the "Master Musicians" series offers biographical and critical study that will supplement the excellent entry in *The New Grove Dictionary of Opera*. You may also want to investigate *Tchaikovsky and His World*, edited by Lesley Kearney (Princeton University Press, 1998). I have not reviewed either of these volumes personally.

Giuseppe Verdi. The standard English language biography is Mary Jane Phillips-Matz's *Verdi: A Biography* (Oxford University Press, 1993). The hardbound copy appears to be out of print, but the paperback reprint of 1996 is currently available. Julian Budden's three-volume study of Verdi's operas is a triumph of musical scholarship and criticism. It is the one absolutely essential resource for any study of the composer's operas. The three volumes of *The Operas of Verdi* (Oxford University Press) were reprinted in quality paper bindings in 1992. The third volume is not currently available, but will surely return in the near future.

Richard Wagner. The dean of contemporary Wagner scholarship is Barry Millington. His comprehensive biography of the composer, *Wagner* (Princeton University Press, 1992, revised edition), includes the composer's life story and individual chapters on each of the operas. Millington also edited *The Wagner Compendium: A Guide to Wagner's Life and Music* (Thames and Hudson, 2001), a collection of stimulating essays by various authors covering major themes in Wagner's life and discussions of each of his musical works.

Carl Maria von Weber. Although currently out of print, John Hamilton Warrack's *Carl Maria von Weber* (Cambridge Univesity Press, 1995, second edition) is the book you should look for. Included in Warrack's biography are musical analyses of each of his operas.

THE CRITICAL WORD

There are many works of music criticism that deal with opera in general. Some of them are of small value and offer no critical comment more perceptive than what you will find in the volumes of plot synopses or the larger opera dictionaries recommended earlier. Some of them, however, make significant contributions to our understanding and appreciation of opera. Here are two choices from the many available that may be of interest to serious opera fans.

Joseph Kerman's *Opera as Drama* (University of California Press, 1988) appeared first in 1956 and immediately whipped up a storm of controversy. It is now available in a revised edition slightly (but only slightly) less controversial than the original, and it remains one of the most exciting, challenging, influential, and wonderfully readable books ever written about opera. Beyond everything else, Kerman insists that listeners and critics should take

opera seriously and not automatically overlook its weaknesses or fail to notice its strengths. His basic premise is that in opera it is the composer who is truly the dramatist. *Opera as Drama* is necessary reading for those who truly love opera and want to understand it more fully, and it should be on the shelf of every library that aims for a worthwhile opera collection.

Carolyn Abbate's *In Search of Opera* is less controversial but more difficult and challenging for the reader. What it shares with Kerman's book is an insistence that we listen and look closely and take opera seriously. Her distinct contribution for readers who can handle her imaginative, often poetic writing style is to open our ears so that we hear opera in exciting new ways. It, however, is not a beginner's book. To read it with understanding and appreciation requires a sound knowledge of the operas she discusses.

PRINTED WORDS ON THE SCREEN: OPERA ON THE WEB

Enter "opera" into one of the search engines available on your computer and you will discover almost six million possible sites. Try instead one of the great operatic composers, "Giuseppe Verdi," for example, or "Richard Wagner," and be certain to use the full name, not just the surname. Otherwise you'll locate the family history of every Verdi in Milan and every Wagner in Berlin. You will still have more sites than you could open in a decade of Saturday afternoon Metropolitan Opera broadcasts, several hundred thousand of them. Try one of the less known contemporary composers. For Harrison Birtwistle there are only 6,870 entries. The key is obviously to narrow the search as much as you possibly can. Request instead "Richard Wagner biography" or a specific opera, perhaps "Harrison Birtwistle Mask of Orpheus."

Another key: go ahead and use the standard printed reference sources for information on major composers and their works. You truly will find almost everything you need in *The New Grove Dictionary of Opera* or *The Penguin Opera Guide*. If you're looking for something truly out of the way, however, the web can be a help. I found at *http://opera.stanford.edu* a translation of the passage from Heinrich Heine's *Memoirs of Herr von Schabelewopski* that served as a source for Wagner's *Der Fliegende Holländer,* and that's a rather specialized bit of operatic knowledge. Just in case you have a patron who is eager to read the libretto for Charles Wakefield Cadman's *Shanewis,* it's there to be found at *www.karadar.com*. You may be thinking that no one will ever ask for *Shanewis,* but someday someone may appear at your library looking for information about Native Americans in opera.

There are many websites dedicated to opera in general. One of the most helpful is *www.operabase.com*, primarily because it provides numerous links to other useful sites and provides them in seven languages. Use the computer's search feature to find entries for significant conductors and singers from throughout the history of opera, often with biographical information, pictures, lists of roles, and discographies.

Almost all opera companies, from the major world houses like the Metropolitan in New York and La Scala in Milan, to the smaller regional companies, have their own web sites. Some of them offer only promotional material for current productions and information for the purchase of tickets. The best of these sites, however, include synopses of operas, interesting production details, often with illustrations, and histories of the company and the house. One of the finest is the Metropolitan Opera web site. It includes detailed plot summaries of many operas, not just those in the current repertoire, and an excellent section devoted to the history of the Metropolitan, with numerous photographs drawn from the archives.

four

KEEPING CURRENT

Library professionals and all the rest of us are aware that we are always "in process." When it comes to an opera collection, if one day we think we have arrived, that we have every resource we need, the next day will hit us with something new and different, and we'll know that we're not there yet. We will always be on the way to where we want to be.

Next Tuesday, the record companies will release a new batch of discs. (Tuesday is the inevitable new release day.) There will be jazz, rock 'n' roll, hip-hop, piano and other instrumental solos, vocal recitals, orchestral programs — and opera. So you already have two superb *Aida*s and the world's greatest *Meistersinger*? Ah, but Tenor "X" has just committed the definitive Radames to disc, that hot-shot young Conductor "Y" has begun his series of Wagner spectaculars, and ancient Memphis and sixteenth-century Nuremberg have never before been bathed in such amazing digitally recorded sound. What's more, those thoughtless composers will go right on composing new operas and producers will go right on recording them.

How, then, can we ever keep current? Here are a few suggestions.

JOURNALS AND MAGAZINES

There are enough enthusiasts for classical music in general and opera in particular to justify the publication of an almost overwhelming number of specialized periodicals. A glance at the entry on "Periodicals" in *The New Grove Dictionary of Opera* lists hundreds of magazines and journals of past and present from around the world. They come in a variety of sizes, shapes, and paper stocks, and each has its own appeal; but all of those listed here are worthwhile, carefully edited publications, and all of them give some attention to recent operatic happenings and recordings. Whatever you do, don't keep them hidden away in the back office exclusively for staff use. The opera lovers among your patrons will await the next issues with all the impatience of a football fan begging for the latest *Sports Illustrated*.

The six recommended here no more than skim the surface of available magazines and journals, but they are all of value in keeping up with what's happening in opera matters, either on stage or in visually or sonically reproduced form. All six of them include reviews of sound recordings. If your periodical budget won't permit subscriptions to all, spring for the first one and either numbers two or three, depending on the relative interest in American or British operatic events. If you can handle it financially, however, subscribing to the whole kit and caboodle will warm the hearts of opera fans.

Gramophone is the granddaddy and the gold standard of recorded music magazines. It has been published since 1923, and it continues to offer reviews and articles by a distinguished group of critics who are not only astute listeners but also bona fide musicologists.

Gramophone is a British publication, a fact that comes through particularly in the advertisements, but it includes musical news of interest around the world. The edition designed for readers in the United States also incorporates a special section with reviews and listings for recordings available on distinctly American labels. The coveted Gramophone Awards, sponsored annually by the magazine, honor outstanding recorded performances and artists. Each issue includes interviews and articles on musical subjects and a regular column that is of special interest to opera fans, "Singertalk" by John Steane. Reviews are divided by genre, one of which is "Opera." There are also evaluations of videos, printed materials, and of sound reproduction equipment. The helpful monthly listing of all new issues of recordings will whet the appetite of the most sated opera collectors.

Gramophone is published thirteen times each year, either with or without a special compact disc that highlights the editors' choices of outstanding recordings. Subscriptions are available either from *Gramophone,* P.O. Box 158, Avenel, NJ 07001–9886, U.S.A., or from *Gramophone*, P.O. Box 280, Sittingbourne, Kent ME9 8FB, United Kingdom.

Opera News, a publication of the Metropolitan Opera Guild, is issued monthly. Like *Gramophone*, it too has been around for a long time, well over sixty years. For many of those years the focus was on performances of the Metropolitan Opera, with particular emphasis on the famous Saturday afternoon broadcasts. There is still extensive coverage of broadcasts and telecasts from the Metropolitan, but *Opera News* has expanded and increased its coverage to include many articles and reviews of opera performances around the world. If you want to know what's happening in opera almost anywhere on the globe, or, even more important, what is going to happen in the future, *Opera News* is a good place to begin. It's worth noting that the magazine is also quite as objective in its critiques of the Metropolitan as it is with any other opera venue and makes a point of reminding readers that opinions in the magazine are not necessarily those of either the Metropolitan Opera or the Metropolitan Opera Guild.

Opera News regularly reviews selected recordings and books related to opera, although the coverage is not nearly so extensive as those magazines devoted to recorded music. Additional reviews and articles, however, are available on-line for subscribers at the *Opera News* website.

Subscriptions are available from *Opera News,* Circulation Department, 70 Lincoln Center Plaza, New York, NY 10023–6593, U.S.A.

Opera is a British magazine, first produced in 1950 and published thirteen times a year. It prints fewer reviews of video and sound recordings than any of the other magazines listed here, but it offers amazingly comprehensive coverage of what's happening in opera worldwide. Planning a business trip to Latvia, a spring break in Graz, a weekend in Palo Alto? *Opera* will provide the schedule for the Riga Opera, the Operhaus, and the Lucie Stern Theatre and tell you where you can inquire for tickets. Miss the first act and wonder how it went? Chances are in the next month's issue you can read a review of the performance.

To identify *Opera* as British points not only to an emphasis on operatic matters in the United Kingdom (although by no means exclusively so), but also to a delightful but almost indefinable quality of urbanity, wit, and a quality of critical acuity in which necessary needling is at once both sharp and genteel. The reviews of both recordings and performances encourage serious thought and often a little smile to go along with it.

Subscriptions are available from *Opera*, 36 Black Lion Lane, London W69BE, UK, or through the website at *operasubs@clara. co.uk.*

The Opera Quarterly, published four times a year by the Oxford University Press, is a leading scholarly journal in the field. Articles are carefully researched and annotated. Some of them, but by no means all, are technical in nature and will appeal primarily to specialists. The majority of the articles, however, are of general operatic interest and are fully accessible to the average reader. Opera lovers will particularly enjoy the surveys of the life and career of both famous and not so famous singers.

A major portion of each issue is devoted to reviews of sound and video recordings and opera-related books. The reviews are long enough to include a great deal of significant information. Often the reviews amount to mini-essays on the opera and the performance under consideration, and frequently there are helpful comparisons with other recordings of the same works. As a quarterly publication, however, *The Opera Quarterly* reviews only a limited number of the recordings and books received each quarter by the journal, and those that are included often have been in release for a great many months prior to the publication of the reviews.

Subscriptions for North America may be secured from the Oxford University Press, Journals Subscriptions Departments, 2001 Evans Road, Cary, NC 27513, U.S.A. For the rest of the world, contact Oxford University Press, Journals Subscriptions Departments, Great Clarendon Street, Oxford OX 2 6DP, UK.

Fanfare: The Magazine for Serious Record Collectors, published every two months, lives up to its title with two hundred or more pages of reviews in each issue. There are articles dealing primarily with recording artists and reviews of opera and other musical performances, but the bulk of the magazine is devoted to thoughtful critical comment on current releases of classical music on disc, including, of course, operatic and other vocal music. As with any collection of performance criticism, readers — and other critics — will often disagree with the opinions expressed, but a generous number of letters-to-the-editor are printed, and often the critics respond with interesting comments of their own. On the whole, *Fanfare* is a valuable and dependable source for information on recent sound recordings.

Subscriptions are available from *Fanfare,* Inc., P. O. Box 17, Tenafly, NJ 07670, USA.

Similar in its coverage to *Fanfare*, the **American Record Guide** is also published once every two months. More attention is given to reviews of current live, often operatic, performances, but the major portion of the magazine, once again two hundred or more pages, is devoted to informed criticism of recently released recordings. No doubt each of these two magazines has its avid advocates, but personally I wouldn't want to be without either of them. A special feature of the *American Record Guide* is the provocative, cantankerous, and thoroughly delightful comments of Editor Donald Vroon.

Order subscriptions from Record Guide Publications, 4412 Braddock Street, Cincinnati, OH 45204, U.S.A.

A PAIR OF UP-DATED GUIDES

Both of the highly respected books suggested here provide information on recordings, including newer issues, available at the time of their publication. They also offer generally sound critiques of both performance and sound quality.

The **Gramophone Classical Good CD Guide** (Gramophone Publications, with Haymarket Magazines) is brought up to date from time to time, the most recent "2003" edition was published in 2002. No doubt others will follow periodically. In addition to basic introductory material and brief essays on the appreciation of music from various periods, there are short biographies of each composer, drawn from **The Concise Grove Dictionary of Music**. The value of the book, however, is primarily in the reviews of recordings, based in large part on the parent magazine. Recent releases are included, but the *Guide* is selective in its choice of recordings for review, so that many newer and older releases are not included. As a summary of some of the best recordings available in a frequently updated form, however, the *Guide* is quite helpful. This is a British publication, and some of the discs listed will be available in the United States only as imports.

The Penguin Guide to Compact Discs, edited by Ivan March (Penguin Books), is also published in revised form on a more or less regular basis. The most recent complete edition that I have seen was published in 2001 and is labled the "2002 Edition." In fifteen hundred plus pages, the complete edition reviews a vast number of discs in brief form. Not every available recording is included, but it is difficult to find a truly worthwhile issue that isn't listed and evaluated. *The Penguin Guide* is also a British publication, and, as in the case of the **Gramophone Guide**, some of the included

recordings will be available in the United States only as imports. The publisher, however, has gone out of the way to accommodate the material for collectors in the United States, so that where domestic issue numbers differ from the British numbers both are indicated.

A COMPREHENSIVE CATALOGUE?

Operatic recordings come and go with all the reliability and predictability of the weather. In other words, what is available and what is not, what's in and what's out of the catalogue is an ever-changing matter governed by laws that refuse to yield precise answers. Recording companies form new alliances with one another, and in the process label names may change. Those companies then decide to discontinue issues almost without warning, and they frequently reissue previously unavailable recordings, often with redesigned covers, remastered sound, and new catalogue numbers. For the record companies and their executives, it's just the regular business of profit and loss. For the collector and the library staff members charged with the responsibility of finding and ordering recordings, it can be a matter of confusion and incredible frustration. How in the world can we possibly keep up with what is or is not "in print" today?

A listing of all the recordings available on any given day would be a tremendous boon, but also an overwhelming task. After all, there are approximately 1,200 different record label names in the United States. I wish there were a single magic answer to how to know precisely what can be found on all of those labels. At least for the moment, no such magic answer exists

You may be familiar with the famous "**Schwann**" catalogue. For many years it was the standard source for information about currently available sound recordings. When publication began in 1949, the catalogue was little more than a pamphlet. After all, the long-playing record, introduced commercially in 1948, was still in its very young infancy. "Schwann," however, grew with the recording industry, and eventually ***Schwann Opus*** and ***Schwann Artist***, the two publications of particular interest to collectors of classical music, became massive volumes of more than a thousand pages of very small, eye-straining print. The parent company, Valley Media, however, has declared bankruptcy, and the new owner of the Schwann data bases has no immediate plans for publication of the catalogues. In the meantime, you may find helpful information on-line at ***www.allmusic.com***, but the entries here are not always accurate and searching the classical section on this website requires patience.

Highly respected catalogues are published in other parts of the world, but they are, of course, designed primarily for use in their own nations. The ***R.E.D. Classical Catalogue*** from Great Britain, however, can prove useful, provided you remember that all of the recordings listed therein may not be available domestically and that label numbers may vary. The main catalogue is published twice a year. It is available either alone or with a monthly up-date supplement in loose-leaf form, and can also be ordered as a monthly CD Rom. Particularly if you intend to add a number of imported discs to the collection, an investment in the main catalogue with the monthly print supplement may prove particularly helpful. Contact R.E.D. Publishing for additional information or subscriptions on-line at ***www.redpublishing.co.uk*** or by mail at R.E.D. Publishing, Paulton House, 8 Shepherdess Walk, London N1 7LB, UK.

You can also find helpful information on available recordings from the on-line dealers and suppliers. In many cases they list in detail the recordings that they have available for sale, including new issues. For suggested websites refer to Chapter Five, "Finding the Recorded Needle in the Haystack."

five

FINDING THE RECORDED NEEDLE IN THE HAYSTACK

Almost fifty years ago, when I began to collect music recordings seriously, the major problem was finding the discs that I knew were somewhere "out there." I puzzled over the marketing strategy of companies that produced records that I could not buy simply because I could not locate them. My local music store would order for me from their one-stop supplier, but more often than not nothing resulted from the order. I recall trying to locate a copy of the then current issue of Mozart's *Don Giovanni* on the London label. The year was 1960, and I waited, not a month or two, but one year, two years, forever. I finally found my London *Giovanni* 42 years later when Decca reissued it in their "Legends" series (Decca/London 466389).

Part of the problem was my small-town location. Part of it was my ignorance, now corrected, of the best sources for recorded music. But part of the problem was an industry equipped to serve major metropolitan areas quite well and willing to let the rest of us struggle along as best we could. Time and, no doubt, experience have changed the situation, and producers and marketers do a far better job today. There are more dealers offering more possibilities for quick mail order and telephone service, and most importantly for on-line ordering. You can still run into problems. After all, it is a big haystack, consisting of thousands of classical discs — and sometimes locating the one you want is like the search for that proverbial needle. The help you need, however, truly is available if you're willing and able to look for it. Success, however, is precisely there — in the patience to turn from one source to another to find the recording you want, and in the energy and the time you put into the search.

Libraries have the distinct advantage of there being dealers dedicated solely to their needs. They depend on your business, and they will try hard to locate the recording you want. You probably already have an account relationship with one or another of the major library suppliers. Baker and Taylor, for example, carries over 135,000 video, DVD and compact disc titles, in addition to an almost limitless number of books, and they promise speedy, efficient service. If you would like to set up an account with Baker and Taylor, you should contact Information Services by telephone at 800-775-1800. Ingram Library Services does not supply music, but they can provide videos and DVDs. You can reach Ingram by telephone at 800-937-5300 or at their website — *www.Ingramlibrary.com.*

If your library moves forward in developing a collection of operatic video and sound recordings, at some point you will probably need a supplier who specializes in music. One of the largest is the Alliance Entertainment Corporation. Open a library account with AEC One-Stop Group and the company will send you their monthly publication, *Connoisseur.* It includes information about new releases, reviews, and a variety of helpful articles. For more information you can dial 800-388-8889, or send a request by e-mail to lauble@aent.com.

There are assuredly many other dealers that specialize in serving the library's music needs. Two that have been highly recommended are the Music Library Service Corporation and Gary Thal Music. On the basis of my personal contact with the heads of both of these companies, I believe that you would receive service that is not only efficient, but also friendly and personal. I don't doubt that they would go that extra mile to help you find what you are looking for. The address for Music Library Service is 502 Compton St., Wilmington, NC 28401. You can reach them by telephone at 800-849-2323, by fax at 910-762-8701, and on their website at *www.mlscmusic.com.* The mailing address for Gary Thal Music is P.O. Box 164, Lenox Hills Station, New York, NY 10021, telephone 212-473-1514. If you request, he will add your name to the mailing list for his newsletter.

There are many general retail on-line sources for video and audio discs and tapes. Enter "compact disc dealers" in your computer search device, and you will come up with a mind-boggling number of possibilities. Most of them promise good service, large inventories, and low prices, but as I have learned from experience, some of them don't deliver on that promise. Sometimes, however, the problem is our failure to provide the necessary information to the dealer. The few suggestions offered here may help you use these on-lines sites wisely and well.

• Unless you enjoy browsing and have time for it, pin down what you're looking for narrowly, but not too narrowly. Be certain that all the information you enter in the dealer's search boxes is accurate. Any inaccurate information will draw a blank. My experience with some of the on-line sites suggests that too much information, even if it is accurate, may not produce the results you're looking for. Too much information can sometimes confuse the computer. Try entering only the composer, the title, and the conductor, but not other artists or label and number data. The conductor is apparently the component that facilitates this kind of limited search. Remember that with a recording you have no practical equivalent of an ISBN number to facilitate your search.

• Once you think you have found the recording you're looking for, on most of these sites you can click on the title or the cover illustration, if there is one, to bring up the full data about the recording. Don't place an order without checking carfully all of the information available to you. Now is the time to look carefully at the names of the other artists involved in the performance, including the orchestra or operatic ensemble. Conductors often record the same musical work more than once, and frequently there may be an even longer list of off-the-air or so-called "live" recordings by the same artists. Check also the label name and issue number, but be aware that companies have been known to change label names and issue numbers when you least expect it. If you need more information than the website reveals, don't take the chance and go ahead and order. Look for the dealer's "contact" frame, click on it, and send a request for what you need to know. I know of one library that has received a number of complete opera recordings as gifts because a local collector, one whom I see in the mirror every day, didn't take the trouble to check the information carefully.

• Pay close attention to any information the on-line dealer offers about the availability of the recording. Many dealers will indicate that the selected item will probably be shipped "within 24 hours," "within two or three days," or "in four or five weeks." If the website tells you that there is "limited" availability, chances are that you won't have it on your shelf any time in the reasonable future. If the chances of receiving what you're looking for within a reasonable time seem slim, try one of the other dealers. One of them just may have exactly what you want in stock for immediate delivery.

• In most cases you will receive e-mail confirmation that your order has been received, and a similar notice will come when it has actually been shipped. You will be given an order number. Hold on to it. You will need it as reference if you encounter any problems.

• More and more on-line dealers offer free shipping on relatively large orders, provided you do not request a special shipping option such as "overnight" or "second day" delivery. If you need the items you're ordering as soon as possible, you may want to choose one of the quick delivery methods, but be prepared to pay for it. Shipping and handling charges are almost inevitably larger than I think they will be, and I'm still trying to figure out why it's more expensive to "handle" a two-disc set than a single compact disc. Many of the dealers that ship by private carrier, such as United Parcel, rather than through the mail service provide a shipping number that enables you to check on the progress your package is making. You won't have your discs any sooner, but you may enjoy tracing their progress across the country.

• Unless you have made a special library account arrangement with these retail dealers, you will need to supply a credit card to which the charges can be made.

Inveterate opera collector that I am, I have developed a personal list of general commercial dealers that offer good, efficient, relatively swift, competitively priced service and can often supply out-of-the-way items. I'm certain there are others equally capable, and I know many collectors who shop on-line regularly and happily at *www.towerrecords.com* and *www.cdnow.com.* The ones listed here, however, are those that I use regularly and whose service I can vouch for from my personal experience.

Amazon is the most familiar of the lot. All it takes is *www.Amazon.com* and you're there. Of course, Amazon sells almost everything, but it's easy to get from the title page to whatever special "store" you're looking for. Sometimes it's a trifle more difficult to find what you want through their search device, but keep trying. (Remember: Composer, Title, Conductor!) If they are not able to supply a recording, they will often direct you to a source for a used copy. The same service applies to books and videos.

Barnes and Noble works much the same way as Amazon, although I personally find their search device easier to use. Provided the material in your order is available, they ship rapidly. I have frequently been surprised with two or three day service when I had expected to wait five or six. Their on-line site is *www.barnesandnoble. com.*

If you're faced with a strained budget (who isn't?), here are three possibilities that offer real bargains. You won't always find precisely what you're looking for, but some of the time you will.

Berkshire Record Outlet Inc. is a major source for budget priced discs. They publish 300 page catalogues and regular supplements throughout the year. The catalogues are the delight of collectors with several hours of free time to browse through the listings, arranged not by composer and work, but by label names. For busy library staff, wisdom dictates a visit instead to their website, *www.broinc.com*, where you can search more easily for what you want. You can also order by mail at Berkshire Record Outlet. Inc, 461 Pleasant St., Lee, MA 01238, or by telephone at 800-992-1200 (the toll-free line is only for orders), but you will need to have Berkshire's own stock numbers before you write or call. I have often been surprised to find new issues listed in the Berkshire catalogue.

Cyber Music is a division of Allegro, one of the import music companies. The specialty here is compact discs and videos at bargain-basement prices, and they have thousands of them in stock. The usual sources are apparently discontinued issues and dealer overstocks. Search here particularly for historical issues of standard operas or recital discs of earlier singers. The web address is *www.cybermusicsurplus.com*, or you can access their site from *www.allegro-music.com*.

There are many sources for used compact discs. Two that I have found particularly helpful are **CD Choice** (*www.cdchoice. com*) and **Parnassus Records** (*www.parnassusrecords.com*). CD Choice gives you the opportunity to search their regularly updated data base of new and used records. Parnassus publishes a catalogue that you can download from the website, order by telephone (845-246-332) or by e-mail at *Parnassus@ulster.net*, or by mail at Parnassus Records, 51 Goat Hill Rd., Saugerties, NY 12477–3008. Parnassus also offers an excellent search service to locate rare and out-of-print compact discs.

From time to time I have suggested recordings that are not available in the United States. Don't let ordering imported discs frighten you. It is as easy as ordering domestically, even though it will probably take a bit longer for delivery. For a quick answer, enter the Amazon website, move to the bottom of the page, and click on **Amazon.UK** or one of the other Amazon locations in Germany, France, or Japan. You will find here many recordings that are not available in the United States, and the only difference you will notice is the price. It's not just that the £ doesn't look like the $; compact discs are more expensive in Great Britain than they are here at home. Otherwise, the search and ordering process is the same as on Amazon's domestic site.

Among the other recommended sources for British issues are **Seaford Music** (*www. seaford-music.co.uk*), **Harold Moores** (*www. hmrecords.demon.co.uk*), and **The Crotchet Web Store** (*www.crotchet.co.uk*). The only one from which I have ordered is Crotchet, and I can vouch for their efficient, helpful service. If you would like to investigate other sites for imported compact discs, check the many regular and classified advertisements in the monthly issue of *Gramophone*.

With all of these possibilities, you should be able to cut the haystack down to manageable size.

SIX

PUTTING THE COLLECTION TO WORK

Now that you have this wonderful collection of operatic material — superb audio and video recordings and excellent printed resources — what are you going to do with it? It surely isn't just to boost the statistical records or to give *your* library bragging rights for having something the others don't have. It may, of course, help those annual circulation figures that you report to whoever it is in your area that demands a yearly accounting. But you know that your library also has a mission well beyond anything the statistics can document, and that mission includes education for the broadest possible range of people and the enhancement of their quality of life. That's truly what your operatic collection is all about, increasing the cultural knowledge and artistic appreciation of your community, and helping the people claim the joy that opera can bring.

Some of your library patrons will already love opera, and will love you for making it available to them. Many will know nothing about opera, and you will have the privilege of building their interest and their knowledge. A few will have already decided that they want nothing to do with opera, and it will become your task to help them change their minds. In a handful of cases, you may even be successful.

Here is a chapter of suggestions. Some of them I have actually tried. Some of them I've heard about. And some of them are products of an active imagination, and I hope to try them some day soon. They are ways of bringing the opera collection to the attention of the library patrons, and once you have their attention, of building their interest and appreciation.

My first suggestion is the simplest and the most obvious one of all.

SHOW IT OFF

Everyone who comes into the library expects to find books and magazines and, usually, computer screens. Computers today are as common in libraries as mustard and relish at a hot dog stand. Many library patrons, however, will not be aware of the rich, wonderful resources you offer in sound and video recordings unless you point them in the right direction.

Perhaps the plan of your building will permit you to house all or part of your collection near the checkout desks or close to the entrance so that everyone who goes in and out will see it, but where and how you shelve your collection of audio and video materials is a decision that must be made for each individual situation. In some cases, security is an issue and the material cannot be safely placed on the open stacks. In other settings, space is the great problem, and merely finding an empty shelf or two is the major concern. Blessed indeed are those rare libraries with enough empty room to last — well, for two or three years, in any case. Whatever the situation, however, don't hide the fact that you have a wonderful collection of operatic resources. Show it off from the beginning, and let people know how and why you are developing this collection.

There are many demands for space in your display cases or on your bulletin boards. With the posters for the latest blockbusters from the superstar authors, exciting material related to the next holiday, the urgent announcement of the Friends of the Library annual meeting, and your spectacular exhibit in support of National Library Week, you may have to push and squeeze to save a little place for opera. But your patrons deserve to know that you are developing a good collection and that it ties in with other interests that the library is promoting.

The arts section of the newspapers will let you know when an opera is to be mounted on the boards in your area. Perhaps a local college or opera group plans to perform Verdi's *Traviata* in a few weeks, a touring organization is bringing Bizet's *Carmen* to town for a one-night stand, or a resident company has scheduled an exciting new production or premiere. Claim that opportunity to let your patrons know that the library has exactly what they need to prepare for an exciting night at the opera. A telephone call to the sponsoring organization will provide all the details and may well produce a few good illustrations for the display board.

Nothing happening on stage in your community this month? Well, then, check the radio and television listings. Almost every week, someone, somewhere is making opera available to the public. Let your patrons know that the library can tell them more about what they will see and hear. Consider also celebrating a few operatic birthdays with appropriate exhibits on the life and works of the great composers. Start with Mozart's on January 27 and work straight on through to Puccini's on December 22. Surely one a month isn't too much to ask.

Singers from your area, both past and present, will attract attention, particularly if you can recommend from your collection recordings in which they perform. If you're in Ohio, try Kathleen Battle. California? I, for one, hope we never forget the glorious sound of native son Lawrence Tibbett, whose father, by the way, was a sheriff in California. You might try a tie-in with *La Fanciulla del West* (*The Girl of the Golden West*), Puccini's "Wild West" opera and one in which Tibbett actually appeared. There's Eleanor Steber from West Virginia and Leontyne Price from Mississippi and Richard Crooks from New York and Clara Louise Kellog, who was born in South Carolina. (That last one may send you to the dictionaries to find out just how important she actually was, and you won't find any recordings of her voice because there aren't any.) The possibilities are almost endless. After all, someone on your library staff dreams up those displays for all the other subjects. Why not for opera?

If you publish a newsletter, you have another wonderful tool. Consider asking local musicians to recommend an opera-of-the-month from among the recordings in your collection. Genuine opera lovers would probably delight in the opportunity and might even be eager to write a paragraph or two to introduce their selections. Unless your library is different from the ones I know, whoever on your staff is responsible for editing the monthly or quarterly newsletter will rejoice in having something to fill up a couple of inches of column space. Wouldn't it be interesting if you ended up with the kind of waiting list that many libraries maintain for the latest bestseller novel, but this time for Wagner's *Lohengrin* or Gershwin's *Porgy and Bess*?

A CENTER FOR OPERA EDUCATION

Libraries truly are educational institutions, and education involves more than providing printed and audio-visual resources. The up-to-date library offers learning experiences beyond the printed page and the video and sound recordings. We do it with visiting authors who discuss and read from their works, with speakers who lead discussions on subjects of contemporary concern, with book fairs and film series and travelogues. Let's do it with opera as well. If the "Center for Opera Education" sounds a bit forbidding, give it another name. Call it "Learning to Listen" or "Listening to Learn" or even "Singing in the Stacks." But remember to claim some of the wonderful opportunities to help your patrons understand and appreciate opera.

An "entry level" program might relate opera to its literary sources. I presented one such series that introduced five relatively brief works of literature and the operas based on them. A grant from a state agency provided enough copies of the printed material to enable each participant to read the literary works in advance. Then, on each of five evenings, the participants reviewed the operas through recordings and discovered how the written word was transformed, and in some cases even deconstructed, for the operatic stage. Here's a list of the five literary works included in that series and their operatic versions: Prosper Mérimée's *Carmen* and Bizet's opera; the brothers Grimm and their retelling of Hänsel and Gretel as seen and heard in Humperdinck's opera; the account of Susannah and the elders from the Apocrypha and Carlisle Floyd's *Susannah;* Pushkin's *Queen of Spades* and Tchaikovsky's opera of the same name; Shakespeare's poetic and Verdi's musical versions of the tragedy of Macbeth.

That list, however, is just a beginning. Check the entries on individual authors in *The New Grove Dictionary of Opera* and you'll find many more ideas. Or sit down together with a musician and a student of literature and the list will quickly grow to monumental length. Other suggestions? Try a series on operatic settings of additional Shakespeare plays or of the great works of classical literature and mythology. The Bible offers some more good possibilities: Rossini's *Mosè in Egitto*, for example, Verdi's *Nabucco* (Nebuchadnezzar), Saint-Saëns' *Samson et Dalila,* or Richard Strauss's *Salome.* Operatic versions of modern literature appear more and more frequently, and readers will have a built-in interest in what the composers have done with the favorite books. There are many from which to choose. Floyd's *Of Mice and Men* is based on John Steinbeck's novel; his recent opera *Cold Sassy Tree* grew from Olive Ann Burns' famous 1984 book. Robert Ward set Arthur Miller's *The Crucible* to music; Benjamin Britten turned to Thomas Mann's *Death in Venice;* Andrew Previn borrowed *A Streetcar Names Desire* from Tennessee Williams; Karl-Birger Blomdahl's *Aniara* introduced operagoers to Harry Edmond Martinson's world of poetic science fiction.

It's not just fiction that finds its way

into opera. Think of the stimulating discussion and even debate that could grow from a consideration of contemporary issues and recent history in opera. John Adams' *Nixon in China* and *The Death of Klinghoffer* might almost have been drawn from the headlines of a few years back. Andrew Davis has found musical expression for *The Life and Times of Malcolm X,* and his opera *Tania* draws on the story of Patty Hearst. If you are looking for ideas and the heated discussions they can inspire, try Jake Hegie's opera *Dead Man Walking,* from Sister Helen Prejean's book. It confronts opera audiences with the controversial issue of capital punishment.

If you have made it through a series of heated contemporary issues, you may want to cool things down with the operatic treatment of events in the distant and safer past centuries. I have prepared and presented a series of five programs, one a week, on "History Set to Music," how opera views the great events of the past. After the Old Testament accounts, we moved to Julius Caesar and Cleopatra, and eventually made our way to the wives of Henry VIII and his daughter Elizabeth, with Nero, King Arthur, Columbus, Ivan the Terrible, Montezuma, and a few other notable and often notorious figures from the past along the way. It's amazing how interesting, and musical, history can become when it's interpreted for us by Handel, Verdi, Schoenberg, Mussorgsky, Donizetti, and the other great composers. George Jellinek's book *History Through the Opera Glass: From the Rise of Caesar through the Fall of Napoleon* (Pro/Am Music Resources, 1994) is an excellent guide to the subject.

If there's no time for a longer series, plan an occasional single program marking a significant opera related anniversary or introducing an opera that will soon be staged in your area or broadcast on television. At my local library we celebrated Gershwin's one-hundredth birthday in 1998 with a presentation on *Porgy and Bess,* the opera and its performance history; and the death of Giuseppe Verdi in 1901 gave occasion for a commemorative program in 2001. Raeburn's *The Chronicle of Opera* (Thames and Hudson, 1998) is an excellent guide to operatic dates. Look forward to the four hundredth anniversary in 2007 of Monteverdi's *Favola d'Orfeo,* the first enduring operatic masterpiece. Three hundred years ago, January 8, 1705, *Almira,* Handel's first opera, had its premiere in Hamburg. He still had some operatic lessons to learn, but it was a good beginning and well worth commemorating. (*Almira* has been recorded in an acceptable performance on CPO, 999 257–2.) Vienna remembers 1805 as the year in which Napoleon's army occupied the city a week before the premiere of the initial version of *Fidelio,* Beethoven's great operatic hymn to human liberty. Caruso first sang at the Metropolitan Opera in New York in 1903, and the Met has never been the same since. The next year in Milan, Puccini's *Madama Butterfly* was greeted with hostile jeers at its first performance. In 1905 Richard Strauss's *Salome* began its scandalous and highly successful conquest of opera houses around the world. There are new possibilities with each new year.

Here's another idea that relates words written and words sung in a manner particularly appropriate for a library. Opera, of course, borrows freely from fiction, but occasionally fiction borrows just as freely from opera. Challenge your literary sleuths to follow the clues to novels that in some significant way include opera and opera singers. Perhaps they'll descend to the underground passageways of the Paris Opéra in Gaston Leroux's *Phantom of the Opera* (1911), a far better story than Hollywood ever made of it. A program could present the music actually referred to in Leroux's novel and let Andrew Lloyd Webber's score rest for a while. Turn to Chapter 15 in *Madame Bovary* (1857) to read about the emotional response of Gustave Flaubert's title character to a performance of Donizetti's *Lucia di Lammermoor*. The music is so clearly delineated in Flaubert's novel that it could easily be keyed to a dramatic reading of the chapter. Or consider the possibilities springing from the opening sentence of Edith Wharton's popular novel *The Age of Innocence* (1920): "On a January evening of the early seventies, Christine Nilsson was singing in *Faust* at the Academy of Music in New York."* Wharton's operatic setting in this chapter is accurate in detail: Nilsson and Victor Capoul, the Faust of the evening, both sang at New York's Academy of Music in the early 1870s, both were noted for their roles in Gounod's opera, and they certainly sang not in the original French, but in Italian, just as Wharton informs us.

Opera singers figure as major characters in more than one good novel — and in a few that aren't so good. Two of the best are Willa Cather's *The Song of the Lark* (1915) and Marcia Davenport's *Of Lena Geyer* (1936), both based in part on the life and career of the famous soprano Olive Fremstad. For a radical change of pace, see what your opera patrons can make of James McCourt's *Mawdrew Czgowehwz* (1975) once they learn to pronounce the name of the diva in this remarkable satirical novel. Reviews of any of these three books, accompanied by appropriate recordings, may send the audience to the shelves looking for both music and novels.

I wonder why opera houses have provided the setting for such a large number of mystery novels. Perhaps a local opera lover who is also a fan of detective fiction can manage to come up with an answer. If so, you are well on your way to what could be a fascinating presentation of good music and investigative logic as your expert explains the relationship of great opera and murder most foul. Take a look at Barbara

Paul's carefully researched mystery novels, including *A Cadenza for Caruso* (1984), *Prima Donna at Large* (1985), and *A Chorus of Detectives* (1987). You can even find some opera singers themselves who tried their hand at fictional operatic detection: Queena Mario, for example, with *Murder in the Opera House* (1934), *Murder Meets Mephisto* (1942), and *Death Drops Delilah* (1944); or the great Wagnerian soprano Helen Traubel with *The Metropolitan Opera Murders* (1951).

A helpful listing of music related fiction is available online at *www.lib.washington.edu/MusicMystery-html.*

In planning and preparing programs, it's important to remember that opera has more to do with words sung than with words spoken. A presentation about opera with only a speaker to listen to is a poor excuse for the real thing — and hardly necessary, given the availability of sound and video recordings. If your library is blessed with an acoustically acceptable auditorium or meeting area, preferably with a piano available, you may want to invite local musicians to perform. Amateur performing groups are often eager for the opportunity. But whether the performance is on record or in person, fill the ears of the audience with great music, and there's a good chance they'll stay around after the program to check out some of the wonderful resources your library has to offer.

I am, of course, aware that libraries, including some of the larger ones, may not always have on hand a staff member with either the expertise or the time to prepare and present programs on opera. It is, after all, a relatively specialized field, even for those with training in music. What the library does have, however, is a surrounding community, and somewhere in that community there are knowledgeable opera lovers who would delight in the opportu-

---

*Edith Wharton, *The Age of Innocence* (New York: Macmillan Publishing Company, 1993), p. 3.

nity to help. Seek them out. Look for faculty members of college and university music departments, private and public school music teachers, trained church and synagogue musicians. Encourage the library staff to spot patrons who bring them reference questions about music in general and opera in particular. Ask the members of the Friends of the Library or other support groups to point you toward good musicians in the community who are also good communicators. Search out the presidents of local music clubs and the leaders of performing groups. Use your community. You are their resource. Now let them become yours. What you will discover is that opera lovers love to talk about opera and frequently know a great deal about it. You may even find one or two who have wonderful collections of rare operatic recordings and who've been waiting for years for someone to give them an opportunity to share their music with other people.

MAKE IT ACCESSIBLE

Sooner or later you'll have to deal with the question of cataloguing and shelving the collection, better sooner than later. Let me share with you a private collector's experience. Back in the 1950s in the ancient days of long-playing records, I began to accumulate operatic recordings. When I had twenty or twenty-five, I could usually find what I wanted, even if it was an individual selection on a recital disc of eight or ten different arias. My catalogue was all in my head. Once the collection grew to fifty discs I began to have trouble. By the time it reached four or five hundred, it had left my memory a long way behind. I couldn't remember where to find Puccini's *Madama Butterfly,* and I certainly had no idea how to locate Maria Callas singing "Un bel dì," one of the arias from the opera. That's when I

began to catalogue my own collection, and to do it in enough detail so that I could find what I wanted. By then, however, it had become a major task not for a few days but for several weeks. The moral of this story is simple: Catalogue carefully and fully from the very beginning, and catalogue in such a way that patrons can find what they're looking for.

Every library will have its own procedures for accessing, cataloguing, and shelving sound and video resources. In some libraries, recordings are shelved incrementally so that whatever the nature of the disc or tape it is simply assigned the next number and shelved accordingly. The result is that Verdi's *Trovatore* may sit on the shelf next to a Stan Getz jazz album, and a Bartók concerto may be assigned number 1004 and Wagner's *Meistersinger* 1005. This system is easy to maintain and probably creates no particular difficulty if the storage area is off limits to library patrons. In an open stack facility, however, browsing through related materials and discovering something you didn't know was there is half the pleasure of a trip to the library. Unless security is a serious issue, a well-ordered collection out in public view and accessible to the patrons will do a great deal more to encourage interest in opera than the same collection hidden away behind locked doors.

You will probably want to catalogue your disc and tape collection much the same way that you do your printed materials. Although you may need to make an occasional adjustment, the standard Dewey Decimal system works well for most audiovisual material and assures that the resources will then be more or less logically arranged on the shelves.

The old-fashioned card catalogue is being replaced rapidly in most libraries by computerized catalogues, often accessible not only in the building itself but also on the patron's own home computer. The usual information is still available: author or composer and librettist(s) for music recordings, title, publishing or issue details, performance data for audio and video recordings, and all the rest of it. An optimum computer system with high-powered search capacity, however, is capable of providing other information that will be of interest to the opera fan. For example, a patron may want to know all of the recordings in your collection by a certain vocalist or conductor. Entering the artist's name — say Arturo Toscanini or Lauritz Melchior — should produce the appropriate list of available recordings if the cast members and conductor have been included in the catalogue to begin with.

A full-service system will also enable the opera lover to find every recording of an individual aria or ensemble included on the recital discs in your collection, provided that information has been entered when the record is catalogued. Patrons looking for a specific aria or ensemble from an opera would be able to find it, much the same way that they could locate a short story or poem in the appropriate index volume. Here is where the wisdom of cataloguing fully from the very beginning truly pays off. Once you have accumulated as many as one hundred recital discs, the task that would have taken perhaps fifteen or twenty minutes for one recording has expanded to twenty-five hours of hard label for an already overworked staff member.

Is all of this effort to make the opera collection fully accessible to the library patrons really worth it? I believe it is, and I hope you'll agree. The more information that is available to the library patrons, the more easily they will be able to find what they're looking for and also discover in the process some possibilities they hadn't thought of before. The opera lover who comes searching either catalogue or shelves for Toscanini's recording of Verdi's *Otello* and in the process also runs into the miracle of his ebullient version of *Falstaff* is bound to love the library more than ever before. Who knows? That may be exactly the person just waiting to give you $10,000,000 for a new building.

seven

A NOTE ON MAINTENANCE

How will your collection, especially the recorded portion, be used?

Staff members know that books sometimes take a hard beating when they are checked out to patrons, and I have seen the damage that has sometimes been inflicted on defenseless vinyl long-playing records. Audio and video tapes also have a way of jamming and breaking when subjected to life in a myriad of ill-behaved home players. The modern compact disc and DVD recordings, however, are somewhat less subject to damage and destruction, particularly if they're handled with just a modicum of care. I hope that will mean for your library that patrons will be able to take the discs home and enjoy opera at their leisure and not be forced to sit with uncomfortable earphones attached in a room of your library through, well, say, four hours of a Wagner epic. After all, we do want opera to be a happy experience, don't we?

The first point you'll need to face is the simple fact that occasionally a music or video disc will be returned damaged. Whether it was damaged accidentally or not is something that even the most sibylline of the staff members will not be able to determine. In any case, if the staff is aware that the disc left the library in good shape and is returned damaged beyond simple repair, it should certainly be the responsibility of the borrower, not the lender, to pay the necessary charges. Of course, if the damage is very small or amounts to no more than a fingerprint or two on the surface, a strong word of caution may be adequate to assure better behavior in the future. Each library will need to generate its own policies to rule in such situations.

The implication here is that every time a disc is checked out, a member of the library staff will check the front and the back of the disc itself to be certain it's in good condition, and that a similar check will be carried out before it is returned to its shelf. Unfortunately, that means extra work for an already overworked staff, but if an opera collection is worth having in the first place, it's worth the extra work it requires to maintain it.

It might be wise to place in each compact disc case a small printed notice that includes rules and suggestions for careful use. It would tell the library patron the policies concerning financial responsibility if the disc is damaged or if it is not returned at all. The notice would also make the usual recommendations for the careful handling of the disc, something like this: 1. Always handle the disc with the fingers inserted in the center and on the edge of the disc. Never touch the surface on either side of the disc. 2. Do not use any cleaning materials on the disc. The library will clean the discs as necessary. 3. Do not expose the disc to direct sunlight or any external source of heat. 4. Do not write on either side of the disc. (I can't imagine why anyone would, unless to make note of the number of a favorite track on the disc.) Whether patrons read and heed the notice is something beyond our ken.

If a disc is returned with fingerprints, they can and certainly should be cleaned as soon as possible. Maxell and Scotch both make disc cleaner kits generally available for less than $13. Use a clean soft cloth and clean from the inside out and not in circles over the disc. If there are light scratches that do not penetrate deeply into the surface, you can use one of a variety of products: the relatively elaborate SkipDr (approximately $30), or the somewhat simpler Pelican Repair and Cleaning kit (approximately $10), and either Maxell or Scotch repair kits

(approximately $13–$15). The investment is minimal, and it makes sense to keep one or more of the products on hand in the library.

If the discs are deeply scratched or gouged, there isn't much you can do unless you want to send the disc out for professional repair (you might try Compact Disc Repairman, telephone, 1-800-FDG-DSL). My recommendation is that you replace a damaged disc rather than sending it for professional repair — unless, of course, the disc is absolutely irreplaceable. You could, of course, invest one or two thousand dollars in a repair and polishing machine (certainly available from many sources, including Skippy Disc in Arizona, telephone 623-825-9003 or e-mail *disc@skippydisc.com*), but you could buy a lot of new compact discs for that amount of money.

Here's one final word that I hope will be a comfort to you. I have over 5,000 compact discs in my personal collection. Admittedly, I handle them with some care, but to my knowledge I have never damaged one. I don't believe I've even left a fingerprint on one.

IMPORTANT OPERAS AND THEIR COMPOSERS

Adriana Lecouvreur (Cilea)

L'Africaine (Meyerbeer)

Aida (Verdi)

Alceste (Gluck)

Alcina (Handel)

Amahl and the Night Visitors (Menotti)

L'Amico Fritz (Mascagni)

Andrea Chénier (Giordano)

Anima del Filosofo, or *Orfeo ed Euridice* (Haydn)

Anna Bolena (Donizetti)

Arabella (Richard Strauss)

Ariadne auf Naxos (Richard Strauss)

Armida (Rossini)

Armide (Lully)

Attila (Verdi)

Aufsteig und Fall der Stadt Mahagonny (Weill)

The Ballad of Baby Doe (Moore)

Un Ballo in Maschera (Verdi)

Il Barbiere di Siviglia (Rossini)

The Bartered Bride [Prodaná nevěsta] (Smetana)

Béatrice et Bénédict (Berlioz)

The Beggar's Opera (arr. Pepusch)

Betrothal in a Monastery [Obrucheniye v monastire] (Prokofiev)

Billy Budd (Britten)

Duke Bluebeard's Castle [A Kékszakállú Vára] (Bartók)

La Bohème (Leoncavallo)

La Bohème (Puccini)

Boris Godunov (Mussorgsky)

La Calisto (Cavalli)

Candide (Bernstein)

Capriccio (Richard Strauss)

I Capuleti ed i Montecchi (Bellini)

Carmen (Bizet)

Cavalleria Rusticana (Mascagni)

La Cenerentola (Rossini)

La Clemenza di Tito (Mozart)

Le Comte Ory (Rossini)

The Consul (Menotti)

Les Contes d'Hoffmann (Offenbach)

Così Fan Tutte (Mozart)

The Cunning Little Vixen [Príhody Ličky Bystroučky] (Janáček)

Dalibor (Smetana)

Les Dialogues des Carmélites (Poulenc)

Dido and Aeneas (Purcell)

Doktor Faust (Busoni)

Don Carlos (Verdi)

Don Giovanni (Mozart)

Don Pasquale (Donizetti)
Don Quichotte (Massenet)
Die Dreigroschenoper (Weill)
Eisnstein on the Beach (Glass)
Elektra (Richard Strauss)
L'Elisir d'Amore (Donizetti)
L'Enfant et les Sortilèges (Ravel)
Die Entführung aus dem Serail (Mozart)
Ernani (Verdi)
Eugene Onegin [Yevgeny Onyegin]
    (Tchaikovsky)
Euridice (Peri)
The Excursions of Mr. Brouček [Výlety Páně
    Broućkovy] (Janáček)
Falstaff (Verdi)
La Fanciulla del West (Puccini)
Faust (Gounod)
La Favorite (Donizetti)
Fedora (Giordano)
Fidelio (Beethoven)
The Fiery Angel [Ognenniy angel]
    (Prokofiev)
La Fille du Régiment (Donizetti)
Die Fledermaus (Johann Strauss, II)
Der Fliegende Holländer (Wagner)
La Forza del Destino (Verdi)
Fra Diavolo (Auber)
Francesca da Rimini (Zandonai)
Die Frau ohne Schatten (Richard Strauss)
Der Freischütz (Weber)
From the House of the Dead [Z mrtvéno
    domu] (Janáček)
The Gambler [Igrok] (Prokofiev)
Gianni Schicchi (Puccini)
La Gioconda (Ponchielli)
Giulio Cesare in Egitto (Handel)
The Golden Cockerel [Zolotoy petushok]
    (Rimsky-Korsakov)
Götterdämmerung (Wagner)
Guillaume Tell (Rossini)
Hamlet (Thomas)
Hänsel und Gretel (Humperdinck)
Hérodiade (Massenet)
Les Huguenots (Meyerbeer)
Hunyadi László (Erkel)
Idomeneo (Mozart)
L'Incoronozione di Poppea (Monteverdi)

Les Indes Galantes (Rameau)
The Invisible City of Ktezh and the Maiden
    Fevronia [Skazaniye o onevidimom grade
    Kitzhe i deve Fevronii] (Rimsky-
    Korsakov)
Iolanthe [Iolanta] (Tchaikovsky)
Iphigénie en Aulide (Gluck)
Iphigénie en Tauride (Gluck)
L'Italiana in Algeri (Rossini)
Jenufa [Jenůfa] (Janáček)
La Juive (Halevy)
Katya Kabanova [Kát'a Kabanová] (Janáček)
Khovanshchina (Mussorgsky)
King Roger [Król Roger] (Szymanowski)
Lady Macbeth of the Mtsenek District
    [Ledi Makbet Mtsenskovo vyezda]
    (Shostakovich)
Lakmé (Delibes)
A Life for the Tsar [Ivan Susanin; Zhizn'a
    tsarya] (Glinka)
Lohengrin (Wagner)
I Lombardi alla Prima Crociata (Verdi)
Louise (Charpentier, G.)
The Love for Three Oranges [Lubov k tryam
    apel'sinam] (Prokofiev)
Lucia di Lammermoor (Donizetti)
Lucrezia Borgia (Donizetti)
Luisa Miller (Verdi)
Lulu (Berg)
Die Lustigen Weiber von Windsor (Nicolai)
Macbeth (Verdi)
Madama Butterfly (Puccini)
The Makropulos Case [Věc Makropulos]
    (Janáček)
Manon (Massenet)
Manon Lescaut (Puccini)
Maria Stuarda (Donizetti)
Martha (Flotow)
The Mask of Orpheus (Birtwistle)
Mathis der Maler (Hindemith)
Mazeppa (Tchaikovsky)
Médée (Charpentier, M-A.)
Médée (Cherubini)
The Medium (Menotti)
Mefistofele (Boito)
Die Meistersinger von Nürnberg (Wagner)
A Midsummer Night's Dream (Britten)

Mignon (Thomas)
Mireille (Gounod)
Moïse et Pharaon (Rossini)
Moses and Aron (Schoenberg)
Nabucodonosor (Verdi)
Nixon in China (Adams)
Norma (Bellini)
Le Nozze di Figaro (Mozart)
Oberon (Weber)
Orfeo (Monteverdi)
Orfeo ed Euridice (Gluck)
Orphée et Eurydice (Gluck)
Otello (Rossini)
Otello (Verdi)
I Pagliacci (Leoncavallo)
Palestrina (Pfitzner)
Parsifal (Wagner)
Les Pêcheurs de Perles (Bizet)
Pelléas et Mélisande (Debussy)
Peter Grimes (Britten)
Porgy and Bess (Gershwin)
Prince Igor [Knyaz' Igor] (Borodin)
I Puritani (Bellini)
The Queen of Spades [Pikovaya dama] (Tchaikovsky)
The Rake's Progress (Stravinsky)
Das Rheingold (Wagner)
Rienzi (Wagner)
Rigoletto (Verdi)
Rinaldo (Handel)
Der Ring des Nibelungen (Wagner)
Il Ritorno d'Ulisse in Patria (Monteverdi)
Robert Le Diable (Meyerberr)
Roberto Devereux (Donizetti)
Roméo et Juliette (Gounod)
Rondine (Puccini)
Der Rosenkavalier (Richard Strauss)
Rusalka (Dvořák)
Ruslan and Lyudmila (Glinka)
Sadko (Rimsky-Korsakov)

Salome (Richard Strauss)
Samson et Dalila (Saint-Saëns)
Semele (Handel)
Semiramide (Rossini)
Serse (Handel)
La Serva Padrona (Pergolesi)
Siegfried (Wagner)
Simon Boccanegra (Verdi)
La Sonnambula (Bellini)
Stiffelio (Verdi)
Suor Angelica (Puccini)
Susannah (Floyd)
Il Tabarro (Puccini)
Tancredi (Rossini)
Tannhäuser (Wagner)
Thaïs (Massenet)
Tosca (Puccini)
Die Tote Stadt (Korngold)
La Traviata (Verdi)
Tristan und Isolde (Wagner)
Il Trittico (Puccini)
Il Trovatore (Verdi)
Les Troyens (Berlioz)
The Tsar's Bride [Tsarskaya nevesta] (Rimsky-Korsakov)
Turandot (Puccini)
Il Turco in Italia (Rossini)
Vanessa (Barber)
Les Vêpres Siciliennes (Verdi)
I Vespri Siciliani (Verdi)
La Vestale (Spontini)
La Vida Breve (De Falla)
A Village Romeo and Juliet (Delius)
La Voix Humaine (Poulenc)
Die Walküre (Wagner)
La Wally (Catalani)
War and Peace [Voina i mir] (Prokofiev)
Werther (Massenet)
Wozzeck (Berg)
Die Zauberflöte (Mozart)

INDEX